Railways in the Niagara Peninsula

Great Western "Niagara" - 1863

Silkscreen print, N. Mika Collection

Railways in the Niagara Peninsula

Their Development, Progress and Community Significance

John N. Jackson, B.A., Ph.D., M.R.T.P.I.

Professor of Applied Geography,
Department of Geography,
Brock University, St. Catharines.

John Burtniak, B.A., B.L.S., M.L.S.

Head, Technical Services Division,
The Library,
Brock University, St. Catharines.

Mika Publishing Company
Belleville, Ontario
1978

Second Printing

Railways in the Niagara Peninsula
Copyright © Mika Publishing Company, 1978
ISBN 0-919303-27-7
HE2809.N52J32   385'.09713'38   C78-001373-5
Printed and bound in Canada

"The material progress of Canada has depended on nothing so much as the means of communication, the facilities for conveying men and goods."

J. M. & Edw. Trout. *The Railways of Canada for 1870-1,* Monetary Times (Toronto), 1871, p. 17.

"People at present have but little idea of the wonderful changes wrought by the railway, from the old stage coach with its slow progress, to the fast train, was a grand step, although many of the great expectations then founded, have not been realized and perhaps never may."

J. P. Merritt, *Biography of the Hon. W. H. Merritt, M. P.,* . . ., E. S. Leavenworth (St. Catharines), 1875, p. 407.

CONTENTS

List of Maps and Diagrams

Abbreviations

The following abbreviations are used in the References at the end of the book.

Journals and Sources of Data

AAG	American Association of Geographers, *Annals*
CHR	*Canadian Historical Review*
CRHA	Canadian Railroad Historical Association
IS	*Inland Seas*
JLA	*Journal* of the Legislative Assembly
LMHS	London and Middlesex Historical Society, *Papers*
NHS	Niagara Historical Society, *Publications*
OHS	Ontario Historical Society, *Papers & Records* and *Ontario History*
PAC	Public Archives Canada, Ottawa
PAO	Ontario Archives, Toronto
WCHS	Welland County Historical Society, *Papers and Records*
WOHN	*Western Ontario Historical Notes*

Newspapers

H.G.	*Hamilton Gazette*
H.S.	*Hamilton Spectator*
N.C.	*Niagara Chronicle*
N.F.R.	*Niagara Falls Review*
N.M.	*Niagara Mail*
St.C.C.	*St. Catharines Constitutional*
St.C.E.J.	*St. Catharines Evening Journal*
St.C.E.S.	*St. Catharines Evening Star*
St.C.J.	*St. Catharines Journal*
St.C.M.	*St. Catharines Mail*
St.C.W.N.	*St. Catharines Weekly News*
T.G.	*Toronto Globe*
Th.P.	*Thorold Post*

Statutes

Statutes are abbreviated. Thus 16 Vic., Cap.136, 1853 means a statute passed in the sixteenth year of Her Majesty, Queen Victoria's reign, numbered Chapter 136 in the volume of statutes for that Session, 1841 to 1867 by the Province and thereafter by the Dominion of Canada.

Introduction and Acknowledgements

This book examines the creation and growth of the railway network in the Niagara Peninsula of Southwestern Ontario from about 1850 to 1900. Spatially, it is concerned with that extent of land which lies between Lake Erie and Lake Ontario, eastward from a line between Hamilton and the Lower Grand River to the international border along the Niagara River. Temporally, it centres upon the Victorian era of steam railway expansion, from approximately 1850 to the end of the nineteenth century. The consideration is therefore of a significant Canadian frontier locality, after its period of primary settlement and prior to the large-scale application of hydro-electricity to its urban and regional landscapes.

The introductory Chapter outlines the salient background features of the railway achievement, including the character of the Peninsula, the furore of hope which greeted each new railway and the mammoth changes which resulted over a few short years in the mid-1850's. The different railway systems are then examined over Chapters II to V, in terms of their sponsoring arguments, the location of the tracks, and the principal features along each route. Discussion examines the Great Western Railway, the Welland Railway, the series of competing American and Canadian railway lines that were constructed in the south of the Peninsula inland from the Lake Erie shoreline, the Toronto, Hamilton and Buffalo Railway, and the initiation of an inter-urban street railway system.

The effects and consequences of the railway system are reviewed in Chapters VI to VIII, emphasizing the bridges over the Niagara River, the urban importance of the new border crossing points, the significance of railways for urban development in Niagara Falls, Fort Erie, Welland and St. Catharines, and their overall role in terms of urban change and regional evolution. The topics covered include their significance for travel, business, industry, agriculture and tourism.

The text is interlaced with historical photographs and documents depicting railway matters and scenes, in their urban context and as an integral component of the regional development process. The majority of these illustrations are taken from the private collection of John Burtniak. Other illustrations, from public or private collections, are credited accordingly.

Acknowledgements are due to many people and organizations who have contributed materially to the final work. These expressions of thanks are due to:

●The Humanities and Social Science Division of the Canada

Council for a research grant to John N. Jackson to examine the evolution and characteristics of urban settlement in the Niagara Region, and to Steve Martin, Elizabeth Dillon and Carole Tolley who so ably acted as research assistants on parts of this project. Gregory S. Stein, Department of Geography-Sociology, State University College at Buffalo, has also provided useful advice.

• The Ontario Arts Council for a grant to John Burtniak to assist with the collection of historical material on the Niagara Peninsula.

• The librarians and research assistants in the Public Archives Canada (Ottawa), Archives of Ontario (Toronto), the Canadian National Headquarters Library in Montreal, Brock University, and the Regional Libraries. Special mention should be made of the assistance provided by Linda Anderson, Government Documents Librarian, Brock University Library; Sheila Wilson, Head, Special Collections Department, St. Catharines Public Library; Alex W. Ormston, Chief Curator, St. Catharines Historical Museum; and J. Norman Lowe, Historical Research Officer, Canadian National Library, Montreal. All other libraries and museums in the Peninsula have provided welcome advice and assistance when approached.

• Phyllis Riesberry, Jenny Gurski, Wendy Cook and their assistants for typing draft and final manuscripts with competence, alacrity and patience.

• Loris Gasparotto, Cartographer, Brock University, and Divino Mucciante, Photographer, Brock University, for their illustrative abilities with maps and photographs.

• Colin Duquemin, Consultant-Outdoor Studies, St. Johns Outdoor Studies Centre, Niagara South Board of Education; James Hogan, University Librarian, Brock Univeristy; Rodolphe Lamarche, Assistant Professor of Geography (Transportation), Brock Univeristy; Francis J. Petrie, Official Historian for the City of Niagara Falls (Ontario); and Alex W. Ormston, Chief Curator, St. Catharines Historical Museum, for reviewing, commenting and improving the draft manuscript.

• Helma and Nick Mika for their kindly encouragement, for the speed, competence and enthusiasm of their publishing activities, and for their excellent hospitality.

It has been our pleasure to work with all the above-mentioned people, to receive their advice, and to benefit by their knowledge and thought, but the final text remains our responsibility.

John N. Jackson and John Burtniak
January 1978

12

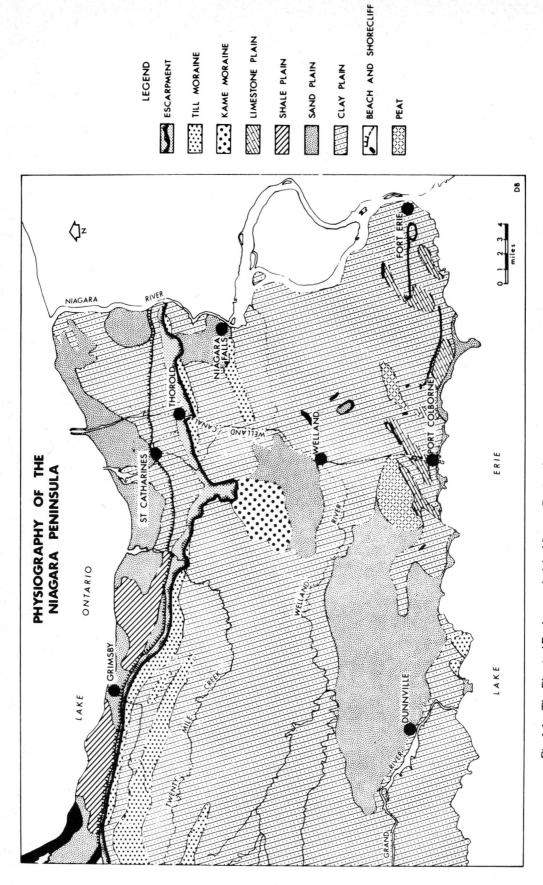

LEGEND

- ESCARPMENT
- TILL MORAINE
- KAME MORAINE
- LIMESTONE PLAIN
- SHALE PLAIN
- SAND PLAIN
- CLAY PLAIN
- BEACH AND SHORECLIFF
- PEAT

PHYSIOGRAPHY OF THE
NIAGARA PENINSULA

N

LAKE   ONTARIO

GRIMSBY

ST CATHARINES

THOROLD

NIAGARA RIVER

NIAGARA FALLS

WELLAND CANAL

WELLAND

PORT COLBORNE

FORT ERIE

TWENTY MILE CREEK

WELLAND RIVER

GRAND RIVER

DUNNVILLE

LAKE   ERIE

0 1 2 3 4
miles

DB

Fig. 1.1   The Physical Background of the Niagara Peninsula.   *John N. Jackson, St. Catharines, Ontario: Its Early Years, 1976*

Chapter I

The Challenge of Railways

The Niagara Peninsula may be defined as that slender projection of land which extends eastwards from Southwestern Ontario towards the international frontier along the Niagara River. It is bounded by Lake Ontario to the north, the Niagara River to the east, and Lake Erie to the south. The western boundary is somewhat arbitrary as the width of land broadens and no pronounced break in topography occurs but, in general terms, the limits are a line from Burlington Bay at the western end of Lake Ontario to Dunnville on the Lower Grand River. Administratively, the Peninsula includes the Counties of Lincoln, Welland and Haldimand, with the two former being amalgamated in 1970 to form the Regional Municipality of Niagara, and the latter being amalgamated with its western neighbour, the County of Norfolk, to form the Regional Municipality of Haldimand-Norfolk in 1973 by the Province of Ontario.

Before considering the development and impact of railways on this area, certain fundamental facts must be introduced. There are the details of terrain over which the routes will cross, the regional context and significance of local landscape features, and the importance of the pre-existing patterns of settlement and their communication links to the outside world. The attitudes expressed by society to the potential of railways as a new and untried venture are also important, together with the government enactments and provisions that made their achievement a viable possibility. These are the background topics of concern that will be considered in this chapter.

The Attitude towards Railways

Modern society is exceptionally mobile, the age of steam has dwindled to a nostalgic memory, and many of its features have been replaced over the past few years.[1] It is therefore difficult for a later age to recapture the almost universal euphoria that greeted the proposals for the first railways. As it was, using the flamboyant style of the period, "the years 1852 to 1857 will ever be remembered as those of financial plenty, and the saturnalia of nearly all classes connected with railways".[2] So wrote T. C. Keefer in 1864.

In the mid-nineteenth century, a strong belief prevailed that railways were the catalyst which provided the urban economy with new opportunities and challenges, induced industrial expansion, attracted population to the cities, and created a new wealth whereby all would benefit through social improvement and economic advancement. Settlements would be bound together with new ties of prosperity, exchange and inter-communication. As Emerson put it, "railroad iron is a magician's road in its power to evoke the sleeping energies of land and water."[3]

The enthusiastic expectations of the period were summarized in the writings of Thomas Coltrin Keefer, Civil Engineer. Born in Thorold, educated at Grantham Academy in St. Catharines and later at Upper Canada College, Keefer (1821-1915) was regarded as one of the foremost engineers of his day, displaying exceptional abilities as an essayist and as a spokesman for the railway. He wrote an authoritative pamphlet, *Philosophy of Railroads* in 1849, which capably expressed the mood of the times.[4] Like many of his compatriots, he believed firmly that the railway provided the panacea for all evils and that the full use of steam technology would advance considerably the material improvement of man. As H. V. Nelles has remarked, Keefer's essential contribution was to describe the revolutionary potential of railroads.[5] He then demonstrated how they acted as the indispensable agents of advancing civilization, and convinced his countrymen that they could afford to build them.

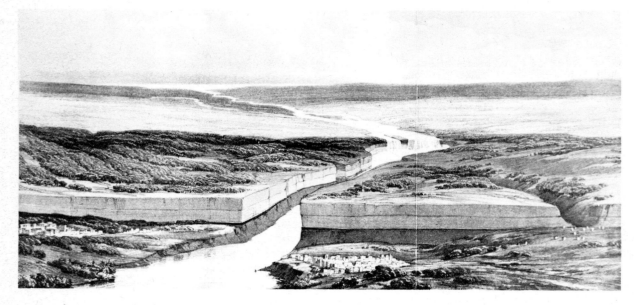

An engraving by John Murray, 1845, shows the Niagara River crossing the horizontal strata of the Niagara Escarpment. The former St. Davids Gorge, later to be followed by the Erie and Niagara Railway, is also prominent.
John Burtniak Collection

His model of achievement was the mythical community of "Sleepy Hollow".[6] The land was well cultivated, the occupants were thriving and independent farmers, the village was limited to a few mechanics, and it contained one store which was the sole forwarder of the district's surplus products. Because of distance, barter and custom, no incentive existed for an increased production. But then everything is changed with exploratory studies by the railway survey gangs. Henceforth, all is expansion and progress:

> "The work has commenced; the farmer is offered better prices for his hay and grain than he ever before received: — even milk and vegetables — things he never dreamed of selling — are now sought for; his teams, instead of eating up his substance as formerly in winter, are constantly employed, and his sons are profitably engaged in 'getting out timber' for the contractors; he grows a much larger quantity of oats and potatoes than before — and when the workmen

have left, he finds to his astonishment that his old friend the storekeeper is prepared to take all he can spare, to send by the Railroad 'down to town'. . . . Is he a farmer? . . . He sees the Railroad . . . carrying his produce for a less sum than his personal expenses and the feeding of his horses would amount to. Is he a blacksmith? he determines his son shall no longer shoe horses, but build engines. Is he a carpenter? he is proud of his occupation as he surveys the new bridge over the old creek."[7]

This thrill of expectation, the so-called "Railway Fever" of the times, generally prevailed. But hope about a glorious future had also to be tempered by many practical considerations. One of these was the legislative provision that enabled the construction of railways. For example, the so-called Guarantee Act of 1849 assured the payment of interest, up to a maximum of six per cent, on half the bonded debt of any railway company with more than 70 miles of track.[8] Payment was subject to certain conditions, principally that half the route had to be built before government support was available. This Act was necessary in a sparsely settled country, with limited capital and with extensive distances between its centres and from these centres to the all-important Atlantic seaboard. A prime function of the railways was to encourage the flow of resource products to harbours for export, primarily to Europe. This, in turn, was deemed to be strongly beneficial for the local market and for the expansion of its business, commercial and trading activities. A precedent for government involvement in the provision of a basic transportation network had been established with the subventions made towards completion of the Welland-St. Lawrence system of canal navigation earlier in the decade. Transportation was deemed too important a factor to be left solely to local initiative.

An enthusiasm for railways is expressed when a cigar manufacturer proudly uses the railway at Niagara Falls for an advertising message.
John Burtniak Collection

Opportunity in the Peninsula at the dawn of the railway era was also affected by the Reciprocity Treaty of 1854. This permitted the free interchange of natural products between Canada and the United States and free navigation of the St. Lawrence River system by American vessels. The treaty was in force over an important operative period for the establishment for railways. It increased international trade, gave an impetus to manufacturing, and provided an added incentive for the railroads which were then opening new territories in their push westwards. The Treaty was rescinded in 1865 by the American Senate, as it is was not thought to be advantageous to that country.

Another important practical consideration was the international border along the Niagara River which provided an invisible but potent administrative divide between two separate and sometimes alien nations. There were hands of friendship and links of kith and kinship across the frontier, but rivalries, tensions and animosities also existed. For example, at the beginning of the railway era, the American invasion of the Peninsula and the sad destruction of life and property during the War of 1812-1814 was still remembered. The presence of American forts and soldiers next to a vulnerable border, was considered to be a serious threat to life and activity in the Peninsula. Furthermore, the seizure of Navy Island in the Niagara River by William Lyon Mackenzie for his "Republic" during the Rebellion of 1837-1838, and the supposed American support for this act, served as a powerful reminder to the Government of Upper Canada that the United States should be regarded as a separate and potentially unfriendly nation. Even as late as the 1860's, the abortive Fenian Raid of 1866 in the Fort Erie-Ridgeway area and the apparent

American assistance of this invasion again underlined the differences between the two nations. Throughout the railway period, there was the threatening spectre of American control and domination, as a precarious balance of sometimes friendly and sometimes hostile relationships existed between the two countries.

Railways in the Peninsula had to cross numerous small streams. These scenes are located on the Great Western line at Grimsby and St. Catharines.

John Burtniak Collection

Topographic Features

Within the Peninsula, two important lowland areas co-exist at different levels,[9] the Ontario Lakeshore Plain next to Lake Ontario and the Haldimand Clay Plain bordering on Lake Erie (Fig. 1.1). There is also the intervening divide of the Niagara Escarpment. This feature, known locally as "The Mountain", is a sharply defined slope that has been described by Lloyd Reeds as "the most striking feature of Southern Ontario."[10] The base of the slope is at about the 350-foot contour and its crest is at about the 550-foot level. Capped by the hard, resistant rock formation of the Lockport dolomite, the Escarpment is composed of nearly horizontal beds of sedimentary rocks, including shales, sandstones and limestones. The scarp face is sometimes almost perpendicular, sometimes ledged into two or more levels, and sometimes mantled by varying thicknesses of morainic or other glacial deposits, but the height difference between the two plains is broadly consistent throughout the Peninsula.

Rivers flow over this formidable barrier. The most important, the Niagara River, has etched back its course from the Escarpment edge to Niagara Falls.[11] Lesser rivers occur along the length of the Escarpment, notably at Decew, Rockway, Ball's Falls and Grimsby, but their deeply-etched rocky valleys presented a severe if not impossible obstruction to north-south communications. Railways seeking to cross the Escarpment from one level in the Peninsula to the other were obliged, therefore, to approach its acute slopes at a gentle angle and to overcome the height difference of 200 feet by long gradients, cuttings and embankments. Each such crossing posed considerable and costly problems for the engineers and work gangs of the period and, naturally, the complex task of crossing the Escarpment was avoided whenever possible by the railway companies.

In terms of communication, the Escarpment effectively separated Lake Erie from Lake Ontario, with the Niagara River providing the only natural route of connection between these two major water bodies. However, only the upper and lower reaches of the River were navigable, to Chippawa and Queenston respectively. The middle section, with the sheer drop over the Falls and the turbulent waters of the Rapids above and the Gorge and Whirlpool below, was quite impassable. These physical obstacles had to be overcome if the necessary links of transportation between Lake Erie and Lake Ontario were to be established.

This important object of inter-lake communication was achieved by a portage road in the 1780's, and later by the construction of the First Welland Canal during the 1820's. The great progenitor and promoter of the Welland Canal project was William Hamilton Merritt (1793-1864) of St. Catharines.[12] Just prior to the railway period, the Government of Upper Canada purchased this private canal undertaking from the shareholders of the Welland Canal Company. An enlargement and reconstruction known as the Second Welland Canal followed. This provided an improved system of navigation from lake to lake, and accommodated vessels with a cargo capacity up to 750 tons.

By these feats of engineering and construction, the Peninsula became a "water-crossing point". The locality must also be visualized as a "land-bridge" between the American and Canadian nations. For example, it provided a prime route for penetration into Southwestern Ontario for many early settlers who left the United States during and after the American Revolution, and it was a major route for the American attack on Upper Canada in the War of 1812-1814.

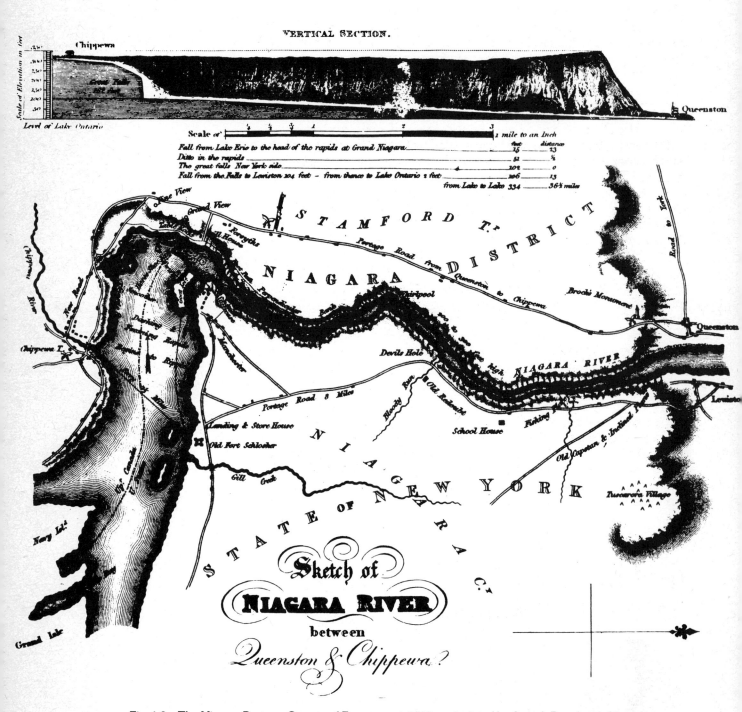

Fig. 1.2   The Niagara Portage, Gorge and Escarpment, 1832, as depicted by Joseph Bouchette. Note the cross-section from Chippawa to Queenston, which emphasizes the height difference between the two lakeshore plains.

John Burtniak Collection

The Peninsula by the Mid-Nineteenth Century

By the 1850's the fertile soils and the favourable climate below the Escarpment had encouraged a greater intensity of settlement than on the heavier, wetter and somewhat less fertile clay soils above the Escarpment. Lincoln County, situated mainly north of the Escarpment, was more densely populated than either Welland or Haldimand Counties to the south of this physical divide. The Peninsula was unevenly settled, with the population being concentrated on the narrow plain next to Lake Ontario rather than on the wider plain next to Lake Erie. This imbalance in distribution is illustrated by the fact that the two major centres in the Peninsula, St. Catharines and Niagara with populations of 4,368 and 3,340 respectively at 1851, were both situated north of the Escarpment.

The Peninsula had been organized into Townships during the 1780's and 1790's. These had been settled by United Empire Loyalists and by later waves of immigrants from Britain, Europe and the United States.[13] They now contained farming and service populations of from 1,500 to 3,000 persons within their respective boundaries. Several distinctive lines or groupings of settlement may be recognized. There were the frontier settlements along the Niagara River, including Niagara (now Niagara-on-the-Lake),[14] Queenston, Chippawa and Fort Erie. Another line of settlement, along the Welland Canal, included Port Dalhousie, St. Catharines, Thorold, Allanburg, Port Robinson, Welland and Port Colborne. A third line, developed to the north of the Escarpment along the Queenston-Ancaster highway, included St. Davids, Homer, St. Catharines, Vineland, Beamsville and Grimsby. In addition, there were Marshville (Wainfleet) on the Feeder Canal from Welland to the Grand River, and the settlements of Port Maitland, Dunnville, Cayuga and Caledonia along this river.

Until the railway challenged this established scene, the movement of people and goods relied extensively on the rivers and lakes, with the Welland River, the Grand River and the navigable lengths of the Niagara River being the more important arteries. Goods were shipped by boat along the Erie Canal and the St. Lawrence River, and also through the Peninsula along the Welland Canal system. There existed also a lakeshore trade to the several small ports on Lake Erie and Lake Ontario.

A bank note illustrating the importance of international railway connections for the economy.

Francis J. Petrie Collection

20

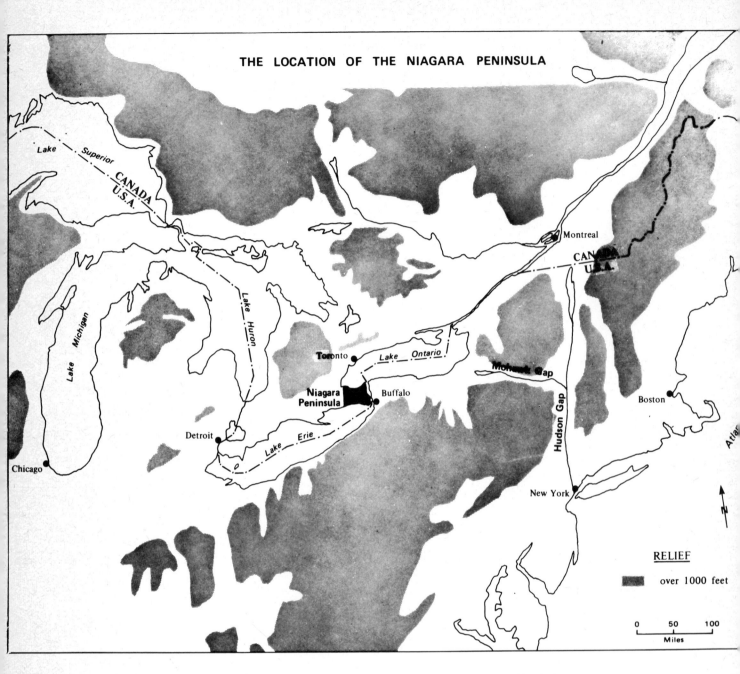

THE LOCATION OF THE NIAGARA PENINSULA

Fig. 1.3   The Location of the Niagara Peninsula in Eastern North America.

In addition, a few rather poor and inadequate road routes existed, with some being sufficiently improved to carry coach and wagon transportation.[15] There were two roads of particular importance, the portage road which avoided the Falls on the Niagara River (Fig. 1.2), and the main road which traversed the Peninsula from Queenston to Ancaster. Railways supplemented this pioneer pattern of water and land communications from the mid-nineteenth century onwards, but the old modes of movement survived and were not immediately supplanted. Gradually and successively, the railways added the strange new factors of mobility, long-distance transportation, and a greater ease and convenience of travel to the pre-existing situation of settlement and communications.

Regional Setting

With the advent of railways, a new set of regional considerations arose. Essentially, the Peninsula became a vital point of interconnection between the Canadian and the American railway systems. The land routes between Detroit and Buffalo, or more significantly between Michigan and New York State, were shorter by land over Canadian terrain through the Niagara Peninsula, than either along a water route via Lake Erie or a land route to the south of Lake Erie on American terrain (Fig. 1.3). Furthermore, as the many ridges of the Appalachian Mountains provided an intransigent barrier between the American eastern seaboard at New York (the most populous American city) and Detroit, Chicago and the opening mid-West, the most convenient trans-continental route of access to serve these rapidly expanding localities was north along the valley of the Hudson River, east through the Mohawk Gap, and then across the Niagara Peninsula towards Detroit or Sarnia.

This Hudson-Mohawk valley route had been followed by the Erie Barge Canal, a major work of construction undertaken by the State of New York and completed in 1825. The route became even more important during the period of avid railway construction. Indeed, as stressed by L. Rodwell Jones and P. W. Bryan, the physical background of eastern North America, to a very large extent, conditioned the larger strategy of spatial evolution and the more important zones of contact between different cultures.[16] The Niagara Peninsula was undoubtedly one such zone of contact.

The two most critical external factors for railway evolution in the Peninsula became the supremacy of New York over Philadelphia and Baltimore from about 1825 onwards, and the physical orientation of the Hudson-Mohawk route leading directly to the land-bridge crossing of the Niagara River. The two height levels existing in the Peninsula, therefore, now took on a radically new significance. In planning a railway to link Toronto, Hamilton or the northern settlements in the Peninsula with the Atlantic seaboard, a route along the Ontario Lakeshore Plain via Rochester and the Mohawk Gap would avoid the complexity and cost of crossing the Escarpment, and lead directly towards the Hudson River and the ocean at New York. Likewise, the Haldimand Clay Plain south of the Escarpment and inland from Lake Erie provided suitable terrain, at 600 feet above sea level, to connect Michigan and New York States. It offered the most direct and convenient railway route from Chicago or Detroit to Buffalo with its links by rail and canal to New York. In either instance, if the necessary connections were to be provided into New York State, then the Niagara River had necessarily to be crossed — a formidable challenge by any scale of the imagination.

The intrinsic regional situation becomes, therefore, of crucial importance when the railway routes, the rival pretensions and the commercial animosities of the various competing railway companies are studied. The account which follows is, therefore, as much the detail of railways *through* the Peninsula as it is of railways *in* the Peninsula. The strategic location of the Peninsula often played a paramount role in the decisions of distant board-rooms in London (England), Montreal, Boston and New York. The Peninsula now lay astride both the railway *and* the water routes to the expanding continental interior.

These pre-emptive facts permeate much of the discussion that follows — the Peninsula lay directly in the line of the advancing tide of western settlement, its distinctive levels offered different sets of extra-regional opportunities and, in the intense power struggle for commercial hegemony between Montreal and New York, the Peninsula was located within their overlapping spheres of competing trading influence. The Peninsula was caught up in a hetic power struggle for supremacy, and it is no accident that it was connected by railway to both Toronto and New York before it obtained a comparable link to either Montreal or the eastern coast of Canada. Because of the Peninsula's location, it became inevitable that the American influence on railway development would be strong, prolonged and, at times, acrimonious and autocratic.

These observations must be taken a stage further. The Niagara River flows into Lake Ontario and then via the St. Lawrence River to the Atlantic Ocean. At first thought, the Lake Ontario-St. Lawrence corridor provided the direct and most suitable Canadian route to the seaboard, either along the north shore on land or by boat along the water system. It certainly offered political advantages, especially after the Act of Union in 1840 (in force from 1841), since it avoided American terrain. Also, the shoals and rapids of the St. Lawrence section, once a severe obstacle to through navigation, had been overcome through a series of short canals by the beginning of the railway era.[17] The St. Lawrence route could therefore be envisaged as having a major importance for road, rail and canal communications.

However, this route also possessed certain negative characteristics. The Lake Ontario-St. Lawrence route, over most of its length, ran approximately parallel to the Atlantic Coast; it did not lead directly towards the Atlantic, but away from the sea and north-eastwards. Furthermore, climatic differences prevailed: New York and Boston had ice-free ports however severe the winter months might be, whereas Montreal and Quebec on the St. Lawrence were winter-locked with ice and impassable from December until April. These advantages and disadvantages were discussed with fervour at the beginning of the railway era. It is not surprising, therefore, that the American Mohawk-Hudson route by rail or by canal was always viewed as a severe rival to the Canadian Welland Canal-Lake Ontario-St. Lawrence water route and a railway to the eastern seaboard via Montreal.

External Urban Centres

The position, significance and relevance of three centres outside the Peninsula should also be noted. Buffalo, Toronto and Hamilton each grew considerably during the late-nineteenth century, and each exerted their marked impact on the Peninsula. Developments within the Peninsula cannot be appreciated without some awareness of the presence of these three cities and their long-term directional pull on the railway routes that passed through the Peninsula.

Buffalo, the county-seat of Erie County, obtained some 14 trunk lines which had terminals at, or passed through, the City.[18] There was also an important lake commerce on Lake Erie, with almost all the great transportation lines on the Upper Great Lakes having an eastern terminus at Buffalo, and the City was the western terminus of the Erie Canal. It was a distributing centre for manufacturing products from the East to the West and for raw products from the West to the East, and became a grain and flour market of first magnitude. Livestock, lumber, iron ore and coal were also handled extensively. Much of the story to be unfolded either seeks to attract some of this commercial wealth to or through the Peninsula on its railways, or is influenced by a strongly stated desire of railways to serve the expanding Buffalo-Tonawanda markets beyond the Peninsula.

Toronto was smaller than Buffalo.[19] It topped the 200,000 mark at the end of the century, compared with a population of about 350,000 in Buffalo. It was important as the Provincial Capital of Ontario and as the second largest city in the Dominion. Railways focussed on this seat of government, and a city which contained important administrative, manufacturing, port, financial, market and trading functions. They were "pulled" from the Peninsula, round the Head of Lake Ontario via Hamilton to Toronto. Links and inter-connections between Toronto and Buffalo were also regarded as important, either wholly by rail on a circuitous land route, or by a shorter distance using some combination of steamer crossing of Lake Ontario and then railway connections to the American centre. Toronto and Buffalo, as well as Montreal and New York, each have their important roles to play when seeking to understand the emergence of railways in the Peninsula.

The Niagara Peninsula, as defined in this book, does not include Hamilton, as its metropolitan, industrial and harbour characteristics vary considerably from the smaller scale patterning of towns and villages and the urban-rural-resource strengths within the Peninsula. Nevertheless, the presence of Hamilton beyond the bounds of the Peninsula, and its active sphere of trading and commercial influence which penetrates into the Peninsula to affect its spatial economy, play an important role in the internal affairs of the Peninsula. Thus Hamilton will enter frequently into the discussion of railways as an important fringe locality.

The First Railways

There were early proposals for railways in the Peninsula. For example, plans for a wooden incline railway were contained in a report prepared by Hiram Tibbet, an engineer who surveyed a possible route for the Welland Canal in 1823. As recounted by E. A. Cruikshank:

> "An Engineer [Hiram Tibbet], who had been engaged in making a survey for a canal around the Falls of Niagara on the New York side of the river, was engaged by Captain William Hamilton Merritt and some of his friends to make a preliminary survey for a canal to connect Chippawa Creek [Welland River] with the West branch [Beaverdams Creek] of the Twelve Mile Creek. An estimate was made for a canal designed for the navigation of large boats, which were to be conveyed up and down the escarpment by wooden railways. . .'The whole expense of the route', the engineer reported, 'exclusive of railways is $34,550, and boats of 20 to 40 tons will navigate it with ease from Lake Ontario to Chippawa in a day or a day and a half at farthest.' "[20]

Tibbet calculated that the construction of locks to ascend and descend the Escarpment would add some $20,000 to the cost of a canal. An objection, that the incline railway "would put a stop to all rafts of timber coming down"[21] was refuted by William Hamilton Merritt. In representing the Welland Canal Company, he stated:

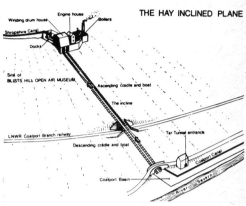
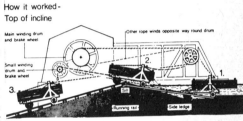

If constructed, a railway incline across the Escarpment could have resembled the Hay Inclined Plane on the Shropshire Canal, England. *Ironbridge Gorge Museum, Telford, England*

"The objection to its proceeding down the Mountain under the construction of the Railway is erroneous in the extreme — is it reasonable for a moment to think that the Directors of the projected Canal would allow this ascent of boats and their contents to interfere with the progress of produce, lumber, &c, coming downward.

It is a very easy matter to construct it upon such a principle, as to prevent [permit] the carriers of various kinds of commodities to pass each other without the least necessity of interfering or meddling one with the other. . .

If it is not convenient to take a boat up bodily the Cargo may follow immediately in a machine adapted for the conveyance of Goods. And may be so arranged that in the event any two (or more) meeting one another, the one may continue on her descent whilst the other is ascending.

This can be done free from any inconvenience or danger.

Should this not meet the approbation of 'A.B.' and his neighbours we can then as a substitute for the Railway have a regular line of locks."[22]

The idea of an inclined railway persisted. It was incorporated into the contract when work on the Canal commenced in 1824, but other circumstances intervened and it was not completed. Instead, the line of the Canal was changed, its dimensions were increased so that it would compete with the American Erie Canal, and locks were constructed to take the Welland Canal over the brow of the Escarpment.

A more successful railway endeavour was constructed around the Falls of Niagara between Queenston and Chippawa. The earlier road portage had been superceded in commercial importance by the Welland Canal. In an attempt to retrieve its dwindling fortunes, a railway company was formed in 1831 and unsuccessful applications for a charter were made to the Legislature of Upper Canada in 1831 and 1832. The proposal was sponsored by businessmen from communities along the Niagara River.

The railway was opposed strongly by William Hamilton Merritt who, on behalf of the Welland Canal Company, regarded the project as one of flagrant injustice to the stockholders. A cooperative scheme with the Welland Canal Company was rebuffed in 1833, the Town of Niagara was also unsympathetic to a route between Chippawa and Queenston, and the military had to be satisfied that the line would not impede their strategic plans.[23]

The application was revived and re-submitted successfully in 1835 when a charter, granted to the Erie and Ontario Railroad Company, empowered the construction of a line from the Welland River to the Niagara River at or below Queenston.[24] By 1839 a route was opened from Queenston to Chippawa. A terminal station and a warehouse were built about 100 feet above the Niagara River at Queenston, with a road connection for horse wagons to a company wharf next to the River. The route then rose up the Escarpment, following the line of Stanley Street in present day Niagara Falls to the bluff above the Falls. It continued on to Chippawa, where a steamboat wharf was constructed on the Welland River. The track was constructed of timber rails covered by iron, and the carriages were similar to those in use on the Stockton and Darlington Railway in England.

As the motive power was provided by horses, this facility can best be described as a horse-operated tramway. It handled freight trucks and also functioned as a rail omnibus service. It attracted a considerable volume of passengers, including the expanding tourist business, with travellers arriving by steamer at Queenston from Toronto and at Chippawa from Buffalo. A timetable of 1842 indicated that: "The cars leave Chippawa for Queenston daily, in time to arrive there for the Toronto steamer, (the *Transit*), at twelve o'clock; reaching Chippawa on return, about 2 p.m., where a steamer will be in readiness to carry travellers on to Buffalo."[25]

The fare from Queenston to Buffalo was $1.00. The line also provided a direct service daily from Toronto to Buffalo, in conjunction with a steamer crossing of Lake Ontario and with river navigation on the lower and upper reaches of the Niagara River. However, the system could carry passengers only during the season of navigation. The line was closed during the winter months and, being unable to compete with the superior abilities of the Welland Canal for freight movement, it fell gradually into disuse.[26]

The Late Arrival of Railways

Despite these early railway considerations, steam railways were late in coming to the Peninsula. This fact requires some explanation, because the brilliant success of George Stephenson's *Rocket* in 1829 on the Liverpool and Manchester Railway in England had attracted the attention of the whole world to the grand possibilities that now existed in this new mode of locomotion and travel. In the United States, the development of the wood-burning railway locomotive occurred at almost the same time as in England. The first American locomotive was built at New York in 1830 for the South Carolina Railroad. In 1831, the Baltimore and Ohio Railway offered a prize for locomotive construction, which was won by the Baldwin Locomotive Works of Philadelphia. In 1840, there were 2,816 miles of track in the United States, which had increased to 9,015 by 1850, slightly more than the British figure of 6,635 miles at that time.

Canada was not in the vanguard of these early railway developments.[27] By 1850, there was less than 70 miles of operative track in the British North American colonies. Some Canadian railways had been chartered in the 1830's and 1840's, but political unrest, economic depression, difficulties over raising capital and a concentration of interest in canals and waterways combined to prevent the construction of other than short routes such as the Champlain and St. Lawrence and the St. Lawrence and Atlantic railways.

Just as the earlier construction of the Erie Canal across New York State had spurred the construction of the Welland Canal and the St. Lawrence works, the advance of the American railway system precipitated action in Canada (Fig. 1.4). There was the fear that inland trade would be diverted to New York or Boston, with their innate geographical advantage of year round traffic to European ports in contrast with the icebound conditions at Montreal during the winter months. One answer was to provide Montreal with railway access to an ice-free port. This solution, it was said, would not compete with but would assist the canals. The prime candidates for a railway terminus were Portland (Maine) and Boston. The outcome was the construction of railway track between Boston and Montreal and between New York and Montreal over a series of routes in 1851 and

ERIE RAILWAY TO CANADA,
VIA
SUSPENSION BRIDGE AND BUFFALO.

A UNITED STATES BONDED LINE
BETWEEN

NEW YORK AND CANADA.

TIME AS FAST AND RATES ALWAYS AS LOW AS BY ANY OTHER ROUTE.

The importance of American-Canadian railway inter-connections is indicated by this poster.
Buchanan Papers, Public Archives of Canada

1852, thereby establishing international railway connections.

By 1853, three lines connected Buffalo directly with New York, and another connected with both New York and Boston via Albany. Buffalo was also the eastern terminus of a railway which was eventually to extend south of Lake Erie westward to Toledo, Detroit, and Chicago. A railroad was also projected to Brantford. The American expectations in 1853 were that this route:

> "will open to the city the whole trade of the rich agricultural valley of the Grand River, with the adjacent lumbering districts, and is destined to connect with the great western road, and thence, via Detroit with all the West, and by Lake Huron with the mineral regions of Lake Superior".[28]

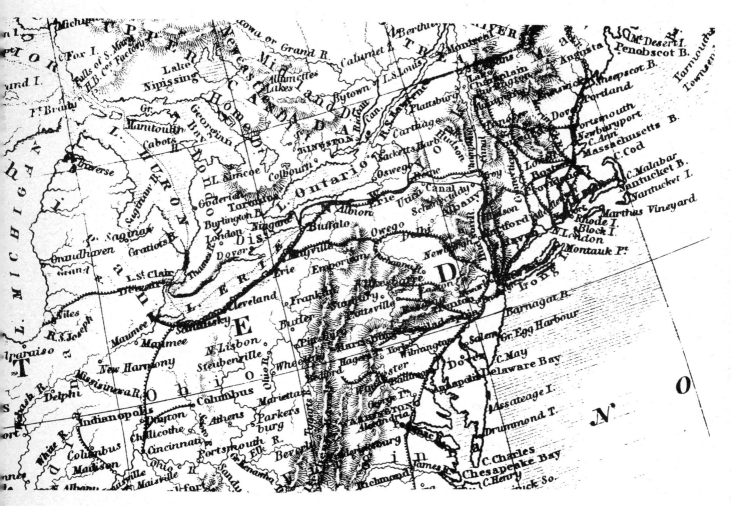

Fig. 1.4   The American Railway Network, from A. K. Johnston, *North America*, 1850. Canada lagged behind the United States in its early railway developments.

Alun O. Hughes Collection

Buffalo was poised to extend its commercial sphere of influence into and across the Peninsula. Using the railway as its weapon, the Peninsula would become subservient in trade to Boston and New York. For instance, the *St. Catharines Journal* advertised in 1843 that three trains left Buffalo daily for Rochester and Albany on the Buffalo and Albany Rail Road.[29] The second class fares were $1.00 and $7.50 respectively. The Peninsula was without a steam railway but it did have stage coach and steamer connections to those elements of the railway network which were currently emerging in the United

States. Doubtless, its citizens were somewhat envious of the superior facilities that existed elsewhere, and meetings to raise support and capital for the construction of railways were attended by enthusiastic crowds.

The Battle of the Gauges

Exemplifying the trans-border cultural differences, Canada West fought a somewhat lonely and futile battle to have a distinctive gauge for its railways. Considerable controversy on this point raged in the Peninsula as elsewhere, and the first major railways were constructed to the gauge of 5 feet 6 inches for the inside width of track. As J. M. and Edw. Trout have tactfully noted, "on the question of gauge several witnesses were heard. We incline to think that the weight of evidence was in favour of a four feet eight and a half inch gauge, while that of five feet six was adopted."[30] The reference is to an Act of 1851, by which the Legislature of the Province of Ontario required the use of a gauge of 5 feet 6 inches for all railways which received assistance under the Guarantee Act of 1849.

A change in gauge at the international border.
John Burtniak Collection

Since Canada and the United States adopted different gauges, there were delays at border crossings and wherever there was a change from one width to another, as well as the obvious expense of transhipment and invonvenience to both passenger and freight traffic. There was also the tremendous expense of converting the entire system when the standard gauge was finally adopted. For example, the Grand Trunk, which gradually absorbed most of the routes in the Peninsula, reached an agreement with the Buffalo and Lake Huron Railway Company in 1863 for the purpose of obtaining mutual facilities for working and interchanging traffic. This involved, in 1864, adding a third rail from Fort Erie to Sarnia so that cars of the American gauge could pass between these points. In 1872, a start was made on converting the whole track to match the general gauge of 4 feet 8½ inches then in operation throughout the United States, and this change was generally completed by 1875.

A third line of track was added to the Great Western railway from the Suspension Bridge to Windsor in 1864. Sometimes trains made up of cars with mixed gauges were run on the line, causing problems in operation. These combined trains were required to carry a large sign marked "N.G." for "Narrow Gauge"[31] (as shown in the frontispiece). Such mixed trains must have looked awkward, and were doubtless dangerous with the imbalance along the centre of drawbar pull. However, despite the costs and the operating difficulties that resulted, the provincial gauge remained mandatory until 1870 when the legislation of 1851 was rescinded. The track to Toronto was narrowed in that year, followed by the removal of the third line in 1871. The Great Western adopted the standard gauge throughout the whole system by 1873.

The double system of gauges, and the railway landscape of poles, rails and wires at Merritton.
John Burtniak Collection

The Expanding Railway Network

The major events of the period are summarized in their chronological sequence in Table 1.1, and are depicted on Figs. 1.5, 1.6 and 1.7 for the years 1862, 1876 and 1907, respectively. This expansion of the network is viewed in the wider contextual situation of Southwestern Ontario on Fig. 1.8, where the years 1860 and 1890 are contrasted. The railway stations that had resulted by 1907 are shown on Fig. 1.9. These maps may suitably be used as reference points,[32] as the various railway lines and their prime features are examined over the ensuing chapters.

Against the somewhat complicated array of physical and human conditions that have been introduced, the mid-and late-1850's witnessed a period of substantial railway construction. For instance, Lovell's *Canada Directory* of 1851 noted only the commencement of operations on the Toronto, Simcoe and Lake Huron Union Rail Road (which was incorporated in 1849)[33] and that the Great Western Rail Road was in the course of construction.[34] Within the short span of six years, the 1857 edition[35] could list *inter alia* the following railway achievements.

Name of Railway	Route	Chartered	Completed	Length in Miles Under Construction
Buffalo and Lake Huron	Fort Erie to Goderich	160	114	46
Erie and Ontario	Niagara to Chippawa	18	18	--
Great Western	Suspension Bridge to Windsor	358	283	55
Welland	Port Dalhousie to Port Colborne	25	5	20
Woodstock and Lake Erie	Woodstock to Suspension Bridge	150	None	None

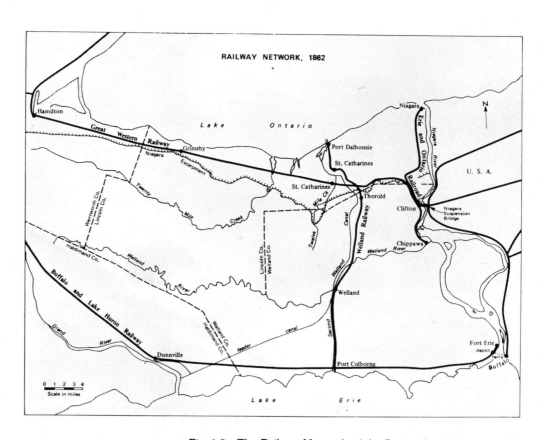

Fig. 1.5   The Railway Network of the Peninsula, 1862.

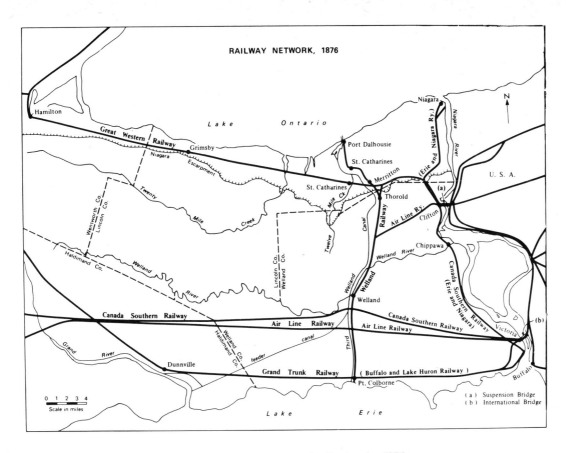

Fig. 1.6   The Railway Network of the Peninsula, 1876.

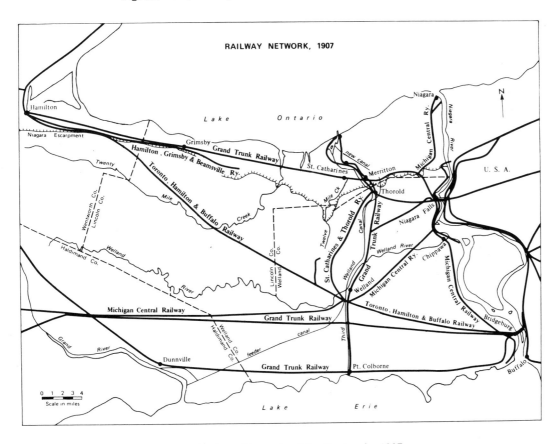

Fig. 1.7   The Railway Network of the Peninsula, 1907.

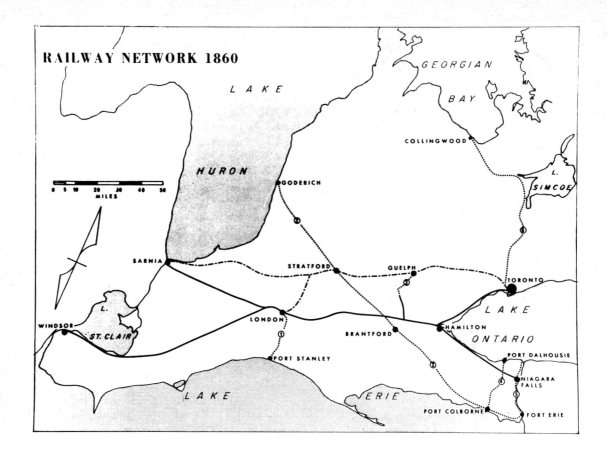

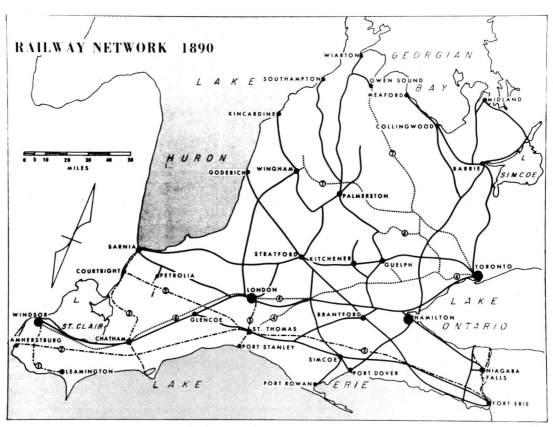

Fig. 1.8   The Railway Network of Southwestern Ontario, 1860 and 1890.

C. A. Andreae, A Historical Railway Atlas of Southwestern Ontario, 1972

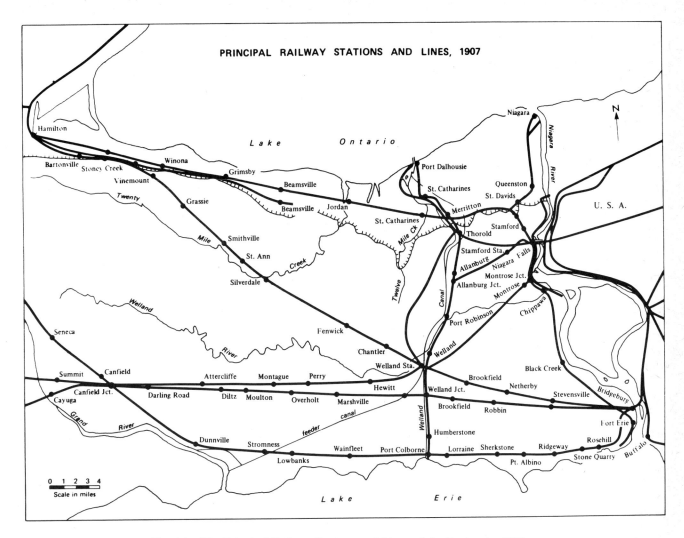

Fig. 1.9   The Principal Railway Stations and Lines of the Peninsula, 1907.

The system of communications in the Peninsula was changed fundamentally by these railway developments. In less than a decade, the mainline of the Great Western system was constructed across the northern part of the Peninsula. At Hamilton, there was a branch line to Toronto, with connections to the Grand Trunk serving the regions north of Lake Ontario from Sarnia to Montreal. At the Suspension Bridge, there were connections to the American railroads.

There was also the Welland Railway, which crossed the Peninsula from north to south. Trains were linked by steamer to Toronto at Port Dalhousie. They also connected with the regular service of boats which plied along the Welland Canal and the feeder canal to Port Maitland and Dunnville.

Another major route was the Buffalo and Lake Huron Railway, which linked Buffalo with Fort Erie by train ferry across the Niagara River and extended via Brantford, Paris and Stratford to Goderich on Lake Huron. At Buffalo, it also linked with the American lines. Within the Peninsula, special tariff arrangements provided for interconnection between the north-south route of the Welland Railway and the east-west route of the Buffalo and Lake Huron Railway. Finally, there was the Erie and Ontario Railway, which ran parallel to the Niagara River and served primarily a tourist function.

The Market Place, St. Catharines, Ont.

The Market, Dunnville, Ont.

The New Market, Welland, Ont.

The old was not displaced by the new. These time-honoured scenes in the market places of St. Catharines, Dunnville and Welland express the continuing reliance of customers and vendors on horse-drawn modes of conveyance.

John Burtniak Collection

Between 1857 and the end of the century, many further changes were introduced. The earlier lines remained, but they had often been renamed and placed under new boards of management. New lines had been added, especially in the south of the Peninsula, where the number of routes parallel to Lake Erie was increased to three competing sets of lines. In the east the Niagara River was crossed by bridges at Niagara Falls and Fort Erie. A new transverse route diagonally across the Peninsula south-east from Hamilton had been inaugurated. In addition to this commanding portfolio of steam railways, an inter-urban system of street railways was initiated with a varied mixture of horse-drawn, steam-operated and electrically-powered systems in their sequence of evolution.

The late nineteenth century was certainly a hectic period of successive developments to the railway milieu, as technological ambition made new forms of locomotion an exciting and feasible proposition. It was also a period of over-optimism, leading to the over-building of lines and to the over-provision of services which did not pay and which barely (or never) repaid their shareholders. The manifest enthusiasm for railways, extending from Keefer's advocacy of their potential to the lurid prose of the railway prospectuses, was certainly not always to be fulfilled. And, unbeknown to the railway promoters, new forms of competition such as the automobile and the truck were also about to be introduced at the end of the nineteenth century. It was 50 years of feverish and pervasive growth, with the temper of the period being based on the shifting and uncertain sands of change, precarious studies of possibilities, and unmitigated rivalries between powerful and antagonistic groups.

Table 1.1
A Chronology of Major Railway Events

1823	Railway incline proposed on the Welland Canal.
1833	Welland Canal opened from Port Dalhousie to Port Colborne.
1834	London and Gore Railroad (later Great Western) incorporated.
1835	Erie and Ontario Railroad incorporated.
1836	Niagara and Detroit Rivers Railroad (later Canada Southern) incorporated.
1839	Erie and Ontario Railroad, line from Queenston to Chippawa opened.
1845	Second Welland Canal opened.
1849	Guarantee Act provides government assistance for railroad construction. T. C. Keefer writes *Philosophy of Railroads*.
1851	Gauge of 5 feet 6 inches adopted.
1853	Great Western Railway, line from Hamilton to Suspension Bridge opened.
1854	Buffalo, Brantford and Goderich Railway, line from Buffalo to Brantford opened. Erie and Ontario Railroad, line from Niagara to Chippawa opened.

1855   Suspension Bridge opened.

1856   Port Dalhousie and Thorold Railway, line from St. Catharines to Port Dalhousie opened.

1859   Welland Railway, line from Port Dalhousie to Port Colborne opened.

1863   Erie and Niagara Railway incorporated.

1870   Gauge of 5 feet 6 inches no longer mandatory.

1873   Air Line Railway, lines from Glencoe to the International Bridge and Suspension Bridge opened.
Canada Southern Railway, line from International Bridge to Detroit opened.
International Bridge opened.

1875   Toronto, Hamilton and Buffalo Railway, line from Hamilton to Welland opened.

1879   St. Catharines Street Railway Company, line opened in St. Catharines.

1883   Niagara Cantilever Bridge opened.

1884   Great Western Railway absorbed by the Grand Trunk Railway.

1885   Fort Erie, Snake Hill, and Pacific Railroad opened.

1887   Third Welland Canal opened.
St. Catharines and Niagara Central Railway, line from Niagara Falls to Thorold opened.
St. Catharines, Merritton and Thorold Street Railway, electrification introduced.

1893   Niagara Falls Park and River Railway, line opened from Chippawa to Niagara Falls.

1894   Canada Southern Railway absorbed by the Michigan Central Railroad.
Hamilton, Grimsby and Beamsville Electric Railway, line from Hamilton to Grimsby opened.

1895   Great Gorge route opened.

1896   Ontario Southern Railway, "Peg Leg" line from Crystal Beach to Ridgeway opened.

1899   Niagara, St. Catharines and Toronto Railway Company (N.S.&T.) incorporated.
Queenston-Lewiston Suspension Bridge opened.

1914   Toronto, Hamilton and Buffalo Railway, line from Smithville to Dunnville opened.

Chapter II

The Great Western Railway

The construction of the first steam railway route between the Suspension Bridge on the Niagara River and Hamilton under the auspices of the Great Western Railway was a crucial event for the Peninsula. It introduced a new mode of transportation to the existing pattern of local urban and rural circumstances. The area, which formerly depended upon a seasonal canal, a horse tramway and roads of poor quality for its internal communications and external links, now had a supplementary means of transportation to meet its expanding freight and passenger needs. Not surprisingly, the event was heralded with favourable anticipation; but it also posed problems of considerable magnitude.

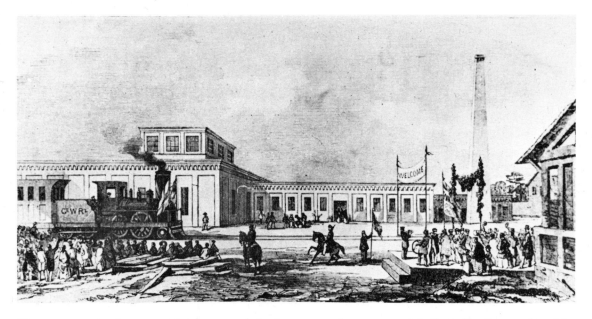

The initiation of railways provided an opportunity for pomp and ceremony, as indicated by the opening of the Great Western Station at London, Canada West, in 1853.   *Illustrated London News 21 January 1854*

The Inauguration of the Great Western Railway

The Great Western Railway had its beginning in 1833 when a Select Committee of the Legislature recommended approval of a petition by Alan (later Sir Alan) McNab and other prominent men in Hamilton and London for a railway across Southern Ontario. This led to the incorporation of the London and Gore Railroad Company in 1834.[1] Its charter allowed for the construction of a wooden or iron railroad, single or double tracked, from Lake Ontario at Burlington

Bay to London and thence to Lake Huron. However, no railway materialized under this Act. The combination of depressed economic circumstances and the fear of war with the United States brought the intended construction to a halt.

THE GREAT WESTERN RAILWAY OF CANADA.

CHARTERED BY ACT OF LEGISLATURE.

Capital £1,500,000 Currency,—£1,350,000 Sterling,

In 60,000 Shares of £25 Currency,—£22. 10s. Sterling. Deposit £3. 5s. per Share, on Account of the Three First Instalments provided by the Act.

DIRECTION IN CANADA.

SIR ALLAN NAPIER MAC NAB, Speaker of the House of Assembly, President.

WILLIAM M. SHAW, Esq.	JAMES B. EWART, Esq.
JOHN O. HATT, Esq.	PETER CARROLL, Esq.
L. LAWRASON, Esq.	GEORGE S. TIFFANY, Esq.

Corresponding Committee of English Shareholders:—

WILLIAM JAMES CHAPLIN, Esq.	JOHN MASTERMAN, Jun., Esq.
CHARLES DEVAUX, Esq.	JOHN MOSS, Esq.
HENRY JOHN ENTHOVEN, Esq.	THOMAS SMITH, Esq.
ABEL LEWES GOWER, Esq.	MATTHEW UZIELLI, Esq.
GEORGE HUDSON, Esq., M.P.	GREGORY SEALE WALTERS, Esq.
SAMUEL LAING, Esq.	

Solicitors in London:—

Messrs. BIRCHAM & DALRYMPLE, 15, Bedford Row.

Bankers:—

LONDON .... Messrs. MASTERMAN & Co., Nicholas Lane.
LIVERPOOL .... Messrs. MOSS & Co.

Consulting Engineer:—

JOSEPH LOCKE, Esq., F.R.S.

Secretary to the Corresponding Committee in London:—

E. AIMÉ, Esq., 62, King William Street, pro tem.

THIS important Line of Railway was sanctioned by the Canadian Legislature, in the last Session.

The Line of the Great Western Railway of Canada, as authorised by the Act, is 245 miles in length, commencing near Fort Erie, opposite to the town of Buffalo, and terminating at Windsor, on the Detroit river, opposite to the town of Detroit. Its whole course lies within the British territory; and it traverses the most fertile and populous portion of the province of Upper Canada, passing through the town of Hamilton, at the head of the navigation of Lake Ontario, and intersecting the Niagara, London, Gore, and other districts, containing numerous towns and villages, with a rapidly increasing population.

The importance of such a line for national purposes, and for the interests of Canada, is so obvious as to have ensured the favor and support of the Government; while at the same time, it forms a direct Trunk Line for the traffic of the principal towns and districts of Upper Canada with one another, and with the seat of Government; and for the stream of passengers and emigration which flow from this country by way of the St. Lawrence to the upper province.

The principal feature of the undertaking, however, as a commercial enterprize, consists in its uniting this character of a main artery for the local and provincial purposes of Upper Canada with that of a completing link in the great system of thorough communication between the North Western States of America and the upper Valley of the Mississippi on the one hand, and the cities of New York and Boston, and the Sea Board of the Atlantic on the other.

The railways, as privately-owned companies, had the prime task of making money for their shareholders.

John Burtniak Collection

When the enabling legislation was about to expire, the proposal was reconstituted. The Company was renamed the Great Western Railroad Company in 1845 and became the Great Western Railway Company in 1853.[2] An important change in intention was also introduced. As stated in the 1845 Act, "the said Company shall have full power to make or continue their Rail-Road, from the Town of London to Point Edward, at the foot of Lake Huron, and to the Detroit River, and to any point of the Niagara River."[3]

The description of the route was phrased in very general terms. It could have applied to an alignment either to the south or to the north of the Niagara Escarpment. More specifically, if the main line was constructed from London to the upper Niagara River, with a branch to Hamilton, then the severe double crossing of the Escarpment would be avoided. This, indeed, would seem to have been the original intention for, as noted in a later Director's *Report* concerned with the cost of the line:

> "It appears that the estimate was framed upon the assumption that the line starting from the Falls of Niagara, about 100 feet below the level of Lake Erie, would keep on that level and so not have much rise to overcome in reaching the Detroit River. It seems also that no detailed survey and estimate of quantities was then made."[4]

It was by no means certain that a southern routing would be followed by the main line. Furthermore, a possible American line between the Niagara and Detroit Rivers provided severe competition, a conflict which will be discussed in Chapter IV. Eventually, a Great Western route from Hamilton and St. Catharines was obtained on a northern routing only because a Canadian railway linking the existing urban centres of the time was seen to offer a greater trading capacity than one traversing the less densely populated land of the Haldimand Plain south of the Escarpment. If Hamilton and its harbour were to be on the direct route from Detroit to the Niagara River, then the railway would have to descend to the level of Lake Ontario and either re-ascend the Escarpment or cross the River at Queenston-Lewiston.

Considerable debate was generated by the selection of a route and its points of eastern and western termination. As stated in the *Hamilton Gazette* in 1845:

> "The charter fixes but two points to and through which the road must pass, namely the towns of Hamilton and London, and this was done for the purpose of securing it as a great provincial enterprise, capable hereafter of extension down the provinces to Montreal. The eastern termination must be somewhere on the Niagara River, and the western termination must be at some point on the Detroit or St. Clair rivers or on both, branching off at London. The precise points of these terminations will be decided on hereafter by the stockholders, all of whom, whether residents or non residents of the province, have a voice according to the amount of stock held by them. The proper course therefore for every interest either in or out of the province, which may be particularly interested in the termini, is plainly to secure the majority of the stock, this will give such interest the power of controlling the termini of the road. The stockholders here [Hamilton] will be satisfied with having the points of Hamilton and London, and are perfectly willing to leave the termini to the choice of the majority of the stockholders — indeed they cannot do otherwise."[5]

The account then assessed the distance between the two American frontiers from terminals at Buffalo, Niagara and Queenston. The length of the line from Niagara or Queenston to Detroit via Hamilton and London was about 240 miles, and from Buffalo to the same place through the same towns about 255 miles. The distance from Niagara or Lewiston to Port Sarnia, through the same towns, was about 190 miles and from Buffalo about 205 miles. With costs being estimated from $12,000 to $20,000 per mile according to the degree of permanency and solidarity of construction required, the relevance of the shortest feasible route became very apparent.

By this time, the railways of New York State were reaching the Niagara frontier and the Michigan Central was linking Detroit and

Chicago. It was obvious that the shortest route of inter-connection between these two systems, from either Boston or New York via Albany to Chicago and the growing mid-West, was through the Niagara Peninsula. The eastern terminus of the Great Western was therefore moved from Burlington Bay to Niagara Falls, a significant change of intention which placed centres such as St. Catharines, Beamsville and Grimsby on a direct through-route of the emerging North American railway system. The pressures behind this decision involved the external spatial relationships of the Peninsula. They were not internal from within the Peninsula.

Jordan Station was established as the railway village of Bridgeport east of Twenty Mile Creek. William Street lay parallel to the tracks, and Main Street connected to the earlier settlement of Jordan.   *John Burtniak Collection*

The Response in St. Catharines

The *Journal* reported frequently on shareholders' meetings and engineering reports as they became available.[6] The reactions usually supported the railway venture. For example:

> "It affords us the greatest pleasure to observe the gratifying tone of letters from England regarding this important Provincial work. Every packet brings us increased assurances of the lively interest felt in the Great W. line of Railroad, and of the active measures taken by the English shareholders and the Agent of the Company now in England to commence operations at a very early day, and complete the same with as little delay as possible."[7]

Given the notion that prosperity, eternal comfort and the improved well-being of society were just around the corner, who can quibble at such propitious hopes? The prospects of great and continuing advantage were supposedly about to be achieved for St. Catharines and its vicinity.

Grimsby March 9th 1848

We whose names are hereunto Subscribed do agree
to pay to Thos Bingle ——————— the Sums Set Opposite
our Several names on the following conditions, that
is to Say in the event of the Great Western Rail Road
be building their Said Road from Hamilton to the Niagara
River, and making a ——————————— Stopping place
and Depot in the village of Grimsby on the lands of William Nelles
being in the first Concession And Lot Number nine. then we
promise to pay the Several Amounts As annexed the one
Half on the commencing of the Said Rail Road, at the Said
village And the remainder on the Completion of
Said Rail Road ——

Names	£.			Names	£.		
T. J. Fairall	15	0	0	John W Lewis	6	5	0
T. Bingle	12	10	0	Wm Wilson	6	5	0
Ann Fairall				Jona Woolverton	6	5	0
Moses Nell	6	5		Dennis Palmer	5	0	0
S. H. Dean	2	2	0	R. H. Allison	6	5	0
McGill	3	15		Sumner & Nelles	12	10	0
John D Burns	12	10	0	Randall	10	0	0
W. Burns	10	0	0	William Nelles	10	0	0
D. Palmer	10	0	0	John Nixon	6	5	0
W Nelles	12	10	0	G. Vandyke	6	5	0
Charles Nelles	6	5	0		75	0	0
	91	0	0		91		
				£166			

A plea of 1848 from residents in Grimsby that the railway be routed closer to the village.   *Stone Shop Museum, Grimsby*

By March 1847 excitement ran high. Survey parties were in the field to determine the precise route for the tracks,[8] and soon the ceremonial cutting of the first sod was held with great celebration in London.[9] In St. Catharines the *Journal* of 21 October 1847 proclaimed with enthusiastic pride:

"It is with very great pleasure that we announce the commencement of this great and important link of communication between the Eastern and Western States. The gentlemen who have the contract for grading this road from the Niagara River to Hamilton, break ground this day, on Mr. Hainer's farm, in this town. This intimation, we have no doubt, will be hailed with delight by the whole community; and the enterprise ought, as we trust it will, receive whatever aid any individual can give to hasten its final completion."[10]

The work of construction brought in the railroad gangs. The men had to be housed and fed, which provided an extra market opportunity for the local farmers to sell their products. The incoming workers also caused some consternation. As William F. Rannie has noted:

"First through [the present town of] Lincoln came the surveyors, followed during the winter of 1851-52 by obstreperous construction gangs. Comprising the largest part of the construction force were the Irish immigrants who had fled the famine in their homeland. They were a rootless, irresponsible lot, suffering under the brutal and dishonest behaviour of subcontractors and straw bosses, and they returned their treatment in like measure. Farmers along the route constantly lost chickens and other livestock to the workers, and payday brawls occurred regularly."[11]

However, hopes for an early completion of the project were soon seen to be premature. The contractors started work at London, Hamilton, St. Catharines, and the Niagara River, but construction was brought to a standstill when funds dwindled because of unexpected pressures in the money market.[12] Prospects improved when the Company obtained further funds. There were also special pleas that towns along the route should subscribe to the undertaking; the meetings for this purpose were generally described as "well attended by the most respectable inhabitants of the town."[13]

The prospect of progress was enhanced by the attraction of American finance in 1851, and further when it was demonstrated that the railway would provide an essential link in the Grand Trunk system from the Atlantic to the Mississippi. The section of line from Hamilton to the Suspension Bridge was included as part of this Canadian "main line" project in 1851, with other constituent parts including the Hamilton and Toronto Railway and the eastern link to Kingston and Montreal of the Grand Trunk.

The concept of a "main-line" is worth noting. It involved government support for the construction of a continuous railway. Several considerations were at issue. Should the work be commenced before all provinces had guaranteed to provide their share of the costs? Should these important railway works be undertaken by private companies? Should the existing public debt be increased and, if so, to what extend? Initially, the concept featured a railway from Quebec City to Hamilton, but in 1851 it was stated that "the Great Western Railroad. . .shall mean and include the whole of the said Main Line of Railway which the said Great Western Railroad Company are authorized to make from the Grand River, by the way of Burlington Bay, to the Detroit River."[14]

By this enactment, St. Catharines, Grimsby and other centres were placed officially on the emerging main line system of Canadian railway developments. The Peninsula was fulfilling its geographical destiny as an important land-bridge for the new route of inland communications. Railway development within the Peninsula cannot be separated from the role and significance of its North American location astride major routes of entry to the continental interior. The urban centres along the line of track were incidental beneficiaries from this spatial position of the Peninsula within its wider context.

The Construction and Opening of the Line

Work was firmly under way by mid-1852, when the *Journal* recorded that "the contractors are making every preparation to secure an early completion of their heavy work, and during the present month two steam excavators will be at work between St. Catharines and the Niagara River."[15] The construction features along the line included several bridges, embankments and cuttings, which were described as follows:

"The bridge to be erected over the Twenty Mile Creek will be 1200 feet in length and 60 feet high and the bridge over the Sixteen Mile Creek 800 feet in length and of the same height. These two bridges are to be built with trusses of 100 feet span, and will contain upwards of one million feet of timber, which is now being prepared and delivered. The valleys of the Fifteen, Twelve and Ten Mile Creeks are crossed by embankments of about the same height, with culverts of sufficient capacity to pass the water of the creeks at their greatest flow. The stone for these culverts, as likewise for the bridge over the Welland Canal, the St. Davids road viaduct and a great number of smaller culverts, are being placed upon the ground: and with three exceptions, I hope to have the masonry on the entire line of road out of the way before next December, and to have the whole completed by June 1853."[16]

The Great Western Railway bridge over Twenty Mile Creek disrupted navigation.

This date, however, was behind the schedule that had originally been contemplated. The engineering works for the line had been delayed by various mishaps, through the inexperience of its main and sub-contractors, by poor understanding of terrain and underground features, and by a harsh winter with deeply frozen ground. As a consequence, on the anticipated date of opening (December 1852), the Great Western was little more than a scar on the landscape. As noted in G. R. Stevens' history of the Canadian National Railways, the construction gangs had everywhere fallen behind their schedules.[17] There were no local personnel trained in any aspect of railway construction. Acquiring the skills needed to build a railway was very much the day-by-day experience of learning on the job, including both the engineering and administrative tasks which were an inevitable part of every project.

The costs of construction were high, greatly exceeding the estimates. As stated in the Director's *Report* of 1854:

> "The original estimate of the cost of the line was made several years ago, when the price of labour, materials, land and everything relating to the construction of a Railway was extremely low in Canada. . .It had always been understood that the Great Western Railway would be nearly as easily constructed as the lines on the Prairies of the West, and that its cost would therefore bear something like a proportion to the cost of these Western Railways."[18]

One costly item was certainly the dual crossing of the Niagara Escarpment, both to the east of St. Catharines and to the west of Hamilton. The cost of the first 18 miles from the Suspension Bridge, without land, rolling stock or any other charge — the mere cost of the line itself — reached the large sum of $17,900 per mile.[19] The cost of the counter-ascent for 24 miles of line beyond Hamilton rose to $21,500 per mile.[20]

Costs were aggravated further by factors other than the terrain to be crossed. The costs of labour, provisions, materials and land all increased radically; for example, the price of lumber and fencing increased by 30 per cent. Contract prices were not based on a defined sum for the construction works; rather, they varied according to the different types of material excavated, which resulted in a series of almost irreconcilable disputes over the exact quantities of the various kinds of material used.[21] The work also employed numerous small contractors with limited capital and with little or no experience in preparing estimates for the work entailing earth removal, bridging and the construction of station buildings. Almost everything had to be undertaken from an inadequate basis of experience.

Bridge construction at St. Davids and Thorold, indicating a varied approach to the art of design when crossing physical obstacles.

John Burtniak Collection

Rails, purchased in Wales, were itemized with no allowance for the cost of their transportation. Materials had often to be transported along miserable roads from inadequate port facilities. The extent of sidings was under-estimated, far below the absolute requirements of traffic. No allowance was made for extras and contingencies. More land, and at a higher cost than anticipated, was required for stations and depots. Additional rolling stock, engines, passenger cars and freight cars were required because the anticipated traffic had been greatly under-estimated. Such factors necessitated frequent applications to Parliament and to the shareholders for further capital.

Despite these exasperations and the continual need to resolve unexpected difficulties, the arrival of the first locomotives must have created a scene of considerable local interest. Undoubtedly, excitement ran high as the inhabitants in the Peninsula caught their first glimpse of the engines, the new and powerful mode of locomotion which would transform their lives. The purchase of locomotives was fraught with great technical difficulties, as shown by the circumstances surrounding the arrival of the first Great Western steam engine, the *Middlesex,* at Winona. It had been purchased in England, shipped across the Atlantic Ocean and assembled at Kingston. It was then taken over Lake Ontario to the Willson wharf at Winona, where a special track was laid to the main line at Winona Station.[22] Only after these several arrangements was it capable of service on the main line that was then being constructed through the Peninsula.

The actual task of constructing the line was undertaken in several divisions, with the eastern division running from the Suspension Bridge to Hamilton. The construction involved 7,602 men in July 1852. They were employed in gangs, together with 210 horses. The track was distinguished by having no level crossing; roads were either taken over it by public and private bridges or under it by culverts, such arrangements being "most favourable for. . .a road intended for frequent trains at high velocities."[23] It was graded for a single line of track, except that the masonry of all bridge structures was sufficiently wide and sturdy to take a double track. The entire line was 228.5 miles in length, of which 42.25 miles were in the eastern division.

One point of difficulty occurred where the Great Western crossed Twelve Mile Creek near St. Catharines. John T. Clark, the Engineer responsible for constructing the length of line from Hamilton to the Suspension Bridge, indeed advised against its opening when the Directors decided to run a train of passenger cars from Hamilton to the Suspension Bridge in November 1853. He warned: "Due to the failure of Culvert at twelve mile creek. . .this would be a premature movement, and if carried out, would be attended with hazard to life and property."[24]

However, Clark was overruled by his superiors. The line had to be placed into operation for it to become a commercial proposition. The sooner it was opened, the sooner revenue would be generated and the shareholders satisfied. On the first day of November 1853 the new line was officially opened, although it was not completely finished. The *St. Catharines Journal* noted quietly, "with astonishment as well as pleasure, that the Iron Horse was seen passing along in all the dignity of steam."[25]

This historic event was an occasion for jubilant celebration. The contractor had extended a special invitation to local dignitaries to ride the inaugural train, a ceremonial event which nearly ended in disaster. As the *Niagara Mail* recorded:

> "A special train containing about 300 gentlemen left Hamilton about half past twelve P.M. for the Falls, which was greeted on the route by loud cheers from the crowds assembled at every convenient point, to witness the first cars drawn by a locomotive, run on the Great Western. The road being yet untried, the train proceeded slowly but without encountering any mishap until it entered the deep cut between Thorold and St. Davids, when the rails being just laid, yielded somewhat on the soft clay, and the fore part of the locomotive run off the track breaking some parts of the coupling. No further damage was done — but unfortunately the train was yet about six miles from the

The opening of railway facilities provided the opportunity for important, festive events.
Mrs. Mary Sullivan Collection

Suspension Bridge where several thousands of people were waiting its arrival and firing guns and making other species of popular rejoicing. It being seen at once that the accident could not be remedied, in any reasonable time, the company got out of the cars and proceeded to walk the remaining distance, being encouraged by Mr. Zimmerman, however, with the information that he had already sent an express [message] to the Falls for the Carriages and Omnibusses there, to come immediately to meet and take up the wayfarers."[26]

The Introduction of Train Services

Despite this mishap, a regular service was opened ten days later over the eastern section of the line. The journey took two-and-one-half hours from Hamilton to the Suspension Bridge. In mid-December, another memorable event took place with the opening of the line from Hamilton to London, followed quickly in January 1854 by the first through train from Niagara Falls to Windsor. The system expanded rapidly to provide a new array of travel possibilities year by year. The Hamilton-Toronto section opened in December 1855. Construction was carried out by a separate company, the Hamilton and Toronto Railway, which amalgamated with the Great Western in 1856. A branch to Guelph opened in 1857.

The Oberon: a narrow gauge Great Western Railway engine.

St. Catharines Historical Museum, from Public Archives of Canada, C-46979

Rapid expansion and successive improvements also occurred to the inter-connecting routes of the Grand Trunk system from Quebec via the Victoria Bridge over the St. Lawrence to Montreal, Toronto and Sarnia. There were a spate of improvements, new extensions, additional facilities and expanded services — Montreal to Brockville in November 1855; Brockville to Belleville in October 1856; Belleville to Toronto in August 1856; and the first train from Montreal to Toronto in 1856. The Toronto station was built outside the downtown area at the foot of York Street; Union Station, described as "capacious and elegant; the handsomest and most commodious structure of the sort in the Dominion", was not opened until 1873. Westwards, Toronto and Guelph were linked in June 1856; Guelph and Galt in September 1857; and the main line from Rivière-du-Loup in Quebec to Sarnia was completed in 1859.

In his prize essay on Canada written in 1855, J. Sheridan Hogan has summarized the contextual situation of these railways. He predicted that the Grand Trunk "will [when finished] present an uninterrupted line from Portland to Michigan, and the distance by this route is fifty miles less than from New York, has a uniform gauge throughout, and will probably be much the cheapest route".[27] He noted that "it has already diverted a large portion of the trade which previously flowed through other channels in the United States".[28] Hogan also lauded the growth of the Great Western, which:

"has enjoyed a success scarcely paralleled in the railroad history of America. For the month of April, 1854, its receipts were £26,735. For the corresponding month in 1855 its receipts rose to £57,684, showing an increase of nearly 120 per cent. . .Passing through the very garden of Upper Canada, and being the connecting link between the Great Michigan Central Railroad, and the New York Roads which terminate at the Niagara River, its success was never problematical;. . .its future prosperity must be even greater than its past."[29]

The *Dakin*: Great Western Railway Engine No. 8., 1864.

St. Catharines Historical Museum, from Public Archives of Canada, C-28860

St. Catharines was certainly not at the focal point of this expanding system. It was but one point along the line of track; nevertheless, the town had been provided with a new medium of direct access to external centres as might be required for its freight flows and passenger traffic. As with other Ontario towns, its horizons of potential interchange and interaction were being broadened substantially and tangibly with each successive addition to the railway network. A comment upon the changes that had taken place is found in a letter written by James R. Benson of St. Catharines to his son:

"The Rail road is now open to Hamilton and the cars run twice a day — the road is not good and they take nearly two hours. . .if the navigation is open at Christmas to Hamilton you may come home that way which will give you an opportunity of seeing the Road; on the first of December they expect to have it open to Ingersoll or London which will enable us to go up and see them often."[30]

As for the locomotives which were used, N. and H. Mika have described the early situation as follows:

"The first passenger locomotives of the Great Western came from different builders in the United States. Among the earliest ones were the *Canada,* the *Niagara,* the *London* and the *Hamilton,* all 4-4-0 type locomotives with inside cylinders and coupled wheels. Eight ballast or shunting engines were purchased for construction and general work from the Globe Works in Boston. From England came twenty freight engines of the 0-6-0 type with coupled wheels, no trucks and inside cylinders connected to the middle axle. Among them were the *Elephant,* the *Buffalo* and the *Tiger.* Twelve engines arrived from Manchester. The *Spitfire,* and *Firefly* belonged to this group of 2-4-0 type locomotives. By the end of 1857 the Great Western already owned more than seventy engines."[31]

Although the track was inadequately constructed, the first main line was open through the Peninsula. New travel opportunities had dawned and, as revenues increased, the deficiencies of the track and its facilities could be improved gradually over time. The imperfect condition of the track at the time of its opening has been described by William Bowman, Superintendent of the Mechanical Department, as follows:

"The road was not in a fit or proper condition to have been opened; I consider it to have been very dangerous to have used the road at all in the then conditions of the works on the line and track. The road was imperfectly fenced; with long intervals between the fencing, it was not ballasted; the ties were laid upon the surface at subgrade in many instances without being in any way secured by gravel; the cuttings were for the most part only channels cut through the bank, without being sloped off, and at all times liable to slide down upon the track or to encumber the track with stones or stumps to the destruction of the next approaching train. The embankments were dangerously narrow at the top, scarcely wide enough to support the ties, and constantly liable to be washed away, depressing thereby the rail on one or the other side, and exposing the passing trains to be thrown off the track and down the embankment."[32]

In winter and spring, mud accumulated on the track up to a depth of three feet because of inadequate drainage: at times, the engine driver even had to abandon his train in the mud. In addition, the number of available locomotives, passenger, baggage and freight cars proved to be quite inadequate. Equipment was poor and not readily repaired as tools, materials and workshops were in short supply.

Accidents were frequent, and it was no uncommon event for the train to leave the tracks.

One severe accident occurred at Thorold in 1854, one mile east of the station and the new railway bridge over the Welland Canal.[33] Around midnight, the westbound express train hit two horses, with the result that the first of the two second class passenger cars was thrown off the track, and the other crashed into the first car. Seven passengers were killed and the injured were attended by Dr. Theophilus Mack, who was summoned from St. Catharines. Accounts vary as to whether the passengers were Norwegian or German emigrants.

Accidents were frequent on the early railway systems.
John Burtniak Collection

Deposition of Dr. Mack, 7th December, 1854.

THEOPHILUS MACK, of the Town of St. Catharines, in the County of Lincoln, Esquire, M.D., being duly sworn, deposeth and saith: that on or about the seventh day of July last past, he was called upon by Mr. Woodward, a Civil Engineer in the employ of the Great Western Railway Company, and by the Conductor of the passenger train, named Matthews, who requested deponent to afford his professional services to attend certain persons who had suffered from the effects of an accident which had taken place near the Thorold Station. Deponent went with them to the St. Catharine's Station, where he found a locomotive engine and one freight car, containing all the surviving wounded; there were seven who had been hurt; found them all suffering from contusions, and one little girl who was severely injured. These parties, with one exception, were Germans—supposed to be Norwegians. Not considering the case of these people to be so urgent as those at the scene of the accident, deponent, after directing that they should be removed to a hotel and properly cared for, proceeded to the spot on the freight car. He found several dead bodies, and one person still alive under the ruins of the crushed car, who died shortly after deponent got there. Directed one wounded child to be brought down in the freight car back to St. Catharines, and returned himself with the engine-driver on the locomotive. On the way conversed with him and his fireman on the subject of the accident. The driver, whose name deponent does not know, stated, on enquiry, that, on approaching the Thorold Station, he saw three horses on the left hand side of the train. Either the driver or the fireman stated that they had whistled to drive off the animals. Driver added, that the horses crossed the track, and, in crossing, the engine struck them both; one was thrown off the track, and the other struck down, run over and killed. In reply to a question from Mr. Woodward, the engineer, who was also on the locomotive, the driver stated that, on striking the horse, he directed his fireman to brake up, which statement was confirmed by the fireman, who added, that he had done all he could; they both affirmed that the way on the train was too great to stop immediately. Did not pull up until they reached Thorold Station. Deponent considers the distance between Thorold Station and the place where marks and cuts on the ties indicated that the car had first left the track, to be about three quarters of a mile. The night of the occurrence was clear moonlight. Returned from the scene of the accident between twelve and two; at this time the night was clear, as above described.

THEOPHS. MACK.

Sworn before us, at St. Catharines,
this 7th day of December, 1854.
WILLIAM F. COFFIN,
M. C. CAMERON.

Another accident occurred five months later within a short distance of St. Catharines, at the eastern approach to the temporary trestle bridge over Twelve Mile Creek. The bridge at each end had a short and sharp curve, where trains were required to proceed slowly and with great caution. In this instance a boy aged 12, employed in carrying water to a work-gang, was hit by an engine and seriously injured. A more serious accident occurred at the same point in 1858. This time a freight train left Clifton, followed shortly afterwards by a mixed train. When the first train reached St. Catharines, it was found that the last six cars had become detached. The second train crashed into these cars, killing the engineer.[34]

Despite the inadequacies of construction and the personal dangers associated with railway travel, every new opening was marked with great celebration. St. Catharines was now linked on land and at all seasons to the Suspension Bridge and the American railway system, westwards across the Peninsula to Windsor, and around the head of the lake to Toronto and eastwards to the Atlantic seaboard. The date November 1853 is therefore as significant as the first "Climbing of the Mountain" by canal boats in December 1829. The earlier feat, accomplished a mere quarter-century previously, had provided a direct navigable route from the St. Lawrence to the mid-west of the continent. There were now, from 1853 onwards, road, rail *and* water routes in combination and in competition. The potential and capability of St. Catharines had been expanded vastly, but so too had the prowess of its adjacent urban centres, including Hamilton. Isolation had diminished, but the scope for rivalry and inter-urban competition in business, customers and markets had been enhanced.

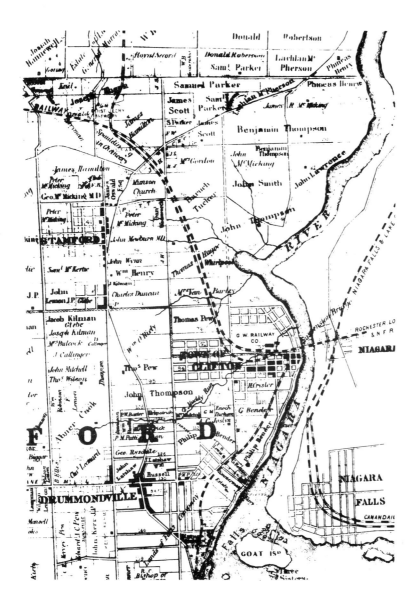

Fig. 2.1 A Railhead Settlement, The Town of Clifton, 1862.

Tremaines' Map of the Counties of Lincoln and Welland, 1862

Clifton Station, ca. 1865, with the Suspension Bridge in the background.
St. Catharines Historical Museum, from Public Archives of Canada, PA-103132

A business card advertises the social facilities that were attracted to Clifton Station.
Mrs. Mary Sullivan Collection

The Major Railway Features

At the eastern end of the line the Niagara River had to be crossed. This was accomplished initially by the ferry steamer *Maid of the Mist,* but this facility was soon replaced by the Suspension Bridge which carried the railway across the River into New York State. The presence of this important bridge (to be discussed in Chapter VI) created a new international border crossing and gave rise to a railway centre (Fig. 2.1) which became the downtown area of modern Niagara Falls. Buildings associated with this railway centre included the passenger station and a restaurant at this changeover stop, terminal facilities, a round house for servicing locomotives, freight storage sheds, customs, and (later) immigration offices.

Trains were staffed and supplied with water and fuel at the Suspension Bridge. A report of 1854 by the Company's Engineer has described some of the difficulties which then existed.[35] The freight house was being enlarged in order to accommodate autumn freight and the buildings and sidings were being re-arranged in order to accommodate the additional traffic which was expected when the Suspension Bridge was opened. Supplying water for the locomotives was noted as a problem because this had to be pumped to the depot, but plans were under way to use a source one-and-a-half miles distant, in order to provide a head of 25 feet and thereby avoid the necessity of pumping.

The station building was of board and batten construction. It has been described as "a long low wooden station of the traditional vertical clapboard style, with wide overhanging eaves and a wood plank platform."[36] It was built on Bridge Street and served until 1879 when it burned to the ground. The station was replaced on the original site by the present brick and stone structure. The new building has been described as "a long red brick and stone building, with a two-storey centre, flanked by two, long, one-storey wings. It had large gothic windows, much Victorian 'gingerbread' ornamental woodwork under its eaves, and massive wood-panelled entrance doors, which, in 1879, made it the envy of the frontier".[37] Internally, there were two waiting rooms, separated by a central ticket office which served both rooms. Like its predecessor, it was larger and more pretentious than might be expected in a centre of small population. But counterbalancing factors included an important frontier location, the Canadian entrance to the Great Western system, its prestigious eastern terminal, and the expectations of an expanding tourist industry. These were deemed of sufficient importance to merit the design and construction of a distinctive structure.

Crossing the topographic barrier of the Escarpment provided a second important feature along the line. The summit level of the Great Western Railway east of Hamilton was located three miles from the Niagara River, above St. Davids on the edge of the Escarpment. The descent here dropped from 362 feet above Lake Ontario to 140 feet at the point where the line crossed the Welland Canal. The maximum grade on this descent was 39 feet per mile. This severe slope had to be overcome by trains travelling east and, as fortune would have it, the direction of heaviest freight traffic. A comparable grade also existed west of Hamilton where the railway re-climbed the Escarpment, but here the change in levels followed the principal direction of freight movement.

To make this eastern crossing of the Escarpment as easy as possible, three deep cuttings were excavated between St. Catharines and the Suspension Bridge. The first was the approach to Twelve Mile Creek, while the other two were situated between Thorold and St. Davids. The latter encompassed the actual rise and the change in levels up the slope of the Escarpment, with one being excavated in hard-clay mixed with boulders and the other in limestone bedrock. The material from these excavations was used for the construction of embankments.[38]

A third feature of interest was to be found at the point where the Great Western crossed over the Welland Canal. This location was to the west of present day Merritton (Fig. 2.2). The railway engineers had proposed a crossing just below Lock 11, using an extension of that lock as the foundations for a swing bridge. The Welland Canal Engineer, by contrast, proposed a bridge in a central position between Locks 10 and 11. As Samuel Keefer has observed:

> "To place the bridge midway between Locks 10 and 11. . .would not only prove an injury to the navigation, but a serious inconvenience to the Road; as regards the Canal, it would divide a most convenient basin into two inconvenient ones, too small to afford the necessary accommodation for passing vessels in both directions at the same time; and as regards the Railroad, it would break up a long straight line 16 2/3 miles in extent, and oblige the introduction of three or four extra curves, increasing the expense and the hazard of running the Road."[39]

Railway locomotive at the American side of the Suspension Bridge.   *Francis J. Petrie Collection*

Fig. 2.2   The Great Western Railway at Merritton, 1876.
H. R. Page, Illustrated Historical Atlas of the Counties of Lincoln and Welland, 1876

A straight line of track passing across the Ontario Lakeshore Plain, now the Niagara Fruit Belt, ca. 1910.

St. Catharines Historical Museum, from Public Archives of Canada, C-38393

This unique point of Railway-Canal crossing was perceived as an extremely important strategic location for industrial development. As Keefer continued: "It must be remembered that the place where the road passes the Canal, from its situation, and the extensive water power at command, is likely to become the seat of a manufacturing Town of some importance."[40] This reasoning provided further weight for retaining a straight line of railway because:

"When this ground is built upon, the approach to a bridge by a curve, will have the view obstructed by the buildings; the engine driver will not be able to see if the bridge is open or shut, and the greatest inconvenience and danger will result from such an arrangement of the crossing. The preservation of the straight line is therefore as important to the Canal as it is essential to the safety of the life and property embarked upon the rail."[41]

A fourth feature was the crossing of Twelve Mile Creek. In 1854 Lowe Reid, the Company's Engineer, stated:

"Two months before the opening of the Eastern Section of the line, the culvert over the Twelve-Mile Creek at St. Catharines broke down, when the heavy clay embankment was being formed over it. It had been unfortunately built on an insecure natural foundation, without any artificial aid beyond a bed of concrete and a double course of planking, and the consequence was, that the immense pressure of the bank over it, added to its own weight, broke the bench walls through the upper crust of the foundation, and caused them to settle 5 1/2 feet into a stratum of soft clay beneath. This culvert was 25 feet span, a heavy structure, began nearly two years before the accident occurred. The Line was opened by means of a temporary trestle structure, built over the spot where this accident happened; and now a more durable trestle viaduct has been built, for a length of 900 feet, on a deviated line, so as to admit, at a future time, of the reconstruction of the culvert, or the substitution of a viaduct built upon to the level of the rails."[42]

A fifth feature was provided by the alignment of the Railway in the vicinity of St. Catharines. It was constructed almost a mile to the south of the developed urban area, and here crossed the valleys of several small tributary streams. This route was part of a long straight length of track from beyond Beamsville to Thorold, cutting diagonally across the survey grid of Grantham Township. The line and the station were also unexpectedly disassociated from the main nucleus of settlement, a point of substance which will be discussed in Chapter VII.

Further east where the track crossed Louth, Clinton and Grimsby Townships, its course ran on a straight west-north-west to east-south-east alignment having negligible gradients. It now lay wholly below the former Iroquois Shoreline, which it had crossed at St. Catharines, and provided no points of great engineering consequence except for the temporary trestle and later stone bridge which were thrown over Twenty Mile Creek. It served the line of settlement that had been established along the Queenston-Ancaster Road, with Grimsby being of particular importance (Fig. 2.3).

Passenger and Freight Traffic

The *raison d'être* for any line must be the train services and the passengers and freight volumes that are carried over the new facility. A schedule of 1854 has provided some fascinating and valuable information about railway operations. As the line was single-track, stations such as Grimsby and Bridgeport (later Jordan Station) were provided with side trackage where trains could pass each other. The regulations read:

"Conductors will not pass these appointed shunting stations with their trains, unless upon properly authenticated telegraph messages, except that freight or mixed trains shall keep out of the way of passenger trains. . .All trains, in shunting, to give preference to the express trains. Gravel trains shall give preference to passenger and freight trains in shunting."[43]

At this time, St. Catharines had five trains running daily in each direction, including those described as freight, accommodation, light express, mail express and night express. Travelling east these left at 3:50 and 6:20 a.m., and at 12:25, 3:40 and 7:45 p.m. Travelling west the comparable departure times were at 12:05, 7:55 and 11:00 a.m., and at 2:35 and 3:05 p.m. The mail and light express trains stopped at the Suspension Bridge, St. Catharines, Grimsby and Hamilton, but the night express did not stop at Grimsby on this schedule. For the express runs, it took 30-35 minutes to reach Niagara Falls, 65-70 minutes to Hamilton, 4-4.5 hours to London, and 8-9 hours to Windsor. There were steamer connections at Hamilton for Toronto, Kingston, Montreal and other places on Lake Ontario and the St. Lawrence River, and stage coach connections at Paris, Galt, Woodstock, Ingersoll and London. St. Catharines is not mentioned for its transfer links, though advertisements in the local newspapers have indicated that horse-drawn carriages from the major hotels met each train. Fares were 1s. 8d. to Suspension Bridge, 6s. 3d to Hamilton, and 32s. 6d to Detroit.

The traffic generated at the St. Catharines station up to 31 July 1854 totalled almost £2,829. Passengers yielded the greatest return, bringing in £2,418 or about 85 per cent of the total. The number of passengers handled (9,733), however, was exceeded by the railway terminals at the Suspension Bridge (53,413) and Windsor (29,656), and was also considerably less than at Hamilton, London or Paris. On the other hand, the St. Catharines traffic, whether passenger or freight, exceeded the combined total from all stations en route from Thorold to Stoney Creek along the Iroquois Lakeshore Plain. These details are summarized in Table 2.1.

Table 2.1

Passenger and Freight Traffic on the Great Western Railway to 31 July, 1854.

Station	Passengers No.	Passengers Amount (£)	Sundries by Passenger Train (£)	Freight and Livestock Tons	Freight and Livestock Amount (£)	Total Traffic Amount (£)
Suspension Bridge	53,413	40,025	502	5,110	9,755	50,282
Thorold	1,932	381	10	194	124	515
St. Catharines	9,733	2,418	31	483	381	2,829
Beamsville	2,718	434	3	45	34	472
Grimsby	3,696	573	9	132	107	690
Stoney Creek	1,129	149	—	2	2	151
Hamilton	39,567	14,646	239	6,005	7,649	22,533

Source: Great Western Railway, Statement of Passenger and Freight Traffic, JLA, v. 13, 1855, Appendix YY, p. 171. The statistics are rounded off to the nearest whole number.

An interesting account of the daily workload at the St. Catharines station in 1861 is contained in the diary of Hugh Neilson, then a lad aged 14 who worked at this station.[44] His routine began at 6:30 a.m. in readiness for the morning freight train which arrived at 8:05. He finished work 12 hours later, or closer to midnight when the trains were delayed. The longer hours were common during the winter months and whenever derailments had blocked the track. His regular monthly salary was $25.00, rising to about $31.00 with overtime.

The frequent issue of timetables attempted to cope with changing circumstances on the line. In February he noted with exasperation that the thirtieth timetable had been brought into operation, the fourth in as many weeks.[45] Many summer excursions and special freight trains are described in his diary, as well as the emigrant and cattle trains. He indicated the number of cars when the train was unusually long; for example, in August, he noted "that Special Passenger Train from Hamilton had 11 first class cars on. It's an Excursion for the Benefit of the St. Georges Society of Hamilton."[46] Trains of 22, 26 and 27 passenger cars are each recorded. Special freight trains became a regular feature — "we have a special freight train, regularly every day now, from Hamilton to Suspension Bridge and back"[47] — and the volume of traffic increased steadily. "We had ten freight trains yesterday, five east and five west, more than ever I saw on this end of the road before."[48] Sometimes the arrival of special goods is noted, such as the supply of large cannon to fortify Port Dalhousie and Port Colborne.[49] The type of goods stored in the freight shed is indicated when thefts are described: "Some person broke into a sugar Hogshead at the Freight House last night and took away 56 pounds of sugar, they don't know who has done it."[50]

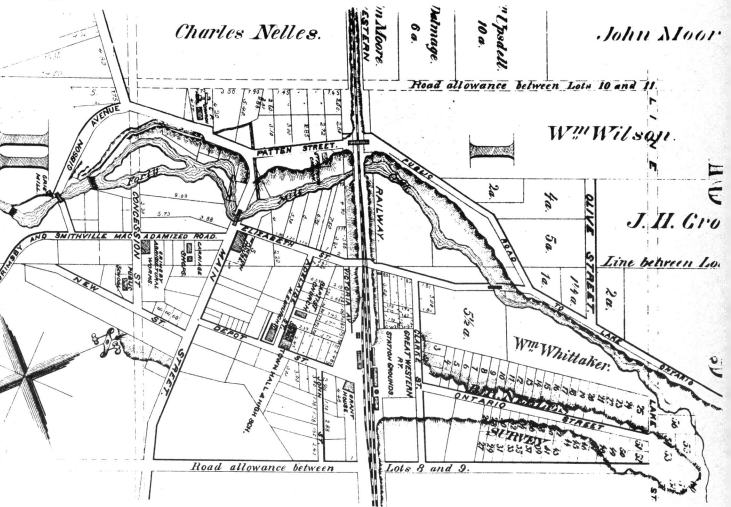

Fig. 2.3   The Great Western Railway at Grimsby, 1876.

H. R. Page, *Illustrated Historical Atlas of the Counties of Lincoln and Welland, 1876*

Reports show that the Railway could not always cope with the amount of traffic that accumulated, because of shortages in rolling stock or locomotives. Also, the single track operations and the use of the provincial rather than the standard gauge, both contributed to the problems. For example, the *Journal* in 1856 carried an article describing the dilemma resulting from a shortage of cars and engines:

"At the present time there are 205,000 tons of goods lying at Detroit, for carriage by that railway. These having, in a great measure accumulated since the ice on the Detroit River obstructed the navigation so that the transit has been interrupted. That immense pile of goods would fill 25,000 cars, and as each train is not, on the average, comprised of more than twenty cars, it follows that it will take 1500 trains to transport the load. But there are only 4 good's trains per day running East from Windsor, and at that rate it will take a period of sixty weeks to clear off the accumulation supposing that no further additions were made to it. The great want of the company at the present time is engine power. In October last, they purchased from the Grand Trunk Co. eight of their fine engines, but as these had to be taken to pieces and conveyed up, some of them are not yet running. Other engines are expected to arrive from England early in the spring, and exertions are being made on all sides to meet the traffic demand, but at the present time it is unable to do so."[51]

WINDSOR TO SUSPENSION BRIDGE (NIAGARA FALLS), &c.

Distances. Intermediate.	Distances. From Windsor.	(GOING EAST.) STATIONS.	1 Freight.	2 Accomo.	3 Light Ex.	4 Mail Ex.	5 Mixed.	6 Mixed.	7 Night Ex.
.....	.....	WINDSOR depart.	Passenger Car attached at Hamilton.	.....	A.M. 7.40	A.M. 11.20	P.M. 3.00	.....	P.M. 7.10
19	19	Rochester.		.....	8.20	P.M.	.....	.....	.....
13½	32½	Baptiste Creek.		.....	.....	12.30	.....	.....	.....
13	45½	Chatham.		.....	9.15	1.00	5.20	.....	8.50
15	60½	Thamesville.		.....	.....	.....	6.20	.....	9.20
13	73½	Wardsville.		.....	10.05	1.50	7.00	.....	9.45
6½	80	Mosa.		.....	.....	.....	7.20	.....	.....
9½	89½	Ekfrid.		.....	10.40	2.25	7.50	.....	10.25*
5	94½	Adelaide Rd.		.....	.....	.....	8.20	.....	.....
5	99½	Lobo.		.....	11.05	2.50	8.40	.....	10.55*
		LONDON arrive.	.....	.....	11.30	3.15	9.15	.....	11.20
10¼	109¾	LONDON depart.	A.M. 6.00	A.M. 7.00	11.40	3.25	.....	P.M. 4.20	11.30
9½	119¼	Dorchester.	.....	7.20	P.M.		.....	4.45	A.M. .....
9½	128¾	Ingersoll.	7.00	7.45	12.10	4.00	.....	5.10	12.10
4¼	133	Beachville.	7.20	8.00	12.20		.....	5.25	.....
5	138	Woodstock	7.45	8.15	12.35	4.25	.....	5.45	12.35
11¾	149¾	Princeton.	8.30	8.50	.....	4.50	.....	6.25	.....
7	156¾	Paris	9.20	9.15	1.20	5.05	.....	6.55	1.20
9¾	166½	Fairchild's Creek	9.45	9.40	.....	5.30	.....	7.25	.....
12	178½	GALT depart.	.....	8.30	.....	4.00	.....	.....	.....
		GALT arrive.	.....	10.20	.....	6.30	.....	.....	.....
10½	177	Flamboro'.	10.25	10.10	.....	.....	.....	8.05	2.00
3½	180½	Dundas.	10.40	10.20	2.10	.....	.....	8.20	.....
5¼	185¾	HAMILTON arrive.	11.05	10.40	2.30	6.25	.....	8.40	2.30
		HAMILTON depart.	P.M. 4.20	10.50	2.40	6.35			2.40
6½	192¼	Stoney Creek.	4.40	11.05			.....	.....	
10	202¼	Grimsby.	5.15	11.25	3.10	.....	.....	.....	.....
4¾	207	Beamsville.	5.35	11.30	.....	.....	.....	.....	.....
5	212	Jordan.	5.55	.....	3.30	.....	.....	.....	.....
5¾	217¾	St. Catherines.	6.20	P.M. 12.25	3.40	7.45	.....	.....	3.50
2	219¾	Thorold.	6.35	12.25	.....	.....	.....	.....	.....
9¼	229	NIAGARA FALLS, (arrive.)	7.20	1.00	4.10	8.20	.....	.....	4.25

* Flag Stations.

A Great Western Time Table, 1854, indicating railway connections and time distances from the Niagara Peninsula. *JLA, 1855*

From Great Western to Grand Trunk Railway

Later events in the evolution of the Great Western Railway are less exciting than the drama of its creation. Nevertheless, they are significant for their ongoing contribution to the regional landscape. For example, many improvements to the track were made over the next few decades, including the adoption of steel rails, the reduction of gauge, the replacement of bridges, and doubling of the track at the turn of the century. One major change occurred when the second enlargement of the Welland Canal was authorized by the Dominion Parliament in 1871. Work commenced in 1873 on this, the Third Welland Canal project. This new route to the north of the Escarpment now bypassed its traditional route in the river valleys next to St. Catharines. The new Canal was aligned on a direct route from Port Dalhousie to Thorold, which necessitated a new rail crossing.

At this point the line ascended the Escarpment at a grade of about 38 feet to the mile on both sides of the Canal intersection. The Railway would not accept a swing bridge because of the anticipated delays and its potential danger. They insisted that a tunnel be constructed for the safe passage of railway traffic. Agreement was reached between the Canal and the Railway that this would be located to the south of the existing track, and that it would be approached by curves of less than 1,443 feet in radius with the gradient nowhere exceeding 42 feet per mile (Fig. 2.4). The tunnel itself, on a gentle arc, was 665 feet long providing a semi-circular arch 16 feet wide and 18 feet high.[52]

The first train, loaded with dignitaries, ran through the tunnel in February 1881.[53] Eventually, after 50 years of usage, it was abandoned and the track was returned to its original alignment when the Fourth Welland Canal was opened in the 1930's. The tunnel, however, has survived as a unique feature of Canadian railway architecture. Where else in Canada does there now exist an abandoned railway tunnel under an abandoned canal? Both the tunnel and canal now posses a significance for conservation.[54]

Amalgamation between the Great Western and the Grand Trunk systems was approved by the Great Western shareholders in 1882. It was legalized by the Canadian Parliament in 1884, when statutory approval was granted for the stock of the Great Western Railway Company to be acquired by the Grand Trunk Railway Company.[55] Somewhat earlier (in 1870), the Grand Trunk had purchased the Buffalo and Lake Huron Railway,[56] and the Welland Railway was sold to the Grand Trunk in 1884.[57] From the point of view of the Grand Trunk, this amalgamation was consolidation; from the point of view of the Great Western the change in ownership represented the end to a significant and noteworthy era of railway achievement.

The railway tunnel under the Third Welland Canal at Thorold exemplifies the stone mason's craft.   *Francis J. Petrie Collection*

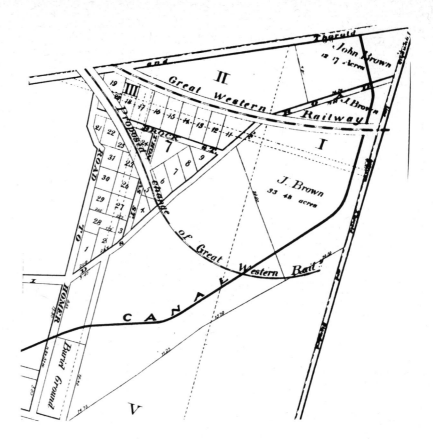

Fig. 2.4   The Great Western Railway and the Third Welland Canal at
Thorold, 1876.   *H. R. Page, Illustrated Historical Atlas of Lincoln
and Welland Counties, 1876*

This union ended a long saga of rivalry, but amalgamation between the two Companies came not as a surprise. The need for some form of closer association had been broached on several previous occasions, in order to improve relations and to effect savings. For example, in 1862, the possibility of combining receipts and placing both under one management had been discussed. This action was accepted by the Companies, but the Legislature was not receptive to the idea and it had to be abandoned. Especially during the late 1860's, a policy of using joint stations wherever possible had developed, which eased the interchange of traffic and reduced the level of operating expenses for the two Railways. Fusion was hastened by the economic depression of 1873 and increasing competition between the Great Western and American railroad interests. The American-owned Canada Southern and the competing Great Western "Air Line" route (to be discussed in Chapter IV) are important in this respect.

The Grand Trunk, like the Great Western, was an important pioneer line. It began life when the Company was incorporated in 1852 to construct a line from Toronto via Belleville and Kingston to Montreal.[58] It provided a serious competitor to the Great Western, with a route on the north shore of Lake Ontario and with sea outlets at Montreal, Quebec City and Portland (Maine). Both Railways had entered into many previous amalgamations and, at the date of union, 825 miles of Great Western track were added to the 1500 miles of the Grand Trunk system. A new possibility for monopolistic price control was introduced to the Peninsula by this union of two major railways (Fig. 2.5).

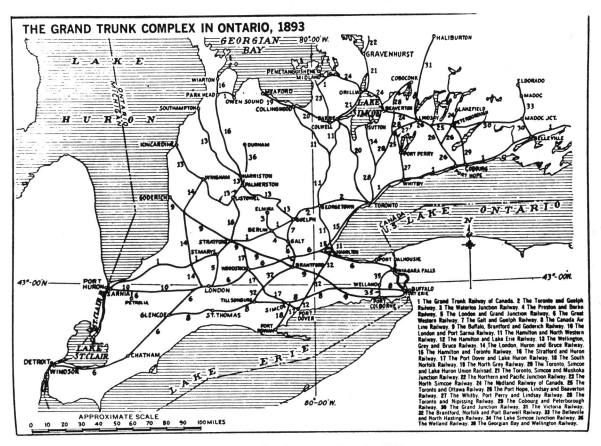

Fig. 2.5 The Grand Trunk Railway System in Southwestern Ontario, 1893.

G. R. Stevens, Canadian National Railways, 1966

As a result of the new ownership, the increasing volumes of railway traffic, and changed attitudes to design by the railway architects, the Grand Trunk in 1882 began the task of reconstructing and remodelling their station buildings along its newly acquired line of track. E. A. Willmot has this to say about the visual consequences of this process, using the station at Grimsby in illustration:

> "The conservative designs used during the 1850s and 1860s were practically shelved, and the new railway stations became more ornamental. Grimsby's handsome station is an example of the imaginative trend which developed in that era.
>
> "Turrets were a popular characteristic of Victorian homes, and railway architects were aware of the prestige they added to any building. The combination of both a conical and polygonal turret gracing one roof was unusual, and the effect was indeed pleasing in the Grimsby station.
>
> "An impression of great height was given to this single story station by the vertical board-and-batten construction, the tall sets of narrow windows, the elongated brackets supporting the eaves, and the steeply pitched planes of the roof. As in most stations, the turrets were purely ornamental."[59]

With these attributes the station was considered to be sufficiently worthy of preservation and, in the mid-1970's it was refurbished and converted into a series of boutique shops. The station at Niagara Falls has received comparable treatment, with a gift shop being established in one part of the building. Such changes are both sad and commendable — sad because the great nineteenth century enthusiam for railways has been eclipsed by new forms of movement, and commendable because these important railway features are likely to remain as reminders of the grandeur of a bygone age. Such links with the past are to be cherished for, as Kevin Lynch has observed, "the rise of industrial archaeology is a hopeful sign...Since we cannot be certain what will be most relevant in the future, we have an obligation to save some characteristic evidence of every major period."[60] Other stations have indeed been saved for new purposes, including those at Stevensville, St. Anns and Jordan Station. Such examples of recycling retain the aura of the railway era and are to be recommended.

The Station at Merritton on the former **Great Western** main line
John Burtniak Collection

Grimsby Station on the Great Western main line of track became the most important between St. Catharines and Hamilton.   *Charles Lamont Collection*

Chapter III

North-South Railway Routes

Two railway routes were constructed across the Peninsula for the essential purpose of providing a link by rail from Lake Erie to Lake Ontario. The first, which became the Erie and Niagara Railway, was the least important of the two ventures. The second, the Welland Railway, was promoted as a project that would assist the flow of traffic through the Welland Canal, to provide a rare instance of unanimity between the canal and railway modes of transportation. The Welland Railway may also be regarded as a railway achievement nurtured from within the Peninsula. It owes particular debts for its success both to William Hamilton Merritt as its prime spokesman and to the Town of St. Catharines for municipal support.

The mouth of the Welland River had to be crossed before there could be a continuous north-south railway route along the Niagara River.   *John Burtniak Collection*

The Erie and Niagara Railway

The Erie and Ontario Railroad, introduced in Chapter I, was saved from oblivion when it obtained a revised charter in 1852. This authorized the company "to vary or alter in their discretion the line or route of their present road. . .and to pass by or near the Niagara Fall's Suspension Bridge, and thence to the Queenston Mountain at the ravine leading to St. Davids,. . .and thence. . .to the said Niagara River at or near the said Town of Niagara."[1]

The line was rebuilt for operation by steam and was opened from Niagara to Chippawa in 1854 using the gauge of 5 feet 6 inches.

The route remained broadly parallel to, but inland from, the Niagara River. At this time, a change in the route was introduced in order to secure an easier grade by crossing the Escarpment further west near St. Davids. Advantage was taken of the buried St. Davids Gorge in "climbing the mountain" and the St. Davids station was located where the track crossed the major east-west highway of the Peninsula, namely the Queenston-Grimsby road. To the south of the Escarpment, the track ran parallel to the Great Western Railway, which had been opened only a few months previously. It then approached closer to the Suspension Bridge than previously so that it could serve the new centres of Clifton and Elgin, before following the rim of the Gorge to Chippawa. There were stations at St. Davids, Queenston and Niagara, each with passenger and freight facilities.

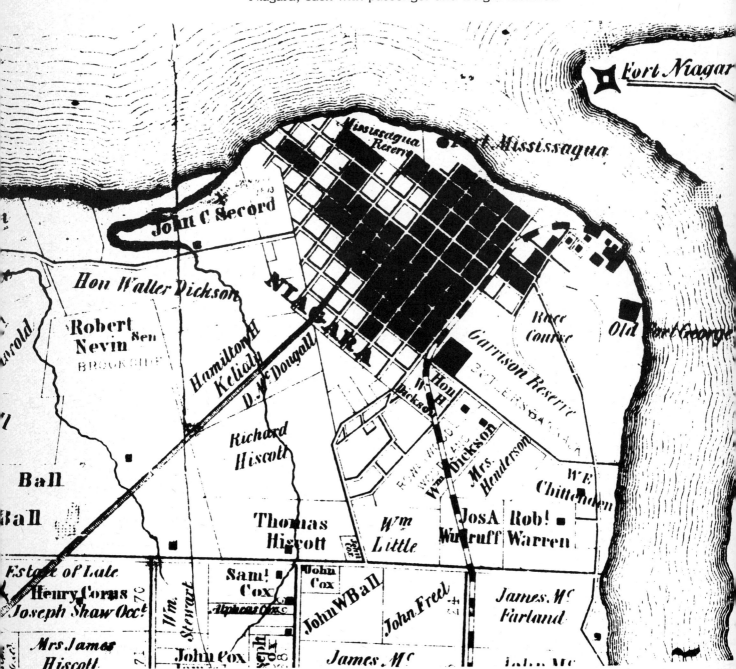

Fig. 3.1   The Erie and Ontario Railroad at Niagara, 1862.

Tremaines' Map of the Counties of Lincoln and Welland, 1862

Macklem's Foundry at Chippawa.   *Francis. J. Petrie Collection*

The Erie and Ontario was the third steam railway to be operated in Ontario, ranking after the Northern Railway and the first section of the Great Western. Its inauguration was recorded in the *Niagara Mail* as follows:

> "The first Locomotive on the Track. A new locomotive called the
> *Clifton* was placed upon the Erie and Ontario Railway yesterday and
> commenced travelling on the road as far as the track is laid. It worked
> admirably and the road is very firm and smooth. The completion of
> our railway will doubtless be made by the time appointed, viz the 1st of
> June next. Niagara will not long remain set down in a corner by her-
> self, but will we trust, soon be in the thick of railway progress."[2]

The engine, probably constructed at the Macklem foundry in
Chippawa[3], provided gallant service. According to a timetable of 1854,
the morning train left Chippawa at 7:25 a.m., and arrived at Niagara
(Fig. 3.1) via Clifton House (Niagara Falls) and the Suspension Bridge
at 8:35 a.m., where it connected with the steamers *Samuel Zimmerman* and *Peerless* for Toronto. Returning, the train left Niagara at 9:00
a.m. and reached Chippawa at 10:05 a.m. The second train of the day
left Chippawa at 2:25 p.m. and returned from Niagara at 4:00 p.m. At
the Suspension Bridge there were connections with the Great Western, Niagara Falls and Buffalo, and the New York Central railways,
and therefore direct lines to Buffalo, Albany, Boston and New York.
The journey from Toronto to the Falls took three and one-half hours.
As no railroad existed round the head of Lake Ontario at this time, a
direct steamer connection to the Atlantic Ocean was important and
profitable because of the increased demand for supplies created by
the Crimean War.[4]

The whistle of a new locomotive must have provided a novel
and somewhat raucous sound if a newspaper comment of 1855 is to be
believed. The *Niagara Mail* then stated that "a new locomotive, called
the Niagara, 'with a scream like a Russian's, in the hands of a Con-
naught Ranger', was placed on the Erie and Ontario Railway on Monday last."[5] Noisy or not, the analogy itself is worth noting as a point of
human interest about railway developments. The steam whistle has
become a nostalgic memory of railways, but was its sound necessarily
appreciated at the dawn of the railway era?

SUMMER ARRANGEMENT!

TORONTO AND BUFFALO

ERIE AND ONTARIO

1855.

RAILROAD

FOUR DAILY TRAINS, SUNDAYS EXCEPTED

FROM CHIPPAWA TO NIAGARA, C. W.   ONE TRAIN ON SUNDAYS.

TRAINS OF THIS ROAD CONNECT AT CHIPPAWA WITH THE

STEAMER CLIFTON

From Buffalo, and at Suspension Bridge with BUFFALO AND NIAGARA FALLS,

New York Central and Great Western Railroads,

FROM THE EAST AND WEST.   At Niagara, C. W., the Trains Connect with the Steamers

ZIMMERMAN & PEERLESS

Which Form a SEMI-DAILY LINE FOR TORONTO, and also connect with the

AMERICAN EXPRESS AND MAIL LINE STEAMERS

FOR KINGSTON, OGDENSBURG AND MONTREAL.

AT TORONTO CONNECTIONS ARE MADE WITH THE

ONTARIO, SIMCOE & HURON RAILWAY

For Collingwood, Sault St. Marie, Lake Superior and all Ports on Lake Michigan.

ALSO, CONNECT WITH ROYAL MAIL STEAMERS FOR KINGSTON & MONTREAL.

With these Connections, this Route affords the Traveler, A QUICK, SAFE AND CHEAP PASSAGE, to all Points in Connection, whilst the UNRIVALLED BEAUTY of the SCENERY makes it the
MOST ATTRACTIVE ROUTE TO THE TOURIST ON THE NORTH AMERICAN CONTINENT.

Passengers purchasing Tickets on the AMERICAN SIDE cross the Great Railway Suspension Bridge Free of Charge. Those coming from the West CHANGE CARS ON THE CANADA SIDE.

BAGGAGE CHECKED THRO' AND NO CHARGE FOR HANDLING BY THIS LINE

FOR FURTHER PARTICULARS SEE SMALL BILLS AND TIME TABLES.

TICKETS can be had at all Ticket Offices of N. Y. Central R. R., at the Clifton House, at the Company's Office, No. 1 International Hotel, Niagara Falls, on the Boats of the Line, or of their Agents

N. D. PALMER, Gen'l Agent, N. Falls.   Clapp, Matthews & Co., Printers, Buffalo.   GEO. B. REDFIELD, Supt.

An Erie and Ontario Railroad poster indicating its railway services and
connections, 1855.

Niagara Historical Museum

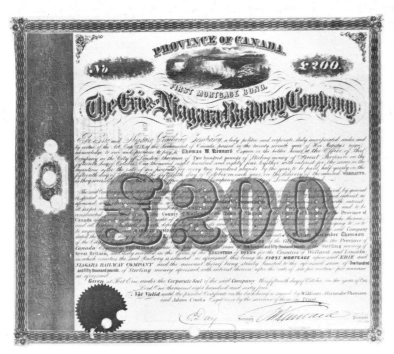

A bond for the Erie and Niagara Railway, 1864.   *John Burtniak Collection*

In 1857, the Fort Erie Railroad Company was incorporated with power to construct a line from Fort Erie to Chippawa. Its charter also permitted "a branch from some point on the said road near the Great Bend of the Niagara River in the Township of Willoughby to Port Robinson."[6] The expectation was, therefore, of a possible connection between the Erie and Ontario Railroad line along the Upper Niagara River and that which was constructed along the Welland Canal. This would have provided a direct railway route from St. Catharines to Buffalo via Port Robinson. In 1863, the Fort Erie company purchased the Erie and Ontario Railroad and changed the name by statute to the Erie and Niagara Railway.[7] Linkage of the two sections, that is, south from Niagara and north from Fort Erie, meant that the Welland River (Chippawa Creek) had to be crossed if a continuous railway along the frontier from Niagara to Fort Erie was to be provided. This was done initially by a low wooden trestle and swing bridge which would not interfere with canal-river navigation. (This structure was replaced by a steel bridge in 1909-1910). The Railway then ran close to the bank of the Niagara River, crossing the several small creeks by wooden bridges. At the southern end of the line there was first a dock on the Niagara River at Fort Erie but, after the construction of the International Bridge at Bridgeburg, the line ran directly into downtown Buffalo.

The track of the Erie and Niagara Railway was leased briefly to the Great Western Railway in 1864. At this time, the Great Western was contemplating the construction of a loop line to the south of the Niagara Escarpment, but this scheme was abandoned by the Great Western for the alternative possibility of using part of the Welland Railway and constructing a new line from the Welland Railway to the Suspension Bridge. By this decision, the Erie and Niagara Railway did not become part of the Great Western system. Instead, it gradually assumed a new role as part of the Canada Southern Railway. This history of an American railroad link between the Niagara and Detroit Rivers will be recounted in Chapter IV. In essence, the Erie and Nia-

DATE	Book No. 34	Ticket No. 55	Buffalo	AM'T PAID
Jan.			Black Rock	Dolls.
Feb.				
March		MICHIGAN CENTRAL R.R.	Fort Erie	1
April		CONDUCTOR'S TRAIN TICKET.		2
May			Victoria	3
June				4
July			Old Fort Erie	5
Aug.				Cents
Sept.			Niagara Junc.	1
Oct.				2
Nov.			Black Creek	3
Dec.				4
			Chippawa	5
				6
1	17		Montrose Jct.	7
2	18			8
3	19		Falls View	9
4	20			10
5	21		Niag. F'ls, Ont.	15
6	22		Wesley Park	20
7	23			25
8	24		Clifton	30
9	25			35
10	26		Stamford	40
11	27			45
12	28		Queenston	50
13	29		Paradise G'e	60
14	30			65
15	30		Assembly Gds	70
16	31	NIAGARA DIV.		75
			Niagara (on the Lake)	80
1889	NORTH o o SOUTH			85
1890				90
1891	Half o Fare		Niaga'a Dock	95

Stopping points along the Niagara River are indicated on this railway ticket of 1889.

Walter F. Parks Collection

gara Railway became successively part of the Canada Southern-Michigan Central-New York Central Systems.[8]

In this struggle for control by competing interests, the strategic importance of the Erie and Niagara Railway lay in the fact that it ran parallel to the Niagara River and connected Lake Erie and Lake Ontario. The regional location of the Peninsula and its physical structure must now be borne in mind, together with an appreciation of Buffalo as an expanding centre of major commercial and industrial importance. It was imperative that the Great Western should consider a route to this American city and port. It was also important that the Canada Southern, serving the south of the Peninsula, should have an option on a line to a port in the north of the Peninsula.

For both Companies, there was the further possibility that either a lateral cut would be dug from the Welland Canal to the lower Niagara River or that the River would become the outlet of an enlarged Welland Canal.[9] These concepts had been studied by W. Shanly in 1854, and had been deemed favourable. The issue of a possible canal was raised frequently by business interests at Niagara,[10] and was again a matter for discussion when routes for the Third Canal were under consideration in the 1870's. A canal would have created considerable trade for the Railway. But it did not materialize and Niagara did not expand. With terminals at Niagara and Fort Erie, and with access to the Suspension Bridge at Niagara Falls and later to the International Bridge at Fort Erie, the Railway became a pawn in the unruly game of political and economic competition between American and Canadian railway interests and between railway and canal modes of travel.

The railway on a street alignment in Niagara.

Francis J. Petrie Collection

Clifton House at Niagara Falls, an important railway-oriented hotel, was owned by Samuel Zimmerman.   *Francis J. Petrie Collection*

Perhaps the most important individual associated with the foundation, promotion and advancement of the Erie and Ontario Railroad was Samuel Zimmerman (1815-1857).[11] He came to Canada in 1842, obtained the contract for the construction of four locks and the aqueduct on the Second Welland Canal system, and contracted for the Great Western line from Hamilton to the Suspension Bridge. In the latter capacity, he realized the potential for development that existed at the terminus and made extensive purchases at Elgin, close to the Suspension Bridge. He converted the Erie and Ontario Railroad into a steam line with iron rails and also extended this route from Queenston to Niagara. He owned the Clifton House, a major hotel at the Falls from 1833 onwards, and developed a large residential estate facing the American Falls.

He met an untimely end in 1857 when he was killed in a tragic railway accident at the Desjardins Canal near Hamilton.[12] Zimmerman is regarded as the founding father of the present City of Niagara Falls. A centennial eulogy has praised his work in the following terms:

Samuel Zimmerman, an early railway personality.   *George A. Seibel (ed), Niagara Falls, Canada: A History, 1967*

"Perhaps no one man in the history of our community did more to further its growth than Samuel Zimmerman. . .He purchased extensive land in the area around Elgin and also much of the village of Clifton. . .In May, 1855, Zimmerman opened the first bank in the community, named after himself, the Zimmerman Bank. . .His building also served as Customs House and Post Office for Clifton."[13]

In a personal vein and reflecting the fact that the railways promoted considerable camaraderie between their employees and the travelling public, it may be noted that the Erie and Ontario line became known locally and affectionately as the "Paddy Miles Express". This popular name was bestowed in recognition of the charm, wit and humour of the Irish conductor who served on the trains.[14] As George V. Taylor has described the situation in a history of Willoughby Township:

"Many interesting stories have been told about the first conductor, George Patrick Miles, who was born in Ireland and made many friends for the railroad by his kind thoughtful acts. . .Then the conductor Paddy Miles, with his blue suit with brass buttons, blue cap with a brass rim, gave the signal and with considerable puffing the long trip started. The road was rough and the dinky locomotive with diamond-shaped smoke stack had to stop at various places. . .The passengers starved and smelling of wood smoke, which often filled the cars for miles, found a good home cooked dinner for twenty-five cents. . .No one complained as it was considerably faster than a horse and wagon."[15]

Paddy Miles, extreme right, at Niagara.   *Francis J. Petrie Collection*

The Paddy Miles Train at Black Creek Station.   *Francis J. Petrie Collection*

Advocacy for the Welland Railway

The Port Dalhousie and Thorold Railway was incorporated in 1853. The Act empowered "the construction of a Railway connecting Port Dalhousie on Lake Ontario and Thorold, with the Great Western Railway, at or near the Welland Canal".[16] The powers were "to lay out, construct, make and finish a double or single iron Railway or Road . . .on or over any part of the Country laying between Port Dalhousie and the Village of Thorold."[17] The Company was also permitted "to construct, own, or employ. . .a steamboat or steamboats for the transportation of passengers and freight from the terminus of their Railway at Port Dalhousie to any point on Lake Ontario."[18]

The Railway was conceived as an ancillary proposition to the Great Western, and it was expected that it would connect with these tracks at Slabtown (near Merritton).[19] It provided a secondary means of access to Lake Ontario and was important for its direct connection with the Welland Canal system at Port Dalhousie. Industrial promotion must also have been in the minds of the sponsors. The route received a boost to its importance in 1856, when parliamentary approval was obtained for an extension of the line to Port Colborne,[20] thus enabling the construction of a railway across the Peninsula from Port Dalhousie on Lake Ontario to Port Colborne on Lake Erie. The name was changed to the Welland Railway in 1857, at the time when an application was made for an increase in capital stock.[21] It was 25 miles in length, and its somewhat distinctive characteristics are suggested by J. M. and E. Trout who stated that "it forms an important link in our great leading route of transportation from the upper lakes to the seaboard."[22] This wording seems more apropos of a canal than a railway. It was indeed a very distinctive railway, with a strong degree of canal orientation in its expectations and achievements.

William Hamilton Merritt, already recognized as the staunch promoter of the Welland Canal, was a prime proponent of the initial railway venture from Port Dalhousie to Thorold and then of its extension across the Peninsula as the Welland Railway. As he opposed railways when they were in their infancy and then continually stressed the advantages of the water mode of transport, his name is more often associated with canals than with railways. However, this reasoning fails to recognize Merritt's full contribution to the development of transportation in Canada. As Donald C. Masters has affirmed:

> "Merritt's ideas have been consistently misinterpreted and his influence underestimated. His entire career was based on a coherent and feasible system which was calculated, by a programme of improved land communications, to make Canada the avenue of trade between Great Britain and the western states."[23]

Merritt opposed the granting of a charter to the Erie and Ontario Railroad in 1835 but, when the inland waterway system to the St. Lawrence was virtually complete, his attitude changed. He wrote in 1845 that: "I have never made any movement, as yet to forward the construction of railroads because I thought the connection of our great waters the first and most beneficial object to attain — that secured in my judgement, that is the moment to commence our railways."[24] His later arguments recognize that the rail and canal modes of transportation could be complementary, with the canals carrying bulk, heavy and long distance cargoes and the railways transporting the lighter and more valuable goods. A railway would also operate during the winter months, when the canals were closed to navigation. In terms of distance and geographical background, he appreciated that a route from Lake Erie to the Hudson River by the Welland Canal, Lake Ontario and the Oswego Canal was both shorter and faster than by the Erie Canal to the Hudson River.

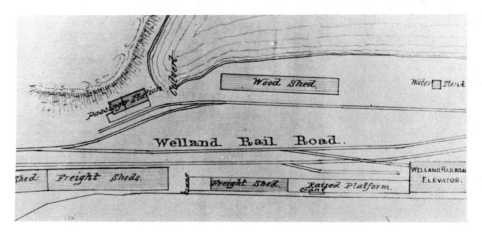

The terminal of the Welland Railway at Port Dalhousie, ca. 1885.

St. Catharines Historical Museum

As for the business association between the Welland Canal and a north-south railway across the Peninsula, Merritt realized that when the Canal was frozen, or especially burdened with traffic, or when overladen ships scraped its bottom, a railway along its bank would prove useful and profitable. By 1845, the Second Welland Canal had been completed. Though undoubtedly an improvement over its predecessor, it was still unable to handle the new, larger size of ships as their beam and depth were greater than the lock capacity. A railway in conjunction with, but subsidiary to, the Welland Canal would receive freight from ships that were too heavily laden to pass through the Canal. It could, therefore, be regarded as essential for the survival and expansion of the Canal. These arguments were presented in a *Prospectus* of 1856, which stated:

> "Immediately on the arrival of steamers at either end of the Welland Canal, light and valuable freight will be transferred by Railway from one Steamer to another in the same line, having previously passed through the Canal, and ready to proceed to her port of destination on the opposite lake. By this arrangement heavy freight will not be subject to transhipment, while light freight will secure speed and certainty."[25]

Further details of business links between the Railway and a regular series of lake and canal steamers appeared in a *Prospectus* dated September 1856. Passengers were now added to the list of light and valuable freight. With each train serving a steamer which had previously passed through the Canal:

> "A continuous line will be opened from every port on and below Lake Ontario, with every port on the above Lake Erie, insuring the same dispatch and punctuality in delivery as if the traffic was entirely conveyed by railway. Passengers, livestock, butter, cheese and valuable merchandise will be transferred to the Railway, while timber, lumber, grain, iron, salt and cheap bulky articles will go through the Canal, and each will add to the business of the other."[26]

This concept of a rapid system of conveyance, operating with clock-work precision, apparently did not take into account some obvious factors that could disrupt schedules. Inclement weather could delay shipping, goods in transhipment might need to be stored, and time and cost factors were involved in the dual handling of the lighter goods. It was also assumed that every ship, once its cargo was lightened, could then pass safely and conveniently through the Canal; perhaps some of the bulkier goods would also have to be removed to permit this transit.

The inter-association of rail and canal was also queried by important voices. Robert Stephenson, the famous railway engineer, pointed out to Merritt in 1856 that the Railway would also be in a competition position with the Canal and that it should attract trade in its own right:

> "You have regarded the Railway as an auxiliary to the Welland Canal, for the purpose of accelerating the conveyance of light goods. You are probably quite correct in taking credit for this portion of the Canal traffic; but independent of this source of revenue, I believe the line of Railway projected between the two Lakes, and nearly parallel with the Welland Canal, will prove a profitable investment of capital."[27]

The realization that the Railway could rival the Canal for carrying heavy freight held intriguing possibilities for the Directors. The *Prospectus* of July 1857 added coal and wheat as two other basic commodities which could be carried. The appearance of coal as a possible freight was due to its discovery in McKean County, Pennsylvania. It was visualized that coal would be transported on a descending grade to Lake Erie, then by boat across the Lake to Port Colborne, across the Peninsula by the Welland Railway, and then by boat from Port Dalhousie to the markets of Southern Ontario. It was argued that this route "would furnish the nearest and cheapest supply for this portion of Canada",[28] and that:

> "The supplying of coal for the use of Canada would form one of the sources of revenue for the Welland Railway, through a short branch at the northern terminus, the altitude would be obtained sufficient to throw it into the holds of vessels."[29]

Arguments for handling the all-important wheat trade were more extensive. Five points were advanced in the *Prospectus* of July, 1857.[30] Firstly, by 1853, the Welland Canal carried one million more bushels of wheat (6.5 million against 5.4 million) than did the Erie Canal. The Erie route was demonstrably longer and more costly than passage via the Welland Canal, Lake Ontario and the Oswego Canal. The Welland Railway was, therefore, proven "to be the shortest, cheapest and best route between Lake Erie and the sea board",[31] a

WELLAND RAILWAY & STEAMBOAT COMPANY.

FROM

PORT COLBORNE, LAKE ERIE,

TO

PORT DALHOUSIE, LAKE ONTARIO:

25 MILES,

Connecting by Steam and Sailing Vessels,

CHICAGO, MILWAUKEE, DETROIT,

AND ALL POINTS ON THE UPPER LAKES, WITH

NEW YORK, ALBANY, TROY, BOSTON, OSWEGO, OGDENSBURGH,

KINGSTON, MONTREAL, AND QUEBEC,

And all other Ports on Lake Ontario and River St. Lawrence.

BOARD OF DIRECTORS.

J. W. Bosanquet, Esq., *Chairman*, Eng.		Thomas Brassey, Esq., England.
Major Kitson,	"	—. Ogilvie, Esq., "
F. C. Gaussen, Esq.,	"	T. R. Merritt, Esq., Canada.
S. P. Bidder, Esq.,	"	R. J. Reekie, Esq., "
L. B. Wade,		

OFFICERS.

T. R. Merritt, Esq., *Chairman, Committee of Superintendence.*
Cornelius Stovin, Esq., *General Manager.*
Hiram Slate, *Secretary.*
C. M. Gibson, *Accountant.*
William Pay, *Car and Track Superintendent.*
William Morrison, *Master of Machinery.*

A commercial advertisement for the Welland Railway.   *St. Catharines Historical Museum*

conclusion of considerable importance given that the American and Canadian Mid-West were then being opened for extensive wheat production.

Secondly, the tonnage of wheat carried on the Erie Canal had diminished since 1853 against increasing consignments carried by the New York Central Railway. The Railway had become the major carrier of wheat. Moreover, these goods were being conveyed by rail during the navigable canal season which, as the *Prospectus* affirmed somewhat smugly, "disposes of the argument *that the heaviest freighting business is done by Railroads when the Canals are closed.*"[32]

Thirdly, it was stated that railroads offered advantages of capacity and speed and could compete directly with canals in the transportation of heavy freight:

> "It is now ascertained that an engine will haul a train containing 150 to 200 tons, (exclusive of the weight of the train), while a canal boat with 150 tons of freight will not ordinarily perform the trip from Buffalo to Albany short of eight days; in this time one engine with a loaded train of 150 tons would run four times each way between the same points, and perform four times the service of a canal boat of like capacity in delivering freight in one way, and eight times as much when loaded both ways."[33]

Fourthly, Buffalo charged a premium of from three to five cents on the shipment of every bushel of grain. To regain this trade for Canada, it was necessary to construct a railway, connecting Lakes Erie and Ontario, along the banks of the Welland Canal. This claim was supported by cost comparisons. The costs per ton mile from Lake Erie to Montreal via the Grand Trunk, to New York via Buffalo and the Erie Canal, and to New York via the Welland Railway and the Oswego Canal were estimated at $11.46, $6.01 and $5.41 respectively. One locomotive and set of freight cars was therefore expected to yield "$98,000 per annum, which on a capital of $1,000,000, gives a dividend of 8 per cent, with a surplus of $18,000."[34]

Fifthly, the advantages of an inter-connected system of communications providing a daily service, were noted:

> "*Fifteen* screw steamers between Liverpool and Quebec, *three* Lake screw steamers between Prescott and Port Dalhousie, and *six* between Port Colborne and Chicago, would establish a daily line of communication between Great Britain and the West, over the Grand Trunk and Welland Railways, in a shorter distance, in less time, and at less cost than any other route. . .during six or seven months of the navigable season, in which the great proportion of the carrying trade is performed. During the remainder of the year the same points will be connected via Portland, which is accessible from sea at all seasons. Therefore, so soon as sufficient capital is procured to establish one line of Ocean Steamers, *the trade of the West is secured forever.*"[35]

Opposition by the Town of Niagara

These somewhat hopeful, and perhaps over-optimistic, commercial expectations were accorded different receptions. The project was opposed in Niagara but it was supported in St. Catharines. Rivalry between the two towns for supremacy was intense, with Niagara remembering its former prime position as the leading service centre and regretting the rise to importance of its upstart neighbour. Niagara was convinced that the projected Railway would compete with the Erie and Ontario Railroad along the Niagara River. Capital raised in Niagara had helped to foster this venture, which had received considerable local commendation. As noted in the *Niagara Mail:*

"The voters of Niagara sustained the £10,000 By Law of the Town Council for stock in the above road, by acclamation. . .Mr. Simpson deserves very great credit for the industry and ability he has displayed in bringing this matter to a head, and we are free to confess that to him we are very much indebted for the present favourable prospect of completing the Erie and Ontario Railroad."[36]

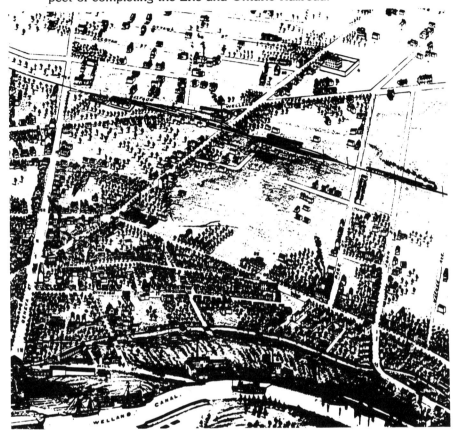

Fig. 3.2   The Welland Railway Station at St. Catharines, 1875. Note its location away from the established core of the town.

H. Brosius, St. Catharines, 1875

At about this time Niagara proposed a railway link from St. Catharines to its own site at the mouth of the Niagara River. The *Mail* observed that "we are fully persuaded that. . .a road to Niagara would be the most advantageous line on the whole to connect St. Catharines with the Lake."[37] As a consequence, the whole concept of the Welland Railway was ridiculed. The *Mail* dismissed the venture by commenting that its *Prospectus:*

"must strike any impartial eye, as one of the finest burlesques on railway bubbles ever seen. We cannot for the life of us believe that the said report is intended for a serious statement — but is meant for a closing laugh (sardonic perhaps) over a laughable undertaking; a sort of Christmas jest for the holidays."[38]

It regarded as absurd the notion that the Railway would act as a substitute for the Welland Canal, attract through-trade from the west, compete with the American railways, and tranship coal from Pennsylvania. It noted the absence of information about locally-generated traffic:

"The mills along the line of the Welland Canal will always use the Canal for the conveyance of their freight; while during winter the railway will have no connection anywhere beyond its termini, its shipping ports being frozen up or inaccessible during that season."[39]

The war of words between the *St. Catharines Constitutional* and the *Niagara Mail* persisted. One vehement comment stated:

"The *Constitutional* is as cankered towards old Niagara, as a Hamilton Town Councillor. Still, we are unchanged in opinion, that the true railway interests of St. C. be in a connection with Niagara Harbor, rather than in the direction advocated by the *Constitutional*. The Port Dalhousie and Port Colborne railway may do by and by, but it is premature as yet — and in our opinion secondary in importance to one which would place St. C. in direct communications with the numerous lines of steamers and the several railways that will centre on the Niagara River."[40]

Obviously, Niagara believed that its former status as the premier centre in the Peninsula could be revived. Its urban fortunes were not yet perceived to be in a state of decline.

A Favourable Reception in St. Catharines

By contrast, within St. Catharines the project of a Welland Railway tended to receive staunch support. One observation in the *Anglo-American Magazine* of 1853 declared that, in conjunction with the many other public improvements which were then taking place, "the future she [St. Catharines] may calmly and confidently contemplate, is one of steady but certain increase and advancement."[41] In addition to its two railways, a company had recently been formed for lighting the Canal and the town with gas, a piped water supply was about to be installed, and business was bustling with optimism. The shipyards, the flour mills, the saw mills, the machine shops, the axe and edge tool factory, the foundries and the various smaller factories were all in active operation. The town was about to be borne forward on the surging crest of prosperity and industry, with the Welland Railway adding its own degree of further encouragement to the expectation of urban expansion.

The *Journal* expressed warm support and endorsement for the railway project which, it felt, would place St. Catharines on the shortest route between Toronto and Buffalo, redress the unfortunate situation of the town relative to the Great Western, and provide an inducement for all interests. This euphoria of optimism was expressed in the following terms in 1853:

"This is a good move for St. Catharines, and as we were not embraced, but passed over as not worth consideration, by the Great Western, we will now tap the travel, and do a little on our own hook. We think this one of the most important moves for the town that has been suggested for a long time. In the age of railroads, the town that is not hitched on must be left behind, wondering at the progress of the age and lamenting its own isolated condition. In such a position we must have been in, had not the charter under which we are now going to act been obtained. . .

"It is better to be out of the world than out of fashion, and we may say, that for our town not to be connected with a railroad is to be both out of fashion and out of the world. Mr. Merritt deserves great praise for his exertions in this matter."[42]

However, the more southerly communities in the Peninsula aligned along the Welland Canal were far less enthusiastic for the project. As stated in early 1854:

> "We have now to report and deplore the act, that the townships have negatived by large majorities, if not by unanimous votes, the projected rail road between Port Dalhousie and Lake Erie. Now we by no means despair, as to the construction of this road, as it is sure to be taken in hand by capitalists, and made private property of. This is not the mode by which the work should be done, and we venture to say, that stock paying as this will do 20 percent will not long remain unsubscribed for. Should the municipalities not change their present position, a day will come when they will deeply regret that they did not secure an investment, which if it paid only 8 percent would have secured the whole stock as municipal property in thirty years."[43]

Despite this lack of external support, the intention to construct a north-south route across the Peninsula persisted, with the initiative, promotion and encouragement of the project stemming mainly from St. Catharines. In January 1854, an issue of the *Journal* carried the announcement that:

> "The Port Dalhousie and Thorold Railroad Co. will apply at the next Session of the Provincial Legislature for an Act authorising the extension of their Charter to Allanburg and Port Robinson, Merrittville and Port Colborne; also from Port Robinson, to intersect the Buffalo, Brantford and Goderich Railway leading to Fort Erie, to that point direct, or to any other part of the Niagara River; and also for power to increase the Capital Stock of the said Company."[44]

Opposition and argument for other routes also existed in St. Catharines. A letter in 1854 under the anonymous signature of 'A Tax-Payer' stated:

> "I notice that the Thorold and Port Dalhousie Railway is about to become a 'living reality'. Many may suppose this is another step on the ladder of fame, which we are so rapidly ascending; but for my part, I fear that it will prove (if ever carried out) far less beneficial to our town than its sanguine projectors anticipate".[45]

The writer suggested a route from St. Catharines to Niagara in order to connect with the steamers and railroads in the Eastern States, and a link to Dunnville connecting with the Buffalo and Brantford Railroad because:

> "Such a road would be productive of far greater advantage and benefit to the town than any other projected. It would place us in direct and permanent communication, not only with the lakes, (with which we are already connected by the canal) but with all the Atlantic Cities . . .We are pretty well in debt already, and I am not alone in imagining that the Port Dalhousie and Thorold Railway will increase our burden."[46]

Three important issues had to be resolved. Should the Port Dalhousie and Thorold Railway link with the Great Western Railway or merely cross this route? Would a short route from Port Dalhousie to Thorold, as one link in the chain from Toronto to Buffalo, be a financial success? Should the route be extended from Port Dalhousie to Port Colborne, given that the municipalities to the south along the line had refused to contribute? Debate was severe, heightened by the fact that St. Catharines was virtually the owner of the road. Work had begun in mid-1854 and by November 1855 St. Catharines had subscribed £25,000 out of the total capital of £26,405 to the undertaking.[47]

In August 1854, a petition signed by 180 taxpayers of the town was presented, praying that the Council would halt work on the road until it was satisfactorily ascertained that it would either be united to the Great Western or continued to Port Colborne.[48] Votes were taken, further meetings were held, and a proclamation was issued in September "for taking the votes of taxpayers in this town, for or against continuing operations on the Thorold and Port Dalhousie Railway."[49] The *Journal* minimized the opposition by stating that "the taxpayers only require some evidence that the work will be accomplished, and their money not expended on a short line that would never pay."[50]

PORT DALHOUSIE AND THOROLD RAILWAY.

(Copy.)—No. 1.

STATEMENT of the AFFAIRS of the PORT DALHOUSIE and THOROLD RAILWAY COMPANY, on the 21st day of March, 1855, prepared in compliance to a circular of the 1st instant, of the Clerk of the Legislative Assembly.

	£	s.	d.	£	s.	d.
This Company was incorporated under a special Act, 14 & 15 Vic. cap. 51, with a capital of Seventy-five thousand pounds (£75,000). The amount of Stock subscribed on the Stock Book is 1,092 shares, £25 each, £27,300, on which there had been paid up to the present moment				18825	0	0
The outlay has been as follows, viz. :—						
To Engineers Department	654	9	2			
do Right of Way	1083	16	3			
do Grading	4800	0	0			
do Superstructure, including 583 tons of Railway Iron	8244	14	4½			
do Incidental Expenses	446	0	0			
				15227	19	9¼
Balance on hand £				3597	0	2¾

With the above expenditure the Company have graded the whole of their line from Port Dalhousie to St. Catharines, which is now ready for the superstructure, and a contract has been entered into to complete the remaining portion between St. Catharines and the Thorold Station on the Great Western Railway.

The Railway Iron already purchased and delivered is sufficient for the entire line up to the Thorold Station, and the Directors are in hopes of placing this section in running order during the coming summer.

(Signed,)   GEO. RYKERT,
President.

(Signed,)   FRANCIS LATOR,
Secretary.

St. Catharines, March 21st, 1855.

—

A True Copy of the orignal on file in the Company's Office.

Attest,   HIRAM SLATE,
Accountant.

A balance sheet for the Port Dalhousie and Thorold Railway, 1855.   *JLA, 1857*

Matters again came to a head in 1855 when additional funds were requested. Some members of the Town Council expressed opposition to the project. For example, Oliver Phelps argued that a short line of road would not pay but that, instead, "a good macadamized road would be of more benefit to the Town than a railroad, since he could convey by wagon a barrel of flour to Port Dalhousie for eight cents, on the present road, and the freight by Railway would be ten."[51] The Council finally decided in favour of a loan of £24,000, but only when the Mayor had to break the tie by voting in the affirmative.

More letters appeared in the newspaper. One correspondent, "H.H.", argued that short lines in the United States and Great Britain had proven unsuccessful[52] and that they did not repay their shareholders; furthermore, it was good generalship to know when to stop rather than to proceed and face further losses. Also, many of the items that had been purchased could still be sold, so that some of the shareholders' investments could be recouped. Anyway, he continued, a macadamized road was the preferable investment whereas a railway would benefit only those who had speculated in land at Merritton, and no reason existed why the citizens of St. Catharines should pay for the personal advantage of these few people. Another point of criticism was the exorbitant amount which had been paid for purchasing the right of way: a line six miles in length had cost £9,135, whereas "the Right of Way from Niagara to Chippawa on a line of eighteen miles in length and averaging a greater width, through lands of equal or not of greater value, was obtained for the construction of the Erie and Ontario Railway for £7,300."[53]

In mid-1855, the ratepayers voted against proceeding with the line. At the same time, the third reading of the Bill to extend the line to Port Colborne was defeated, with staunch opposition being led by Zimmerman and other interests from Niagara Falls. The *Constitutional* thought "that the check thus given will be but momentary, and that the ever active genius of its projector will devise some means to effectuate its successful accomplishment."[54] After further discussions and meetings, the by-law was again submitted in late-1855. This time, a further £25,000 was voted for the Railway, an action which was supported by the *Journal:*

> "There is no use now in any party regretting this investment on the part of the town. It is now the interest of the taxpayers that the work be promoted and finished as soon as possible...The sooner the road and boat are put into operation, the better."[55]

Whilst this debate over funds and possible extension of the

Railway to Port Colborne continued, work was progressing on the northern length of track. In November 1855, the Company's Engineer stated: "Iron is laid down; we have got the right-of-way to Thorold Station, nearly 6 miles; 9½ acres, to St. Catharines, cost $824, and 10 acres more, cost $1200".[56]

When requests were received in early 1856 for additional funds to complete the works, even the *Journal* baulked. The issue of 22 May 1856 included a three column diatribe, signed "Anti Railway Mania", which roundly castigated the Directors: "They scattered their money freely, spent it profusely and finished it quickly."[57] The second vote was referred to as "a bare majority of the pigmy votes polled", and the extent of construction was described in tones of perturbed despair:

> "The road today is unfinished and if appearances indicate anything, it will not be done for a twelvemonth yet. There are no *engines* or *cars* to be seen on the road, and but little work...You can *see* a scratch along a *part* of the line, and an unfinished road with black ash ties, and iron rails laid on them, on another part of the line; you can see also a *hen-coop depot* at this station."[58]

The paper even posed a cryptic conundrum for its readers:

> "Why is the Port Dalhousie and Thorold Railroad like the *wood* in the St. Catharines Market? Do you give it up? Well, because it is considerably short at both ends, because it won't pay, and because it is for sale."[59]

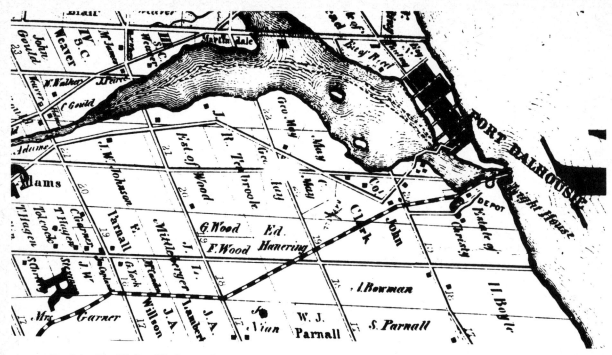

Fig. 3.3   The Welland Railway at Port Dalhousie, 1862.   *Tremaines' Map of the Counties of Lincoln and Welland, 1862*

The paper urged that no more money be paid, the Railway men must be checked, and therefore the taxpayers were adjured to:

> "*Bar* hence-forward, any more Loans to this road! *Stop* any more supplies, and *veto* any more such appropriations! You have the power, *use* it. You have been gulled enough. . .Avoid it, as you would the extortioner, who catcheth and keepeth all he can get."[60]

Perhaps remarks of this ilk served to spur the Directors to greater achievement because, in June 1856, the long-awaited event occurred: the first length of track was opened from St. Catharines to Port Dalhousie (Fig. 3.3). This propitious happening received eulogistic applause from the *Journal*:

> "On Monday last, our Railroad to Port Dalhousie was opened for the first time, and we were pleased to see the admirable arrangements made by this Municipality duly appreciated by a large number of passengers, and but for the omission of due notice by advertisement the cars would have been crowded. When the public are duly informed that our cars start every morning at 8:30, and join the boat at Port Dalhousie, only waiting for their arrival, and that Toronto can be reached in so much shorter time than by any other route, we doubt not but that this admirable line will be well patronized.

> "Hurrah for progression! We are now hitched on the rail, and conveyed from our town to the boat in ten minutes, and in 2 hours forty minutes we make our appearance in Toronto."[61]

Opening the Line and Its Service Facilities

Against this background of slow progress and civic confidence, approval was obtained in 1857 for an increase in capital stock. The name was also changed to the Welland Railway Company,[62] and the line was opened successively southward from St. Catharines. It had been extended to Thorold by July 1858.[63] By September the track had been completed and tested with trial trains and, though no station buildings had yet been erected, the hope was that the whole length would be open for traffic by April 1859.[64] But some disturbing news appeared on the financial horizon at this time. An unexpected development was noted in anxious words:

"It is with Buffalo that we have to compete for the trade of the West and it is only with the works completed or projected that connect that city with this trade that it is prudent or advisable to compare this road. The contemplated International Bridge to be erected over the Niagara River will unite the Buffalo and Huron Railway with Buffalo and the railway system of New York State."[65]

As the only existing rail crossing of the Niagara River was at the Suspension Bridge, the contemplated crossing provided dire competition and a severe threat to the aspirations of the Welland Railway. The *Journal* had no doubts but that the capital necessary for the construction of International Bridge would be raised:

"We are strongly inclined to believe that our enterprizing neighbours will experience less trouble in getting the capital for their Bridge than the promoters and friends of the Welland Railway encountered."[66]

Milwaukee: a Welland Railway locomotive, 1866.   *St. Catharines Historical Museum*

However, as it turned out, a bridge was not built at this crossing until 1873.

In April 1859, the first freight train passed over the full length of the Welland Railway. The *Journal* commented that:

"On Tuesday last, the first load of wheat from Lake Erie to Lake Ontario, per Welland Railway, was conveyed over the track, and the result of the trial, we understand has been eminently satisfactory, in every particular. The elevators at Port Colborne will elevate 5000 bushels of wheat per hour with ease. . .The Co. have now four loco-motives on the road, and a fifth will be here by 1st May. It is calculated that eight locomotives will be enough to do the work of the line."[67]

The simple but effective architecture of Allanburg Station.
Mrs. Harry Vanderburgh, A History of Allanburg and Area, 1967

Freight facilities on the line included, by June 1859, two cranes at Port Dalhousie, with three more expected. Each was capable of handling 300 tons per day, or 120,000 tons for the season of 200 days. At both Port Colborne and Port Dalhousie:

"Elevators capable of transshipping 4,000 bushels per hour, or from 4 to 5 millions of bushels per annum, have been erected and, including Flour and other rolling freight the road, with its erections at either terminus, will have sufficient capacity to convey 500,000 tons of traffic, from Lake to Lake during the season."[68]

In June 1859 trains commenced running regularly across the Peninsula. The first public notice announced two trains a day in each direction, connecting at Port Dalhousie with the steamer *Peerless* to Toronto and at Port Colborne with the Buffalo and Lake Huron Railway to Buffalo.[69] Trains departed from Port Colborne one hour after leaving Buffalo. They crossed the Peninsula to Port Dalhousie in one-and-a-quarter hours, and the passengers reached Toronto by steamer two-and-a-half hours later. The St. Catharines Station was, therefore, about three hours from Toronto and two hours from Buffalo. It was also possible for passengers arriving in St. Catharines to connect with the Great Western at either the St. Catharines or the Thorold stations; a timetable in 1859 suggested a two hour visit to the baths in St. Catharines to offset the waiting period.[70] It was also possible to travel from Toronto to Buffalo, spend three hours there, and return on the same day.

By 1861, the schedule had increased to three trains daily in each direction.[71] The time-distances from the station at St. Catharines to other stopping points on the Welland line across the Peninsula were, as follows: Port Dalhousie, 20 minutes; Thorold, 25 minutes (a slow journey because of the rise up the Escarpment); Allanburg, 35 minutes; Port Robinson, 43 minutes; Welland, 55 minutes; and Port Colborne, 80 minutes. The down-trains crossed the Peninsula in 1 hour and 30 minutes, 10 minutes faster than those running in the up-direction across the Escarpment.

These new passenger and freight facilities were viewed with considerable local satisfaction. An issue of the *Journal* in 1859 noted with pride that traffic on the line was increasing:

"On Friday last, seven vessels arrived at Port Colborne loaded with grain to pass over the road, the smallest of which contained 15,000 bu. Seven more are on their way. The trains are running day and night and yet, so fast does the freight offer, they are scarcely capable of keeping up with the business. The Buffalo and Lake Huron Railway is in the same position and this is solely owing to its connection with the Welland. Before the completion of the latter road the former never carried a barrel of flour, but since then the business in this line has been steadily increasing and now it can boast of as large a traffic in proportion to its length as any road in Canada. . .The Welland Railway is destined to become the best paying railroad in the province, and through its influence the Buffalo and Lake Huron will be the next."[72]

Welland Railway.

Connecting with Great Western Railway at Merritton and Welland Junction.

HAMILTON, TORONTO, LONDON, SARNIA, DETROIT, CHICAGO, BUFFALO, NEW YORK, BOSTON, &c.

	Going North.				Going South.		
Miles from Pt Colborne.	STATIONS.	EXP.	PASS.	Miles from Pt. Dalhousie.	STATIONS.	MAIL.	EXP
		a.m.	p.m.			a.m.	p.m.
	Pt. Colborne........dep.	7 45	2 27		Pt. Dalhousie.........dep.	9 55	5 40
1¼	Humberstone............	7 50	2 32	3	St Catharines............	10 15	5 56
4¾	Welland Junction...arr.	7 58	2 42	5½	Merriton ....arr.	10 27	6 11
							p m.
	Cayuga................arr.	9 40	5 37		Chicago..............dep.	....	9 10
		p.m.					a.m.
	St. Thomas 20..........	12 35	8 30		Detroit 11................	....	8 35
					Sarnia 22...................	.. ..	11 25
		a.m.				a.m.	p.m.
4¾	Welland Junction...dep.	7 58	2 42		London 8................	6 00	1 55
7¼	Welland	8 10	3 00		Toronto 12..............	7 10	3 30
11¾	Pt. Robinson............	8 22	3 13		Hamilton 4..............	9 10	5 00
14½	Allanburg................	8 32	3 23			p.m.	p.m.
17	Thorold	8 40	3 35		Boston	3 00	6 00
19½	Merriton 3............arr.	8 50	3 50		New York................	7 30	8 30
						a'm.	
					Buffalo..................	9 00	2 30
	Clifton 2..............arr.	10 50	6 30		Clifton 2..................	10 10	3 30
		p.m.					
	Buffalo......................	12 50	8 35	5½	Merriton 3............dep.	10 27	6 11
		a.m.	s.m.	8	Thorold	10 40	6 21
	New York	7 15	10 30	10½	Allanburg	10 53	6 30
			p.m.	13¼	Pt. Robinson............	11 03	6 39
	Boston	9 20	2 40	17¼	Welland	11 16	6 50
		a.m.		20¼	Welland Junction........	11 35	7 00
	Hamilton 4................	11 25	5 00				
		p.m.					p.m.
	Toronto 12................	1 15	6 45		St Thomas 20.......dep.	7 10	3 30
	London 8..................	1 55	8 40		Cayuga	10 20	6 55
	Sarnia 22.................	4 30	....				
	Detroit 11................	6 30	....				
		a.m.		20¼	Welland Junction...dep.	11 35	7 00
	Chicago	7 30	....	23¾	Humberstone............	11 45	7 08
		a.m.		25	Pt. Colborne............	11 50	7 13
19½	Merriton ....dep.	8 50	3 50				
22	St. Catharines........arr.	9 00	4 00				
25	Pt. Dalhousie............	9 10	4 10				

NOTE.—Train leaving Port Dalhousie at 9 55 a.m. makes close connection at Welland Junction for Buffalo.

The Welland Railway, a time table of 1879.

Regional Collection, D. B. Weldon Library, University of Western Ontario

These grand expectations were not realized. The Railway, as an auxiliary to the Canal, transferred 11 million bushels of grain from Lake Erie to Lake Ontario in its first four years of operation. In 1862, over half a million bushels were "lightened" from one end of the Canal to the other (that is, transferred from grain vessels which were laden too deeply to pass through the Canal), out of total movement of four million bushels from Lake Erie to Lake Ontario.[73] But there were also competitive routes, including the Erie and Niagara Railway along the frontier and lines to Hamilton from other ports on Lake Erie. The Welland Railway did not enjoy a monopoly, and more was at issue than solely the route. There were the grain storage facilities, harbour works, competitive prices, and the need for a regular flow of activity in order to meet the overhead and running costs and to generate sufficient money to permit expansion when required.

Most of the shipments of grain received in the Upper Great Lakes continued to flow to Buffalo and then by way of the American railways or the Erie Canal to New York, rather than via the Welland Canal or the Welland Railway to Lake Ontario, the St. Lawrence and Montreal. Ships were purchased to work on the two lakes in conjunction with the Railway and the Canal, but the actual total activity generated neither matched expectations nor covered the operating expenses and construction costs. As A. W. Currie has observed:

> "The Company hoped to handle 10,000,000 bushels of grain per annum which at one per cent per bushel would cover all operating expenses, interest and dividends. Actually the Railway seems never to have hauled more than one-third of this tonnage."[74]

Although the expectations of through traffic were not fulfilled, the Welland Railway answered a local purpose as traffic was generated from points along its route. For example, at Thorold in 1880, "outward freight traffic included 164 carloads of flour, water, lime and stone, having a total weight of 3,564,730 lbs. The weight of goods received during the same period amounted to 397,689 lbs. The amount of freight shipped out was the largest that has ever been shipped from Thorold in one month."[75] Passenger traffic also became important, a fact which is obvious from the timetables. These soon scheduled regular services with up to eight arrivals and departures across the Peninsula each day. Especially significant were the boat connections across Lake Ontario to Toronto, and the promotion of tourist traffic from within the Peninsula for day excursion trips to the lake beach at Port Dalhousie.

Construction Details

The Welland Railway, constructed to the provincial gauge of 5 feet 6 inches, followed the Second Welland Canal closely for 25 miles in a parallel alignment along its eastern bank. This route and its relationship with the Canal are of particular urban significance. It meant that those industries which had been attracted to locations along the Canal now had the supplementary transportation advantage of railway access from the rear. This new role was applied with particular intensity from Thorold to Merritton across the brow of the Escarpment. Here, a typical cross-section from west to east included the Canal towpath, the Canal, the reservoirs supplying water to the locks, the hydraulic channel inter-connecting the supply reservoirs, the riparian industry which was generally powered from the hydraulic raceways, and then the Welland Railway and/or road access.

Somewhat to the dismay of its residents and business leaders, St. Catharines was almost by-passed by the Railway of its own creation (Fig. 3.2). The tracks were located on the eastern fringe of the developed area rather than through the town. They followed a straighter and more direct route from Thorold and Merritton to Port Dalhousie than the serpentine meandering of the Welland Canal, along which St. Catharines and its industrial activities had developed. Despite its persistent and firm support for the Railway, the expectations of a new impetus to its growth pretensions were largely unfulfilled. St. Catharines did obtain the office of the Welland Railway, which was located over the post office on Ontario Street, but it was physically as separate from the Welland Railway as it had been avoided earlier by the Great Western. The municipal efforts and financial support on behalf of the Welland Railway, though not in vain, were not to benefit to any great extent that community which had been

81

primarily responsible for nurturing the venture into existence in the first place.

Construction details of the Welland Railway are available in the records retained by Francis Shanly,[76] who was appointed Engineer to the Company in 1856. He was born in Ireland in 1820 and emigrated with his parents to Upper Canada in 1836, where he pursued a career in engineering. His office correspondence, note books, plans and contract specifications provide abundant detail about the works for which he was responsible. They include information about the provision of fencing and cattle guards; grading; clearing and grubbing the track; the construction of culverts, ditches, cuttings and embankments; ballasting and track laying; masonry for road crossings and small bridges, larger bridges and their foundations; the delivery of ties, rails, fuel wood and all other materials; estimates from contractors and suppliers of machinery, equipment, buildings and rolling stock according to defined specifications; the award of contracts; and arrangements about the times and points of delivery.

A postcard showing the railway crossing of the Welland River at Port Robinson.

John Burtniak Collection

The numbers employed on the project varied from month to month, and included many Irish labourers.[77] The maximum labour force consisted of 1,595 workers in 1857 on the two divisions of operations, 190 in the north and 1,405 in the south. The payroll for grading included 1,358 men working in gangs of about 15 persons each under 95 foremen and using 280 horses. Tradesmen included masons, stone-cutters, carpenters and blacksmiths. Those working on the construction of fences were enumerated separately. A carpenter as a skilled craftsman received a daily rate of $1.75 compared with a foreman who received only $1.25 and a labourer, $1.10. By contrast, the monthly rates for the more permanent "office staff" included assistant engineer, $80; draftsman, $60; station master, rodman and inspector of timber, $40 each; tapeman (surveyor), $34; office keeper, $30; and clerk, $26.

The principal engineering works and other structures built along the line of track included:

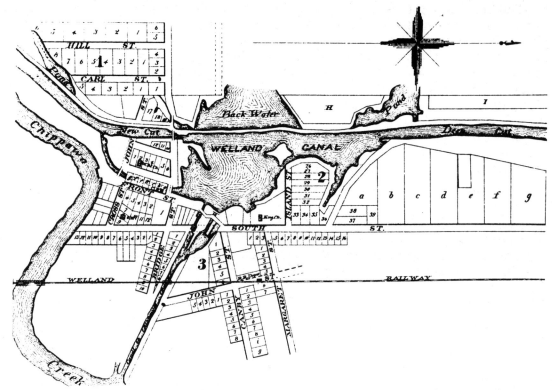

Fig. 3.4   The Welland Railway at Port Robinson crossing the Welland River and the Canal Cut, 1876.

H. R. Page, Illustrated Historical Atlas of the Counties of Lincoln and Welland, 1876

wharfing and foundations at Port Dalhousie and Port Colborne, with the former being more costly as dredging, piling and excavation were required.

grain warehouses and their machinery, at both terminal ports.

a timber-arched bridge over the Welland River (Chippawa Creek), at Port Robinson (Fig. 3.4). This had four 60-foot spans, supported at the ends by stone abutments and set upon three stone piers built in the river.

a swing bridge over the Chippawa Cut of the Welland Canal system at Port Robinson.

a bridge over Ten Mile Creek at Brown's Quarries, next to the Niagara Escarpment.

crossings to take the Welland Railway over the Great Western at Thorold, and over the Buffalo and Lake Huron Railway at Port Colborne.

stations, of similar design and constructed of timber, at the major road crossing points next to the principal communities along the route. The typical station measured 60 feet in length and 22 feet in width. It was built on piled foundations, with a shingle roof projecting prominently on all sides.

cuttings and embankments necessary to surmount the change in levels, approximately 300 feet in all, across the Escarpment.

two bridges over the St. Catharines hydraulic raceway. The *Constitutional* stated that "at the time of railway construction, the canal authorities were constructing a new hydraulic aqueduct, and permission was given to the Welland Railway for the line of their railway to cross over it."[78]

The most contentious of these features was the point of meeting between the Welland Railway and the Great Western. The provisions of the charter had indicated that there would be a direct connection between the two routes, and this intention would seem to have prevailed until about October 1853. As J. P. Merritt later noted, "the arrangements for a connection between the G.W. and Port Dalhousie R. R. Companies seem to have broken up at this time, so that a direct line to Buffalo, or some point on Lake Erie was to be built."[79] The *Journal* commented: "It appears that the Directors of the Great-Western Railroad have, contrary to a distinct understanding, withdrawn their proposition to unite with the Port Dalhousie road, after arrangements had been made to that effect."[80]

By 1855, an agreement between the two Companies stated that "the point and mode of junction and crossing between the two lines [were] to be determined solely by the Engineer of the Great Western Railway Company".[81] Various scissor arrangements for this junction and crossing of the Great Western track were proposed by the Welland Railway, but strong opposition to these arrangements was received from the Great Western. They viewed with concern a "level crossing, occurring as it does at the foot of a gradient of 85 feet in the mile *down* which all your *loaded* trains will come,"[82] obviously envisaging a horrifying accident involving two trains.

The canal system at Merritton.

The final solution was a bridge with approaching embankments to take the Welland Railway over the Great Western tracks. This was selected as the safest method for coping with an otherwise potentially dangerous crossing, but it was a costly solution in terms of the construction requirements for a lengthy approach on flat terrain. It also meant that the two lines did not inter-connect until the construction of the Third Welland Canal in the late-1870's. By that time, the pressure for a link between the two routes had become acute because of the need to carry loads of stone and other equipment to the Canal works. The Welland Railway, on an alignment close to the Canal, was ideal for this purpose and sidetracks were laid to facilitate the Canal construction. As the two lines did not connect, the possibility of a direct route from the Great Western to Port Dalhousie was lost and this, in its turn, might have spawned some industrial advantages. In this instance, Merritt seems to have been less successful than in many of his earlier negotiations.

Equipment and Rolling Stock

Agreement was reached in 1857 between the Welland Railway and the Boston Locomotive Works for the supply of a locomotive engine. This was built for a gauge of 5 feet 6 inches. It had four connected driving wheels of cast iron, each five feet in diameter, and four truck wheels. The tender sat on eight wheels and contained 1,500 gallons of water, and the boiler had two domes finished on the outside with plain brass casings. The contract details of its general finish read:

"The whole of the materials and workmanship to be of the very best description, and all the valve, gear, guides, and working parts to be of best wrought iron, case hardened and cleaned up.

"The Axels, connecting rods and braces, principal bolts, nuts and rods to be of the best hammered iron.

"The Engine is to be furnished with a Cab of neat pattern, and a foot walk and hand railing of iron is to run around the boiler. It is to have a pilot or Cow catcher of wood, well braced with Iron, and brackets for a head light fixed to front of boiler. The painting and finish generally to be neat and plain.

"The name of the Engine "CHIPPAWA" to be in neat brass letters, on each side of Boiler, and the number ("2") conspiciously in front of Smoke Stack, and the Tender shall bear on each side 'Welland Railway No. 2'.

"The Tender is to be made of good substantial Iron plates, well rivetted and braced...It is to be furnished with double breaks, and two Tool Boxes with Locks, and shall be painted a good plain green, without ornament, the lettering and numbers gilt."[83]

The specifications of the station building slated for construction at Port Dalhousie were described as follows:

"The building is to be of Timber on a Piled Foundation — and shall be 60 feet long — and Twenty-five feet wide outside. The Roof to be covered with Shingles and to project 9 feet at each Side and 3 feet at the Ends. It is to be divided into two Equal Compartments — that at the South End devoted to Freighting business provided with Two Sliding half Sash doors — one opening on Each of the Platforms. These doors to be about 8 feet wide and 9 feet high.

"The other Compartment is to be divided into three rooms viz 'Office', 'General Waiting' and Ladies Rooms. The latter to be furnished with Water Closet."[84]

The piles were of oak timber, one foot in diameter, and placed six feet apart. The roof was of truss construction, the building was enclosed with tongued and grooved upright boards, and the surrounding platforms were eight feet wide. For this, too, it was required that "the whole of the Workmanship and Materials must be of the very best description."[85] The choice of colour for the external paint was left to the Engineer, but the contract did specify that three coats were required and that the colour on the doors, window frames and sashes was to contrast with the walls. Construction was to be undertaken in six weeks after the award of the contract.

The first stations on the Railway were often inadequate in size, and additions were required as passenger and freight volumes increased above the original expectations. For example, in 1857,

Your Friends in

Port Robinson

Would Like a Glimpse of You

A decorative postcard of the station at Port Robinson. *John Burtniak Collection*

tenders were invited for enlarging the station at St. Catharines. This called for 30 feet to be added to the east end, "to be finished in every respect like the present building, with the exception of the doors (of which there are to be two, back and front)".[86]

Changes to the Welland Railway

In 1872, when the Great Western Railway lost the opportunity to use the Erie and Niagara Railway as part of its southern loop line concept, it negotiated running privileges over the track of the Welland Railway. The agreement stated that the Great Western could use 15 miles of track north from the Welland Junction in order to connect its southern route to the Suspension Bridge at Niagara Falls. As railways were now changing from the gauge of 5 feet 6 inches to the standard gauge of 4 feet 8½ inches, it was stipulated that the Great Western would lay a steel rail, keep the track in good running order, maintain cattle guards and fences at their expense, and pay the Welland Railway $9,000 a year for 21 years.[87]

Soon thereafter, the gauge of the line southwards to Port Colborne was reduced, because the ballast required by the Great Western for the construction of their Air Line route was to be supplied from 11 acres of land that had been purchased on the Lake Erie shore. The implications and the resultant work have been described by William Pay, the Superintendent of the line, as follows:

"The Welland railway having the wide gauge, five feet six inches, they could not run their trains to Port Colborne. . .I then began to get ready for it, and on the second day of April, 1873, the road was narrowed up from 5 feet 6 inches to 4 feet 8½ inches. No.1 train, No.2 and 3 were cancelled, and No. 4 ran to Port Colborne at night on the narrow gauge all right.

"On July 14th, 1873, the last of the 150 cars were narrowed up to 4 feet 8½ inches at a cost of $4,961.66. This includes the narrowing of the track. The Great Western now began to run their ballast trains to Port Colborne and paid the Welland railway fifty cents for every loaded car amounting to about $350 a week for five months."[88]

At this time, too, the five old locomotives were scrapped, because of age and because they could not be reduced in width. Three replacement units were purchased from Rhode Island for $42,675.[89] The boilers of these dismantled locomotives were used by the contractors on the Third Welland Canal, then under construction. The extensive reliance of the Canal works upon the Welland Railway is also clearly indicated in the Pay narrative, for example:

"In 1873 I put in a siding at Port Dalhousie for Larkin and Connolly to lock 1, new canal, and we took from Merritton 1,950 cars of stone, 50 cars of cement, and 38 cars of long timber, at $4.50 a car.

"Belden and Dennison had locks 2, 3, 4 and 5; I put in a siding for them, reaching over to Ontario street. I made arrangements with the Great Western railway to run their train of stone over the Welland railway to the locks from Merritton, paying the Welland 50 cents for every loaded car for the right of way. They run in 11,000 cars. The Welland railway put in 200 cars of cement from Thorold at $4.50, 142 cars of long timber from Merritton at $3.50 a car."[90]

A whole series of tracks were laid from the Welland Railway to the construction works in progress on the route of the new Canal. These temporary lines were found mainly to the north of the Escarpment. They ran to the beach of Lake Ontario for ballast, to Locks 6 and 7 near Geneva Street, to Lock 10 near the cemetery in St. Catharines, and to the aqueduct at Welland.

Railways were used to a considerable extent to assist with canal construction.

As the Third Canal was constructed on a new alignment, the spatial arrangements between the Welland Railway and the Welland Canal were necessarily changed. The Canal forsook its long established channel along the valley of Twelve Mile Creek next to St. Catharines, and was re-routed along a straight diagonal cut from Martindale Pond to the brow of the Escarpment east of Thorold. The line of the Welland Railway was dissected twice by this new channel. The first point was between Port Dalhousie and St. Catharines at Scott Street, east of Martindale Pond. The second point was between Thorold and Allanburg, after both the Canal and the Railway had passed over the brow of the Escarpment. At both points, swing bridges were provided for the Railway to cross over the Canal. In addition, the Railway had to be re-aligned for about a mile where it crossed the Escarpment to the east of Thorold, as its track was required for the new Canal works. With this double crossing of the Third Canal, the Welland Railway no longer paralleled the Canal on its eastern bank for the whole length.

However, the Railway retained its position next to the now abandoned Second Canal route, and this stretch of the Canal over the Escarpment from Thorold to St. Catharines now offered new advantages for industrial development. The point of particular importance to be noted here is that this portion of the Second Canal had been abandoned in favour of the Third Canal because its winding and constricted route was not able to handle the increasing Great Lakes-St. Lawrence shipping trade. But the Second Canal did retain its status as a water body; it still carried its regular flow of water, the changes in level as it crossed the Escarpment still provided an abundance of opportunities for harnessing the water power potential, and the water could still be used for industrial purposes (Fig. 3.5).

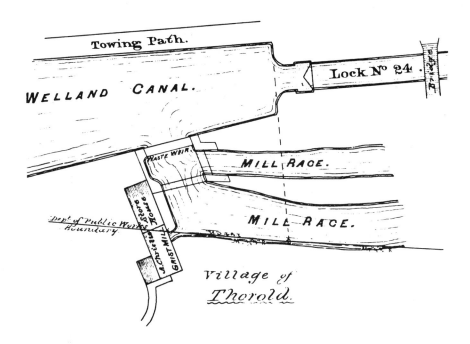

Fig. 3.5 A cross-section of the Welland Canal at Thorold, ca. 1850, indicating the tow-path on the east and the hydraulic-power facilities on the west of the Canal. *Shanly Papers, Archives of Ontario*

Thus, in 1887 there were two distinct Canal routes from Port Dalhousie to Allanburg — the Third Canal, with a depth of 14 feet, larger and fewer locks, and a straight alignment; and the Second Canal, with a limited depth of ten feet, smaller and more locks, and a circuitous route. The Second Canal between Port Dalhousie and Thorold remained open for barge traffic until about 1915.

The railway tracks which paralleled the Second Canal therefore retained their usefulness in serving the industries already located on the Canal banks; and, as the potential for industrial location along the abandoned section was realized and developed, the significance of the railway was increased considerably. Industrial sites from Thorold through Merritton to St. Catharines still possessed a fourfold set of inter-related advantages: railway access, water for power, access by barges and water for industrial purposes. This important array of beneficial circumstances contributed materially to the advent and expansion of the pulp and paper industry and other manufacturing enterprises along the line of the now abandoned canal across the Niagara Escarpment. The development of the paper industry started in Merritton in 1863 when John Riordon, "the father of the Canadian pulp and paper industry",[91] and his brother Charles began the production of wrapping paper in a property leased from Thomas R. Merritt, just below Lock 6 on the east side of the Welland Canal. In 1867, a new mill was established between Locks 17 and 18 for newsprint production, which was sold mainly to the *Toronto Globe*. Other companies followed — the Lincoln Pulp and Paper Mill in 1871, the Garden City Paper Mill in 1890, the Montrose Paper Company in 1902, the Lybster Paper Mill in 1908, Interlake Tissue in 1911, and the Ontario Paper Company in 1912.[92]

The paper industry in Thorold-Merritton developed because of the combined advantage of rail and Canal modes of transportation.

John Burtniak Collection

Railways played a positive role in this cumulative process of industrial location and advancement. A half-century after the Riordon venture, the Ontario Paper Company chose to locate in Thorold. The combination of reasons that were involved has been described by Carl Wiegman. There were the advantages of cheap hydro-electric power, the community had a paper-making tradition and a supply of trained paper-makers, "it was on a canal connecting two of the Great Lakes, which opened the possibility of shipping pulpwood and paper by water. It was served by several railroads. It was not far from the coal mines of Pennsylvania and Ohio. And it was near a settled community."[93] This succinct type of statement could be repeated for many other industrial decisions. It underlines the relevance of railways in the process of industrial location, not as a factor in isolation but as an important inducement when coupled with other locational features.

These changes to the Canal also had a signal effect on the Welland Railway because, conceived as an auxiliary to lighten its more ladened ships, this function became redundant when the Third Canal was opened from Port Dalhousie to Allanburg in 1887. As the depth of water over the lock sills had been increased from 9 to 14 feet, the width from 26.5 to 45 feet, and the length between the gates from 150 to 270 feet, ships of increased draught and capacity were now able to use the Canal. The potential cargo capacity of vessels using the Canal had been increased approximately four times, typically from about 750 tons to 2,700 tons.[94] These major improvements provided a re-invigorated form of competition to the Welland Railway for the carriage of heavy goods across the Peninsula. Indeed, the supplementary system of a railway link between Lake Erie and Lake Ontario was no longer required as an adjunct to the Canal, and its importance (already in jeopardy because of alternative routes) waned rapidly. The line was no longer required to meet the purposes for which it had been built.

But the route was not yet dead. In 1876, when the Welland Railway moved its Thorold depot from Chapel Street to a new station at Regent Street, the *Thorold Post* wryly noted: "The new station presents a very neat appearance, and is a decided contrast to the rickitty cramped up place they had before".[95] Also, freight services at Merritton were improved considerably when the Welland Railway was linked directly with the Great Western Railway; for example, after 1877, freight could be booked directly to all Great Western stations from Thorold instead of only from Merritton as previously.[96]

The saga of the Welland Railway as an independent Company culminated in 1884 with the sale of its assets to the Grand Trunk Railway.[97] This event ended three decades of independent existence. Previously, the Great Western had offered to buy the Railway, but this was rejected because the price was too low. The later successful bid was £166,592, which included £26,000 for the capital improvements which had been expended by the Great Western on the line. As for the reason for this purchase, A. W. Currie has concluded that, "since . . .the Grand Trunk got only a broken-down, unprofitable road, its main objectives must have been to keep the Welland out of the hands of the Canada Southern".[98] This was, indeed, a sad end for what may be regarded as St. Catharines' prime civic contribution to the Canadian railway era.

The Riordon paper mills at Merritton, 1898.   *John Burtniak Collection*

Chapter IV

Railways in the South of the Peninsula

The south of the Peninsula provided not only the most direct route but also one with no topographic constrictions for linking the American railway systems between Buffalo and Detroit. It lay on the direct route from the principal seaports of Boston and New York to the expanding western interior of the continent. As a result, by the end of the 1870's, three parallel and competing routes had been constructed inland from the Lake Erie shoreline (Fig. 4.1). Admittedly, the southern portion of the Peninsula comprised a larger area than the northern section but, as no major centres of population then existed, this was an inordinate number of separate tracks. The surfeit can be explained in terms of regional location, the economic-political circumstances of the time, and by the exigencies of inter-company rivalry. Then, in the 1890's the Toronto, Hamilton and Buffalo Railway was added, again largely south of the Escarpment, and a few small but interesting and provocative tourist lines were also constructed.

The Buffalo and Lake Huron Railway

From the heat of polarized debate, the first railway to be constructed inland from Lake Erie was initiated as the Buffalo, Brantford and Goderich Railway by the Brantford and Buffalo Joint Stock Railway Company, which had been authorized in 1852 to build a line from Fort Erie to or near Brantford.[1] This was American competition financed by American capital. As viewed by T.C. Keefer in 1864:

> "This road originated in a desire, on the part of the populous city of Buffalo, to render tributary to herself the rich peninsula of Canada West; and also to divert the stream of eastern and western travel and freight away from the Suspension Bridge route to her own hotels and stations."[2]

This Railway also received considerable support in Brantford, where it was visualized that it would provide a viable alternative to the inadequate steamer service which plied along the Grand River and across Lake Erie to Buffalo. It also offered redress for the slight received when the Great Western line running between Hamilton and London by-passed the town.[3] Funds were subscribed by Brantford, Bertie Township and Buffalo, and construction was underway in Humberstone Township by 1852, while the major task of raising a bridge over the Grand River near Paris was in progress by 1853. The track was opened from Buffalo to Brantford in 1854 with the usual celebrations:

> "Shortly after 2 p.m., the trains arrived and were received with loud cheers, firing of cannon and every demonstration of joy. There were three locomotives, the first with one passenger car, the second with

five, and the third with one, all well filled. About 500 we understand came over from Buffalo, including a large number of Buffalo firemen who made a very good appearance in their splendid uniforms."[4]

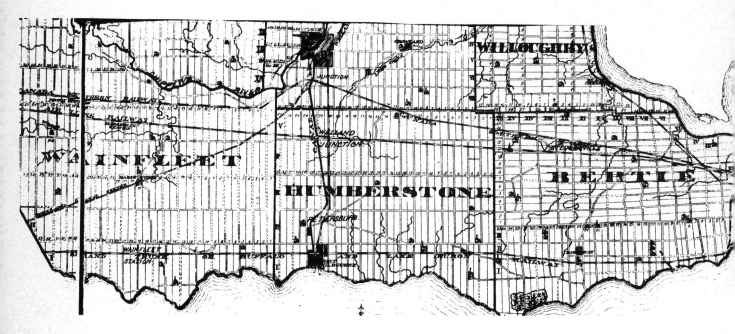

Welland County, 1876.

H. R. Page, Illustrated Historical Atlas of the Counties of Lincoln and Welland, 1876

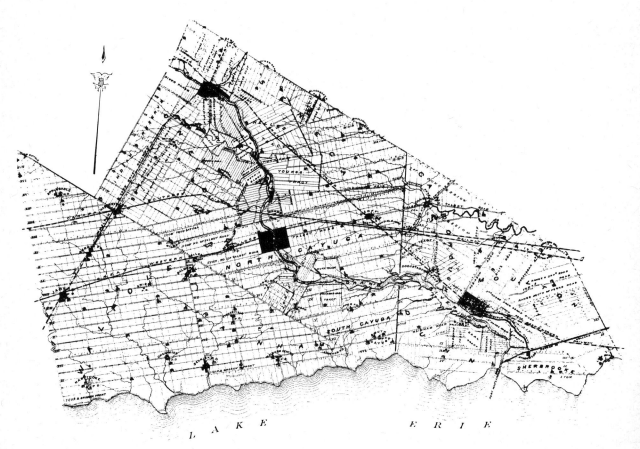

Haldimand County, 1879.

H. R. Page, Illustrated Historical Atlas of the County of Haldimand, 1879

Fig. 4.1   Competing Railway Lines in the South of the Peninsula, 1876 and 1879.

Sherkston Station on the Buffalo and Lake Huron (later Grand Trunk Railway), ca. 1880.   *Ernest F. Ott, A History of Humberstone Township, 1967*

The lonely yet commanding Station at Lowbanks.   *John Burtniak Collection*

Initially, there were stage connections from the main line to Port Dover, Hamilton and Paris, but the line was soon extended. In 1854, it reached Paris, where it linked with the Great Western. It thus obtained a part of the substantial flow of passenger traffic between Detroit and Buffalo. However, the Company ran into financial difficulty in attempting to complete its track from Paris to Goderich, and was unable to complete to "the more perfect finishing and equipment of the portion from Fort Erie to Paris". Labourers working on the road were not paid regularly, resulting in riots at Ridgeway in 1855, with one person being killed and several wounded in the fracas.[5] Faced by these difficulties, the line was purchased and incorporated as the Buffalo and Lake Huron Railway in 1856.[6]

The line was formally opened to Goderich in 1858. At the Niagara River, Buffalo and Fort Erie (then Waterloo) were linked by a ferry crossing. The first boat, the *International,* is presumed to have been constructed at Chippawa; it weighed almost 500 tons, had a length of 160 feet, a beam of 32 feet and a depth of 10 feet.[7] The ferry did not carry railroad cars; the passage from Black Rock to Fort Erie took 25 minutes. This vessel burned in 1854; it was replaced temporarily by two chartered ships in 1855, the *Sandusky* and the *Troy,* until a second *International* could be constructed by a Buffalo company. This operated from 1857 until 1873, when the International Bridge was opened for railway traffic.

The transition in size between the two vessels provides an interesting commentary on the rapid rate of technological advance and change during the late nineteenth century. As described by Eric Heyl:

> "The new ferry boat was a wooden side-wheeler, 226 feet long, 40 feet 8 inches wide, 13 feet depth of hold, 1,121 gross tons register. Two sets of tracks, capable of holding eight passenger cars, were laid on the main deck. The machinery consisted of two engines placed thwartship. Each engine was connected to the side-wheel on its side of the hull and was operated independently of the other engine. This permitted the greatest flexibility when maneuvring the vessel."[8]

After crossing the entrance to the Niagara River on this shuttle ferry, the Railway then followed closely the north shore of Lake Erie via Ridgeway and Sherkston to Port Colborne, Wainfleet, Lowbanks, and over the Feeder Canal to Dunnville. It then angled north-west across Haldimand County to Caledonia, and thence via Brantford and Stratford to Goderich, thereby connecting Lake Huron with Lake Erie (Fig. 4.2). Because of the location of its two terminals, the line could carry through traffic only during the ice-free season of navigation, though local traffic between the way stations could operate on a year-round basis. As its terminus was in a foreign country, trade was also liable to fluctuate through international trading and currency regulations. T.C. Keefer offered this interpretation in 1864:

> "The great want of this road is a terminus on Lake Ontario in order to obtain the grain traffic. . .This railway has a value in its power of mischief, for it furnishes, in connection with the Grand Trunk, via Stratford and Sarnia, an opposition to the Great Western, and as it has at present no legitimate orbit, it may become merged in one of these larger bodies."[9]

This prophetic statement was to be fulfilled within a few years. Working agreements were arranged with the Grand Trunk in 1866 and 1867, followed by absorption into the Grand Trunk network in 1870.[10] An important feature of the Buffalo and Lake Huron-Grand Trunk route was that it resulted in a second crossing of the Niagara River, to supplement the previous crossing at the Suspension Bridge. An agreement for use of the new bridge was made between the two Companies in 1866.[11] The bridge, from Bridgeburg (near Fort Erie) to Black Rock (near Buffalo), was under construction by 1870 and was opened for traffic in 1873. A new line, 3.5 miles in length, was constructed to connect the previous line of track to the bridge, and the former line to the ferry crossing was abandoned. These new circumstances proved to be to the detriment of Fort Erie, but gave birth to the new settlement of Bridgeburg at the crossing point of the Niagara River. The details of this bridge are discussed in Chapter VI, and its urban significance in Chapter VII.

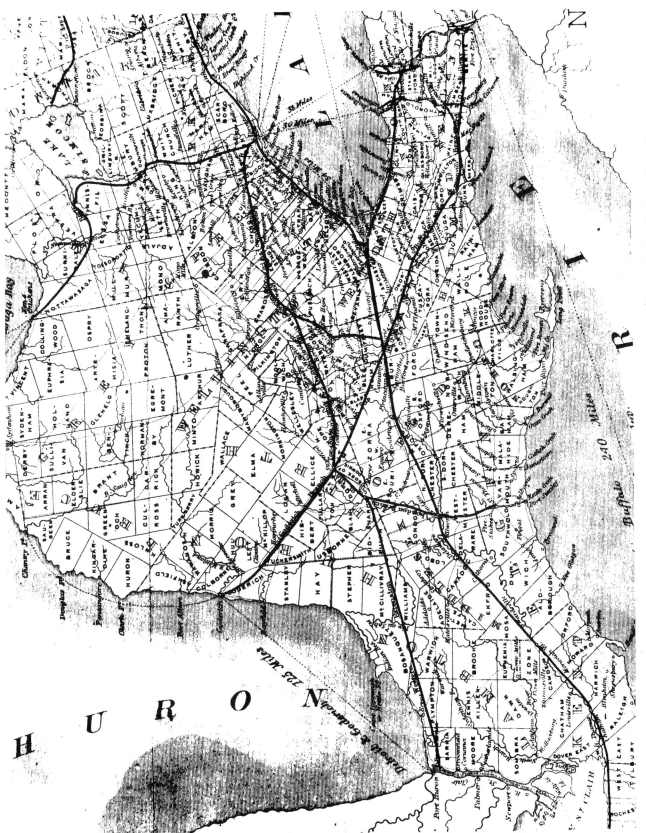

Fig. 4.2 The Railway System of Southwestern Ontario, 1857. This part of Maclear & Co, *Railway Map of Canada West*, shows how, by the construction of the Buffalo and Brantford Railway, the north and south of the Peninsula were connected to the wider Provincial railway system that then existed.

W. H. N. Hull Collection

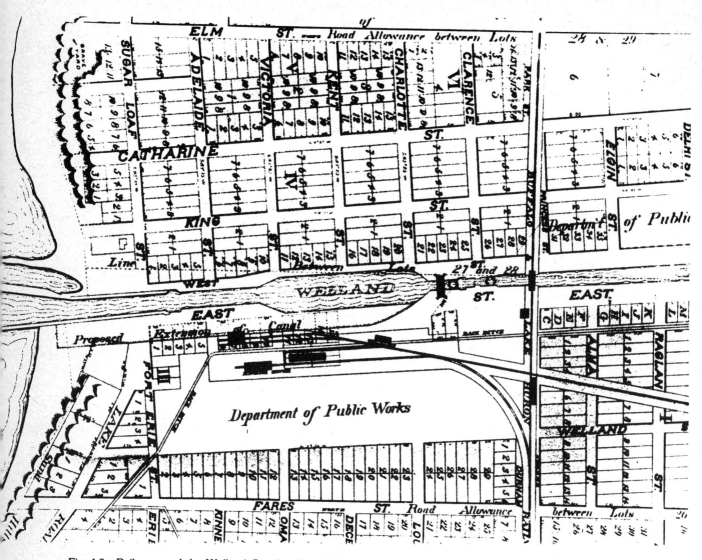

Fig. 4.3   Railways and the Welland Canal at Port Colborne, 1862.

Tremaines' Map of the Counties of Lincoln and Welland, 1862

Another important feature was the strengthening of Port Colborne which, by 1859, had also received the Welland Railway to supplement its industrial and trading ability as the southern port of entry to the Welland Canal system (Fig. 4.3). The two lines here crossed at grade and were connected to each other by a one-way railway line, towards Buffalo. Regretfully, the Railway also had one immediate adverse consequence. It put out of commission its direct forerunner. Inevitably, virulent competition existed between the several modes of transportation in the Peninsula, and the fate of the Grand River Navigation Company as a result of the Buffalo and Lake Huron Railway illustrates the supremacy of the railway endeavour. As B. E. Hill has indicated: "The official opening of the steam rail connection between Brantford and Buffalo sounded the death knell of the canal [the Grand River Navigation Company]. This cheaper, speedier and more efficient mode of transportation soon was drawing away much of its freight and passenger traffic."[12] The exhilaration of the local citizens at the progress wrought by the railway must have been mitigated with a certain degree of regret. The Navigation Company had played a significant role by opening up the lower and the middle sections of the Grand River valley to settlement; it had also fostered its towns and cities, including Dunnville (Fig. 4.4), Cayuga and Caledonia in the Peninsula. It was now swept aside as an unwanted asset as railways in the Peninsula progressed.

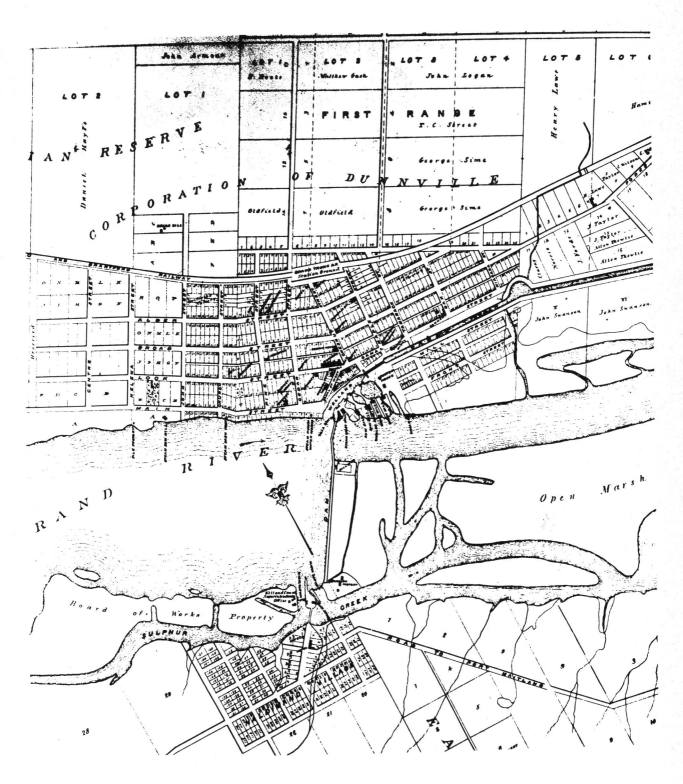

Fig. 4.4   The Buffalo and Lake Huron (Grand Trunk) Railway at Dunnville, 1879.
H. R. Page, Illustrated Historical Atlas of the County of Haldimand, 1879

Leaping forward to the present, the station later constructed at Ridgeway (west of Fort Erie) has been described as "one of the prettiest ever built on the line".[13] With this aesthetic attribute it is fitting that, during the 1970's in an era of railway decline, it should have been moved to Fort Erie as one component of an historical railway museum. Its architectural characteristics have been described by E. A. Willmot as follows:

"This station could well qualify for a study in window design. On the west end of the building which contains the waiting room, the curved glass in the windows matches the contour of the building, and the windows are protected by the overhanging eaves of the conical roof. A rectangular fan transom was placed above the waiting room door, and on each side of the entrance, narrow sidelights are glazed in delicately tinted pink pebbled glass. Above the bay window of the operator's office, an ornate square turret rises beyond the roof ridge. A Palladian window was built on its front elevation, with complementing oval windows on the east and west sides of the turret."[14]

The Canada Southern Railway

An American route inter-connecting the American systems could have been achieved somewhat earlier than the Great Western in the north of the Peninsula. Such a railway was first envisaged as early as 1836, when the Niagara and Detroit Rivers Railroad was incorporated to construct a line from Fort Erie to Sandwich on the Detroit River.[15] It was intended to provide a direct means of connection between the states of New York and Michigan, primarily to assist the considerable western emigration which was then taking place and to accommodate the expected high volumes of freight and passenger traffic. The shortest route was through Canada and:

"Although the portion of country through which the proposed Railway is intended to pass, does not, at present, possess the wealth necessary to enable the inhabitants to complete a work of such magnitude: the object is, nevertheless, attainable by means of the assistance that will be promptly afforded by persons resident in the adjoining portions of the United States."[16]

The impetus was external. The proposal was essentially an American venture, crossing Canadian terrain to connect American railway systems, and financed by American capital to meet American needs. Within the Peninsula, as J. P. Merritt later noted:

"The subject of a through line of railway from the Niagara to the Detroit River, had for some time occupied the attention of the people on our Western frontier. . .[In June, 1836,] a large and influential meeting was held at Sandwich. . .[at which] Stock books were opened throughout the country, those for the Niagara district being placed in the hands of Mr. [William Hamilton] Merritt."[17]

Dunnville, as an established port and market centre, was encouraged in its patterns of urban growth, first by the Buffalo and Lake Huron Railway and later by the Toronto, Hamilton and Buffalo Railway.   *John Burtniak Collection*

This selection of Merritt for the promotion of American interests was a good choice. He was a leading and respected citizen, he had been elected to the Upper Canadian Assembly for the Haldimand Riding in 1832, and was re-elected in 1834 and 1836. Through marriage, travel and business connections he had considerable knowledge about people, affairs, trade and commerce in the State of New York. He was capable of identifying the local advantages which would result from a through link between the Niagara and the Detroit Rivers.

Capital was raised, and lines were surveyed across the

Peninsula from the Falls at Niagara and Fort Erie. But competition from the London and Gore (Great Western) Railroad, the economic depression from 1837 onwards, and the unrest of the Mackenzie Rebellion restricted its further promotion. Even so, discussions about possible railway routes continued, with Merritt being an active participant.[18] In 1845, when the charter was about to expire:

> "Mr. Merritt thought it a fitting opportunity to attempt to revive the scheme, and consequently opened a correspondence with some of the leading capitalists in Boston. Meeting with encouragement, he made a personal visit, explained the scheme, and was agreeably surprised to find the leading capitalists there in perfect accord. The stock was instantly taken up, and influential contractors, who were also large shareholders, agreed to finish the work within the time and before the expiration of the charter".[19]

This former station at Ridgeway has been moved to Fort Erie, where it now provides a central feature of the railway museum.
John Burtniak Collection

Merritt's energetic efforts on behalf of a railway across the Peninsula to New York were considerable. His diary has indicated the busy schedule, the wide-ranging contacts, and the extended discussions that were necessary in the cause of railway promotion:

> "July 12th. Met C. C. Trowbridge of Detroit, called on Jacob Riddle, president of the New York and Albany Railroad, Garden G. Howland, president of the Utica Railroad, Davis, Brooks and Co., Sedam and Sage, W. B. Astor.
>
> 21st, The last day in New York. Met with Mr. Fisk, president of the Long Island Railroad, and James J. Shipman, the engineer, who constructed it at a cost of $8,500 a mile, he thinks as good a road, similarly situated, can be made for $7,500 a mile.
>
> Some of the names in Boston, with whom we transacted business, were Hon. George Bliss of Springfield, president of the Western Railway, Joseph Quincy, Thayer and Bros., Francis Young, A. Gilmour, W. F. Wild, A. Lawrence."[20]

In 1845, the Board of Directors assembled at Windsor. They acknowledged Merritt's progressive exertions and passed a laudatory resolution: "That the sincere thanks of this meeting be offered to Wm. Hamilton Merritt, Esq., M.P.P. for his unceasing, strenuous, and successful exertions in calling public attention, and particularly the attention of capitalists, to this patriotic and profitable enterprise."[21] Other consequences were less favourable. Regard, esteem and respect in certain quarters was countered with antipathy, fear and distaste elsewhere. For his American efforts, he was dubbed by some of his own people with the unwelcome sobriquet of the "Honourable Member from New York".[22]

Recent research has suggested that Merritt had a capability and a vision beyond the narrower viewpoint of many of his contemporaries. In the assessment of Donald C. Masters, Merritt:

A steel-engraving portrait of William Hamilton Merritt, a vital figure in both canal and railway developments.
John Burtniak Collection

> "had a constructive railway policy in that he understood the possibilities of a through line from Chicago and Detroit to tidewater. . .The Niagara and Detroit project was a perfectly legitimate attempt to divert through Canada trade which would otherwise be transported by American railways south of Lake Erie; but [in addition], as early as 1845, Merritt was willing to combine it with a Canadian trunk line [that is, from the Maritime Provinces through Quebec and north of Lake Ontario to the border at Detroit]. . .Similarly his advocacy in 1854 of a railway from Amherstburgh to Niagara was by no means prejudicial to the interests of the main Grand Trunk line."[23]

The Grand River was the major physical barrier on east-west railway routes in the south of the Peninsula.

John Burtniak Collection

Main Street (looking west)
Stevensville, Ontario.

Stevensville, as a small rural centre, obtained two railways because of railway competition in the south of the Peninsula.

John Burtniak Collection

With Merritt's re-invigoration of the Niagara and Detroit Rivers project, a *Prospectus* was issued in 1845 which explained clearly the purpose of the line and the attraction of the Canadian route. These features were described in the *Journal* as follows:

> "The Niagara and Detroit Rivers Rail Road is designed to connect the eastern with the western parts of this continent, by one continuous line, which as regards *cost of construction,* direction, elevation and economy is unrivalled by any road for a similar distance. It will be nearly in a straight line, having only two gentle curves in a distance of 222 miles.
>
> The grade is in no place over fifteen feet for short distances, and averaging less than two feet in the mile. . .
>
> *Wayfare through Canada* — This part of the line is left to balance the repairs of the road and the expense of management. Although no remuneration is estimated, the route intersects the Welland Canal, Grand River Navigation, the Port Dover and London Plank Roads; also various other communications leading from numerous villages and a dense agricultural population in the interior; the travel and freight from which, in addition to what will pass direct from Buffalo to Detroit and vice versa, is likely to yield the same returns as other lines for the like distance".[24]

A bill to extend the time allowed was presented in 1846, followed by further bills in 1847, 1849 and 1850. Petitions for the renewal of this charter were supported *inter alia* by the councils of Bertie and Wainfleet Townships and the Niagara District. They were opposed by the City of Hamilton, the Village of Beamsville and, most strongly and ardently, by the Great Western. This, of course, was the period when the Great Western was also actively considering its route, and rivalry between the two Companies and their adherents was intense. As the *Toronto Colonist* noted in 1845:

> "The Niagara and Detroit Railway will be essentially a work, if carried out, for the *benefit of American travelers,* offering no particular advantage to the Province through which it will pass, but the great disadvantage that it will be along the line of an extended frontier, without protection, and entirely at the mercy of our neighbours."[25]

Merritt's argument was that only one line should be built from Detroit, with branch lines as necessary, rather than attempting to support the costly duplication of two competing lines. In 1845 his diary noted: "I proposed the directors of the Great Western Railway unite their interests with the Niagara and Detroit River Railroad on the following terms: — First, that a line be run to a point, where they diverge to Hamilton and Buffalo by the shortest and most direct route."[26] He was not without support in this feeling. George S. Tiffany of Hamilton wrote in 1845: "My sincere wish is that a union of interests of the two roads should be affected, and I see no difficulty in the matter."[27]

However, the response from the Great Western was non-committal. The Company resolved: "That the termination of the Great Western Railroad on the Niagara River shall be at or near Fort Erie, and that the point of interaction between the branch and the main trunk from Hamilton to Windsor shall be at such place as on proper investigation will be found most conducive to the interests of the stockholders."[28] These sentiments were quite unacceptable to Merritt. The resolution made no mention of the imperative need for union between the two companies. Merritt replied with concern:

"The Resolution proposed did not, in my judgment, clearly and fully meet the intention of the parties. I therefore proposed the following:

Resolved, That the Directors of the Great Western Railroad Company agree to unite their interests with the Niagara and Detroit Rivers Railroad Company on the following terms: — First, that a line be run from Detroit to a point where they can diverge to Hamilton and Buffalo on the shortest and best route. That in case the above be agreed to, we will join.

My reasons for preferring the latter, is, that it places the two companies on precisely the same footing. Without this recognition, any attempts at negotiation would be idle. It also clearly expresses the object and intention of diverging as soon as practicable from Detroit — which will be in the vicinity of Burford [near Brantford] (as we suppose) and the stock will be subscribed with this view".[29]

In the meantime, the relative merits of one or two routes across the Peninsula were given avid coverage in newspaper columns. The *Journal,* in 1845, noted that "there can be no sort of good policy in the construction and maintenance of two long parallel lines of road, not many miles distant from each other, and having the same primary end in view, namely the traffic between the eastern and western states."[30] However, within four months, the *Journal* took the opposite viewpoint: namely that the Peninsula could sustain two routes, including one line in the south and one line in the north. A line in the south was thought not to be prejudicial to the northern route, but would attract traffic which would otherwise flow to the south of Lake Erie. Thus it was argued:

"The object in constructing the Niagara and Detroit Rivers Rail Road is to secure the commerce between Buffalo and Detroit to the north side of Lake Erie in opposition to any that might be constructed on the other side; and not, as is supposed by some, to rival any undertaking having a similar object in Canada."[31]

By 1847, Merritt also seemed to have accepted the proposition of two routes when he stated in a letter to Sir Allan McNab:

"Two routes offer from the Falls — above [south] and below [north of] the mountain. The first lies most direct from Detroit; the latter passes the most extensive manufacturing location in the western part of America, (the Welland Canal); passes through numerous villages, and branching from Hamilton to Toronto. The Western road through Chatham, Delaware, London, Brantford to Hamilton, will take as many way passengers and some more way freight than any one of the roads named; connecting Stoney Creek, Grimsby, Beamsville, Jordan, St. Catharines, and the great manufacturing towns which must spring up on the Welland Canal, to the Falls there can be little doubt in this but the way passengers and freight will pay for cost of construction. . .

Again, suppose the road on the north side of Lake Erie, to intersect the Great Western on or about London, was made; it would not only successfully compete with the south side of Lake Erie, and draw far more travel over the western part of the Great Western than it would take from it on the East. I do not consider the Canada Southern road will affect it, terminate where it may. The southern population being inconsiderable, travellers are more likely to pass over this than to travel on the other."[32]

A compromise agreement was reached between the Niagara and Detroit Rivers Railway and the Great Western in 1847. The terms stated:

"The Eastern terminus of the Great Western Railroad shall be on the Niagara River, and that the road shall go to the Town of St. Catharines, and to the City of Hamilton, and then to Chatham, Sandwich and Windsor. If such arrangements were not commenced and intended for completion before 1855, then the Directors of the Great Western would not oppose the renewal of a charter by the Niagara and Detroit Rivers Railroad Company."[33]

When this agreement was communicated to the House of Assembly, the application for a charter by the Niagara and Detroit Rivers Railway was withdrawn. Even so, the matter persisted with proposals and counter-proposals continuing to be made. A huge tangled jungle of interests, principles, facts, and arguments had to be resolved. For example, in 1850 when the Standing Committee on Railroads and Telegraph Lines examined evidence for the incorporation of a company to construct a railroad between the Niagara and Detroit Rivers, careful calculations were made of through versus way business. Through business required the shortest and most convenient route, whereas way business involved linking the greatest number of centres in order to encourage and promote their traffic. The former involved a direct route, which was wholly above the Escarpment and relatively inexpensive to construct; the latter involved a lengthier route *and* the ascent and descent of grades if Hamilton was to be served.

Charles Lamont Collection

The financial-business interests agreed that:

"The projects must be viewed with reference to their financial merits; whichever road can be more cheaply built, and will pay better, that is the one to which the capitalists will give the preference. It is obvious that the road *via* Hamilton presents the heaviest cost, and consequently, the prospect of being less profitable and less inviting to the capitalist. Here it is, the question arises: How much gain would it be to any road traversing your Peninsula, to visit Hamilton, and secure the business of Lake Ontario? Would the business be an equivalent for the additional cost?"[34]

Specifically, as the cost of the Great Western was estimated to be at least a million dollars more than the Niagara and Detroit Rivers Railroad, then its business would have to yield annually about $130,000 extra in order for the route to be economically viable.

The station and its unprotected crossing at Attercliffe

John Burtniak Collection

The Great Western continued its strong objections. It resisted the proposed charter for a Niagara and Detroit Rivers Railroad and opposed any suggestion which involved co-operation between the two Companies. The Great Western regarded a main line along the direct route of easy gradient, with a branch line from Brantford to Hamilton as the virtual abrogation of its charter. The outcome of this insistence was twofold: confirmation of a route across the north of the Peninsula for the Great Western and deferral of railway construction in the south by almost a decade. The Peninsula was caught in a battle of words and of conflicting aspirations. Its destiny was being determined in the board-rooms of distant railway companies against the financial merits of conflicting routes.

For instance, in 1847, the Woodstock and Lake Erie Railway was incorporated to build a railway from Woodstock to Port Dover and Port Burwell.[35] It was provided with a time extension and was allowed to extend its line to Dunnville in 1853,[36] followed in 1855 by an extension line to the Suspension Bridge on the Niagara River and to St. Thomas.[37] In the same year the Amherstburg and St. Thomas Railway was incorporated to build from Amherstburg to St.

Thomas.[38] Three years later, in 1858, these two Companies were amalgamated to form the Great Southwestern Railway, a name which was changed immediately to the Niagara and Detroit Rivers Railway Company, with permission to alter the line from Simcoe to the Niagara River "so as to cross the Grand River at such point or points as they may deem expedient."[39] Next year, 1859, the Niagara and Detroit Rivers Railway Company was authorized to construct a railway from the Niagara River at Clifton through Simcoe and St. Thomas to the Detroit River at Windsor or Sandwich, and also a railway "from some point on the aforesaid line of Railway. . .to the Niagara River at or near Fort Erie."[40]

Buffalo to Niagara Falls and Toronto.

Miles from Buff.	STATIONS.	Express. Daily.	Toronto Express. Ex. Sun.	Atlantic Express. Daily.	Toronto Express. Ex. Sun.	Express. Daily.	Excursion Sundays only.
..	BUFFALO, Exchange St. Depot	....	7.55A.M.	....	3.30P.M.	....	9.30A.M.
3	BLACK ROCK......	....	8.15 "	....	3.50 "	....	9.50 "
4	FORT ERIE........	7.15A.M.	8.25 "	11.45A.M.	4.00 "	7.55P.M.	10.00 "
5	VICTORIA.........	7.20 "	8.30 "	11.50 "	4.05 "	8.00 "	10.05 "
7	NIAGARA JUNC....	7.25 "	8.35 "	12.05P.M.	4.10 "	8.05 "	10.10 "
12	BLACK CREEK.....	....	8.42 "	....	4.18 "	8.12 "	10.23 "
18	CHIPPAWA.........	7.43 "	8.51 "	12.22 "	4.29 "	8.22 "	10.38 "
21	NIAGARA FALLS....	7.52A.M.	9.02 "	12.40 "	4.43 "	8.33 "	10.45 "
22	SUSPENSION B'GE,	....	9.09 "	12.45P.M.	4.52 "	8.35P.M.	10.50 "
28	QUEENSTON........	....	9.35 "	....	5.15 "	....	11.05 "
35	NIAGARA CITY	....	9.45 "	....	5.30 "	....	11.15A.M.
..	TORONTO, via Stm'r,	....	12.00 noon	....	7.15P.M.	....	....

Toronto to Niagara Falls and Buffalo.

Miles from Niag.	STATIONS.	St. Louis Express. Daily.	Buffalo Express. Ex. Sun.	Pacific Express. Daily.	Buffalo Express. Daily.	E
..	TORONTO...........	....	7.30A.M.	....	‡ 3.00P.M.	
..	NIAGARA CITY	....	10.15 "	....	* 6.00 "	
7	QUEENSTON	....	10.27 "	....	6.12 "	
13	SUSPENSION B'GE,	....	10.45 "	1.00P.M.	6.32 "	
14	NIAGARA FALLS....	8.00A.M.	10.50 "	1.05 "	6.37 "	
17	CHIPPAWA.........	8.14 "	11.05 "	1.18 "	6.54 "	
23	BLACK CREEK......	8.24 "	11.20 "	....	7.10 "	
28	NIAGARA JUNC....	8.35 "	11.35 "	1.35 "	7.25 "	
30	VICTORIA	8.50 "	11.40 "	1.45 "	7.30 "	
31	FORT ERIE.........	8.55A.M.	11.45 "	1.50P.M.	7.35 "	
32	BLACK ROCK.......	....	11.55 "	....	7.45 "	
35	BUFFALO, Excha'ge St. Depot	....	12 15P.M.	....	8.05P.M.	

* Daily.   ‡ Except Sundays. Toronto Boats do not run on Sunday.

From Buffalo to Toronto by the Canada Southern Railway, 1880.   *John Burtniak Collection*

These two lines were not constructed. The plans of the Niagara and Detroit Rivers Railway Company lay moribund until the late 1860's when, after the American Civil War, they emerged under a new guise and new auspices. The promoter, this time, was William A. Thomson (1816-1878) of Queenston. He had incorporated the Fort Erie Railroad Company in 1857, and purchased the Erie and Ontario Railroad in 1863. He now promoted the Erie and Niagara Extension Railway Company, which was incorporated in 1868 with powers to construct a direct route across the Peninsula from Fort Erie via St. Thomas to Sandwich or Windsor.[41] The name of this Company was changed to the Canada Southern Railway in 1869.[42]

This extended concept of a railway across the south of the Peninsula from the Niagara River was opposed strongly by the Great Western and by the communities which it served. An example of hostility was expressed in the pages of the *St. Catharines Constitutional:*

> "The line is not at present required, as there are three parallel lines already in existence; that the road, if built, could not by any possibility pay its working expenses, as even the Great Western does not now do so from the proceeds of local traffic; that it would be unfair to detract business from the Great Western, which was built with English capital under Acts of the Canadian Parliament."[43]

The reason for the opposition to the Canada Southern, as was so frequently and ardently stated by its promoters, was that it would provide the shortest route between Buffalo and either Detroit or Chicago and their expanding hinterland areas. The proposal was, therefore, in direct competition with the Great Western and the communities served along its line of track. The route was surveyed between the three points of Buffalo, St. Thomas and Detroit by F. N. Finney, the Chief Engineer. It had low grades and easy curves. The route crossed the south centre of the Peninsula, with stations at Fort Erie, Stevensville, Welland Junction, and across the Welland Canal to Marshville (Wainfleet) in Welland County. It then entered Haldimand County, traversing the centre with stations at Moulton, Attercliffe, Darling Road, Canfield, Deans Station and Hagersville. It crossed the Grand River between these latter two stations. The first train passed over this track in 1873. By an Act of 1875,[44] the Canada Southern Railway was given permission to acquire the holdings of the Erie and Niagara Railway, which consolidated its competitive position against the Great Western and provided ownership of track and facilities from north to south across the Peninsula. The extent of its system in Southwestern Ontario by 1880 is shown on Fig. 4.5.

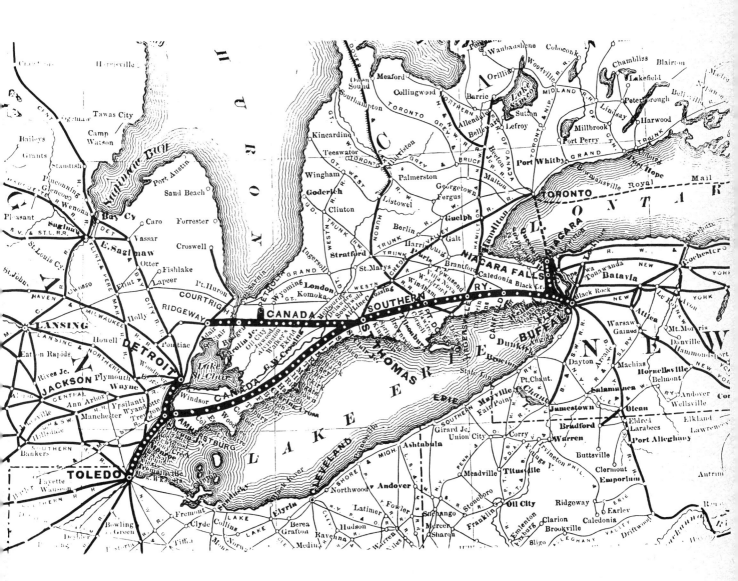

Fig. 4.5 The Canada Southern Network, 1880. This map from a Company time table depicts the oft-repeated statement that it provided the shortest route between Detroit and Buffalo.

John Burtniak Collection

The International Bridge replaced the ferry crossings over the Niagara River.
John Burtniak Collection

The Railway had to use a ferry crossing of the Niagara River, as the International Bridge north of Fort Erie was still under construction. It then made use of the completed bridge, until the Niagara Cantilever Bridge was built south of the Suspension Bridge at Niagara Falls in 1883. A double track was laid from Welland to Niagara Falls to serve this new structure, and this route then received the greater amount of traffic flow. Yards were located at Montrose to the north of the Welland River near Chippawa in 1883.

As already noted, the Canada Southern had taken possession of the Erie and Niagara Railway in 1875, which then gave this American-controlled railway both an east-west and a north-south route across the Peninsula. Interestingly enough, a Dominion Act of 1875 confirmed that the Canada Southern Railway was of general benefit to Canada, an enactment which justified the earlier mediation and overtures of William Hamilton Merritt on its behalf. The line was operated by the Michigan Central Railroad from 1894,[45] and by the New York Central from 1929.[46] To add confusion to confusing confusion in the sequence of railway names that have been mentioned, the Canada Southern-Michigan Central line is also sometimes referred to as the Pere Marquette Railroad. This name is derived from the fact that, in 1904, this Company was granted rights to use portions of the Canada Southern Railway.[47]

John Burtniak Collection

The Canada Air Line Railway

The Great Western responded vigorously to the threat posed by the Canada Southern. It feared that American competition would jeopardize its monopolistic position as the only east-west route within the Peninsula. To counterbalance this situation, the shareholders in 1870 authorized the construction of a competitive loop line. This was known as the Canada Air Line Railway, so named because the air line distance is the shortest route between two points on the earth's surface. The proposed route (alternatively called the Great Western Loop Line) called for a supplementary Great Western line from Glencoe west of London, via St. Thomas and Tillsonburg to Canfield in Haldimand County. It met the Buffalo and Lake Huron line here, and it was anticipated that rights of passage would then be obtained over this line to the International Bridge that was then under construction near Fort Erie.

The main street of Cayuga.

John Burtniak Collection

In the north of the Peninsula, the existing route of the Great Western from Hamilton to the Suspension Bridge involved a double crossing of the Niagara Escarpment. If the severe grades near Hamilton and St. Catharines could be avoided, there would be savings both in distance and in operating costs. The proposed Air Line Railway had no relief *impedimenta* along its route. The track could be laid on a nearly straight line across the flat terrain inland from Lake Erie. Cost estimates were comparable at $25,000 per mile, either for constructing the new route or for doubling the existing main line. The Air Line route was favoured because it was shorter. There was also the expectation that trade, created from opening a route across land not previously served by the Company, would produce more revenue than from doubling the present length of track.

However, the rights of access over the Canfield-to-Fort Erie section on the Buffalo and Lake Huron Railway were refused because this Railway was then leased to the competitive Grand Trunk. Accordingly, a different scheme for traversing the Peninsula had to be developed. This had three components — a track parallel to the Buffalo and Lake Huron line in the south-west of the Peninsula from Canfield to the International Bridge at Fort Erie, a lease with the Welland Railway to use their track north from Welland Junction to Allanburg, and the construction of a link from Allanburg to the Suspension Bridge. By these means, the Air Line was connected to the former main line, and the Great Western was then able to operate two routes across Southern Ontario between the Detroit and Niagara frontiers. The first train passed through in 1873. A new station, Allanburg Junction, was built to the south of the hamlet of Allanburg where the track to the Suspension Bridge diverged from the Welland Railway. In Haldimand County, the Railway served Jarvis and Cayuga, crossing the Grand River by an imposing bridge at the latter place (Fig. 4.6).

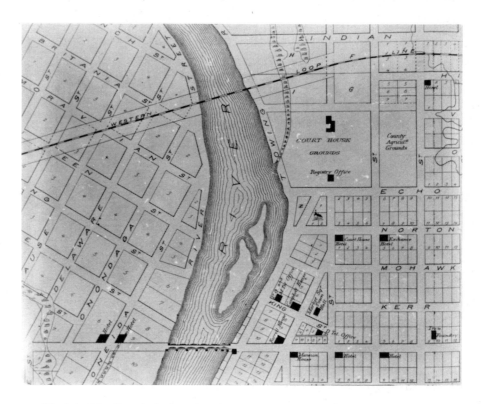

Fig. 4.6   The Canada Air Line Railway crossing the Grand River at Cayuga, 1879.   *H. R. Page, Illustrated Historical Atlas of the County of Haldimand, 1879*

The multiplicity of railways in the Peninsula brought about rate wars and severe competition for trade, with the result that many railways were amalgamated into the Grand Trunk network. The Canada Air Line became part of this larger system in 1882. The Grand Trunk had previously obtained control of the Buffalo and Lake Huron Railway in 1870. The Welland Railway, as a subsidiary of the Great Western, and the Great Western itself were also incorporated into this larger union of railway enterprises. The only lines in the Peninsula not incorporated into the Grand Trunk system were those of the Canada Southern and its associate, the Erie and Niagara Railway. As a result, by 1890, the railway map of the Peninsula depicted one east-west Canadian line north of the Niagara Escarpment, and three lines (two Canadian and one American) south of the Escarpment. In the north-south direction there was a Canadian line along the Welland Canal and an American line along the Niagara River

The general store at Canfield.   *John Burtniak Collection*

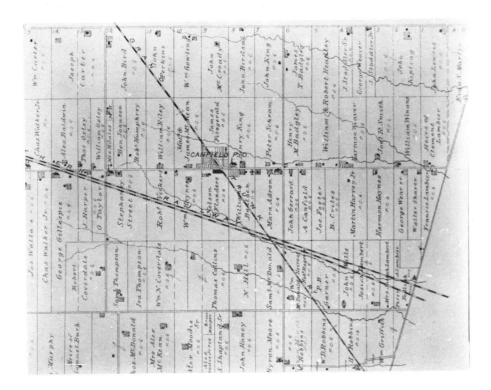

Fig. 4.7   A Meeting Point of Railways at Canfield, 1879.
H. R. Page, Illustrated Historical Atlas of the County of Haldimand, 1879

The sparsely populated areas of Haldimand and Welland Counties thus received three sets of competing lines to nurture their small rural settlements. Canfield (Fig. 4.7) was boosted, as was the Township of Wainfleet. This township, with a population of less than 2,000 in 1851 and about 3,000 residents by 1885, was centred on the

110

Village of Marshville (now Wainfleet). Though the Village was not on any of the main lines, it had the Marshville and Perry stations to the north on the Air Line and Canada Southern railways, and Wainfleet Station to the south on the Buffalo and Lake Huron (Grand Trunk) route. Similarly, there was a large number of stations further east in the County. For example, the hamlet of Stevensville (Fig. 4.8) in Bertie Township obtained the Canada Southern to the north and the Air Line Railway to the south, resulting in a road link between the two stations.

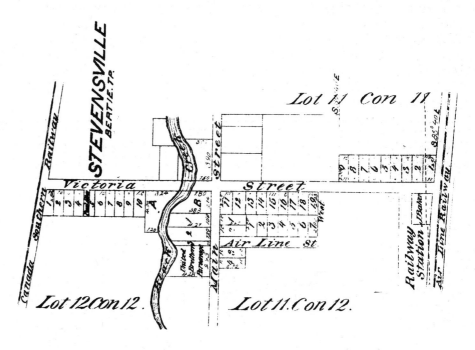

Fig. 4.8   Two railways at Stevensville, 1876.
H. R. Page, Illustrated Historical Atlas of the Counties of Lincoln and Welland, 1876

The Toronto, Hamilton and Buffalo Railway

The complexity of railway lines in the south of the Peninsula was augmented by one further major line before the end of the nineteenth century (Fig. 4.9). This was the Toronto, Hamilton and Buffalo Railway (popularly known as the T.H. & B.), which was incorporated in 1884 to build a line from Toronto via Hamilton to the International Bridge on the Niagara River.[48]

As Andrew Merrilees has written:

"The one man who more than anyone else was responsible for its promotion and construction, and who for many years was in charge of its operations, was the late John Newton Beckley of Rochester, New York. Mr. Beckley was president of the Dominion Construction Co. which promoted, built and operated the line for a short time."[49]

The original intention was to construct a line from Welland, where it would connect with the Michigan Central, through Hamilton to Toronto. There was to be a branch line from Hamilton to Brantford and Waterford, where it would again connect with the Michigan Central. The Toronto to Hamilton section of these proposals was abandoned in 1896, when running rights over the Grand Trunk line from Toronto to Hamilton were obtained by the Canadian Pacific Railway.[50] The joint owners of the line were the New York Central, the

Michigan Central, the Canada Southern and the Canadian Pacific Railway Companies. With the merger of the Michigan Central and the Canada Southern into the New York Central, the New York Central gained 72.9 per cent and the Canadian Pacific 27.1 per cent of the working control of the T.H. & B.[51] A double line of track, surmounting the Niagara Escarpment south of Stoney Creek, was constructed and opened for operation from Hamilton to Welland in 1895. A through service from Toronto to Buffalo was initiated in 1897. Of the three daily trains, one went by Niagara Falls and two by Fort Erie. At first, the three Companies provided their own locomotives on their own tracks, and the engines on all trains were changed at Welland and Hamilton, but agreement for a through engine service was reached by 1912.[52] Through passenger traffic was heavy, with the bulk of the passengers riding from Toronto and Hamilton to New York, Boston, Cleveland, Pittsburgh, and Cincinnati during the summer season.[53]

Fig. 4.9   The Toronto, Hamilton and Buffalo Railway in Lincoln and Welland Counties, 1907.

Lincoln and Welland Counties, Ont., The Scarborough Company, Hamilton, 1907

Grassie Station on the T. H. & B. line.
Charles Lamont Collection

Within the Peninsula, the importance of the T.H. & B. lay in the fact that it provided the shortest route on land from either Toronto or Hamilton to Buffalo. It introduced a new transverse route from north-west to south-east, and provided railway access to an extensive area not previously served. Stations were constructed at Hamilton, Stoney Creek, Vinemount, Grassie, Smithville, St. Anns, Silverdale, Fenwick, Chantler and Welland. At Welland, it connected with the Canada Southern-Michigan Central line to Niagara Falls, the International Bridge and to Canfield, and with the Grand Trunk (formerly Welland Railway). With the addition of the T.H. & B. to its already commanding repertoire, Welland certainly became the railway hub of the Peninsula. It now had important connections in all cardinal directions, especially eastwards to the frontier and onto the American railway system.

It is interesting to compare the sentiments that were expressed at the news of the coming of a railway with those which had prevailed when railways first arrived in the Peninsula in the 1850's. The hamlet of Smithville, in the west of Lincoln County, has provided a suitable example. Prior to 1895, Smithville was an isolated village with no railway connections. The journey by rail began with a ride in a stage coach or by horse and carriage to Grimsby. With news of a railway all things changed. The village historian, Frank E. Page, has recorded the response:

> "At last the air became charged with news of the coming of a railway. Would it touch our village? How soon would it come? Perhaps it was just rumor like lots of other things which had been promised to put life into the sleeping old village. Some said: 'Would it not kill the town?' Some said it would cut up the farms and kill the cattle. Others said it would never be built. There were those who believed that a railway would be detrimental to Smithville, and some actually canvassed voters against the project...The route contemplated was to run a mile or more north of Smithville, which was strongly opposed...A bonus by-law of $5,000 was passed by the Township. It has been stated to have carried by the small majority of 9 votes. In advancing this bonus certain concessions were obtained from the Railway Company, guaranteeing a specified number of trains daily each way to stop at Smithville."[54]

These arguments carried a familiar ring, displaying the thrill of expectation, honest but conservative doubts, and the fervour of local initiative seeking a railway to improve existing facilities and conditions:

> "And so the work of the cuts and grades began. There were wheel scrapers, slushers or hand scrapers, and plows at work everywhere along the proposed route. There were bridge gangs and workmen of various trades, and skilled and unskilled laborers. A few farmers undertook to stop the construction of a railway on their farms by the use of pitch forks, axes, etc., but in spite of this formidable opposition, the grades began to fill and the cuts to open up a clear view of roadbed ready for ties and rails. Soon the track-laying began; work trains loaded with rails, spikes and ties appeared. The rails were lifted by many strong Italian arms and placed into position, followed by the spike drivers, after which the locomotive moved forward foot by foot."[55]

Page concluded with words of typical enthusiasm; the "railway is the big factor which is going to play its part in making our native village into a good-sized prosperous town."[56] Railways, 40 years after their introduction to the Peninsula, were still perceived as the great transforming agency in urban evolution. The growth pretensions were such that every hamlet wished to become a village, every village a town, and every town a city. In reality, Smithville became a railway junction. Negotiations for a T.H. & B. branch line from Smithville to Dunnville began in 1910; the line was constructed in 1914, and it was extended to Port Maitland on Lake Erie at the mouth of the Grand River in 1916. Thus, Hamilton was now connected by rail to Lake Erie. A ferry, *Maitland No. 1,* was established, crossing Lake Erie to Ashtabula, Ohio. Its main cargo was coal destined for the steel works at Hamilton; mainly newsprint was shipped in the southbound direction. A coal dock was constructed, and metallurgical and fertilizer plants were attracted to railway-owned land at the terminal.

The notable station at Smithville on the T. H. & B. line.

John Burtniak Collection

Smithville gained little from these railway developments. The expected urban transformation did not occur, though the spatial form of settlement did change as the village was pulled north from its former nucleus to the station and the line of track. However, of importance, was that the station at Smithville was also designed with some distinct features. It has been described by E. A. Willmot as: "possibly the most decorative station in the Niagara Peninsula, and certainly the most whimsical ever built by the Toronto, Hamilton and Buffalo Railway Company."[57] A full description of its unique qualities reads as follows:

"The exquisite little railway station in Smithville with its Hansel and Gretel quality has the appearance of an illustration taken from the pages of a child's fairy-tale book. Its clean white clapboard walls are relieved by the fresh green of the shingled roof and trim around the windows and eaves-troughing. A small circular waiting room is contained in the area below the turret, and bell-cast eaves projecting over the doorway, protect travellers against the elements. A tidy geometrical pattern is formed in green and white in a running band below the eaves of the turret, and is repeated below the gable over the baggage room.

"A beautiful sunburst effect has been created in the small square glass panes above the narrow double-hung windows of the waiting room. A frosted sunburst is centered on the clear glass, and radiates to the finely etched detail in each frosted corner."[58]

Crystal Beach, Canada, Buffalo's Coney Island.

The Midway, Crystal Beach, Canada, Buffalo's Coney Island.

Recreational scenes at Crystal Beach

John Burtniak Collection

Crystal Beach: A favoured resort for summer visitors from Buffalo.

John Burtniak Collection

Tourist Lines

Mention must be made of two rather distinctive, tourist-oriented railway routes, which catered specifically for the seasonal and weekend holiday trade from Buffalo to the sandy shores and warm summer waters of Lake Erie. The first is the "Peg Leg Railway", so called because its track consisted of a single T-shaped rail carried on oak posts.[59] There was a central rail which supported most of the weight of the car and two guide rails on either side of the central rail. The whole structure extended from 10 to 30 feet above the ground level. It carried a train of two cars, with power supplied initially by batteries, and in 1898 with power from an electric cable. A major problem was the difficulty of anchoring the upright posts, which yielded in the soft ground against the weight of passing trains. The cars were built by the firm of Stuart and Felker of Thorold.

The route ran for one-and-a-half miles from Crystal Beach to Ridgeway, where it connected with the Grand Trunk to Buffalo. The Crystal Beach Amusement Park was conceived as a religious assembly ground, but it became a recreational resort by 1890. It was served mainly by boat from Buffalo, with this principal mode of transportation being supplemented only temporarily by rail. The purpose of the Peg-Leg route, known officially as the Ontario Southern Railway, was essentially to accommodate the summer tourist traffic. It operated for only three years, from 1896 to 1898, more as novel railroad curiosity than as a viable venture. Revenue did not meet the operating expenses.

CASINO AND SWIMMING POOL, FORT ERIE BEACH, ONT.

LAKE FRONT, FORT ERIE BEACH, ONT.

The Casino and Lake front at Fort Erie Beach.

John Burtniak Collection

A tourist handbill has described the distinctive characteristics of this Railway in these glowing terms:

"Save time by riding on the Ontario Southern Railway. Its novelty will please you immensely. The wonderful bicycle railroad. The one and only road of its kind on earth. The perfection of safe rapid transit. No dust, no cinders, cool and delightful. Elegant view of the Lake, Buffalo and the surrounding country from an elevation of over 50 feet...Take a ride over the tree tops...Fare five cents. Trains each way every 15 minutes".[60]

A second and longer-lasting tourist route served the Erie Beach Amusement Park at Fort Erie.[61] This resort, known originally as Snake Hill Grove, was founded in 1885 to provide a picnic ground for the residents of Buffalo. A merry-go-round, casino-dance hall, outdoor swimming pool, athletic stadium, parks, promenades, and a zoo were added, attracting crowds of up to 20,000 on summer weekends. It was served by a narrow gauge steam railway, which began operation in 1885, until a pier was built about 1910 which enabled boats to land at the beach. The tracks were constructed along the shoreline of Lake Erie from the old ferry landing in Fort Erie, where ferries crossed the Niagara River to Main Street in Buffalo. The line was known as the Fort Erie, Snake Hill, and Pacific Railroad, but less elegantly and perhaps more appropriately as the "Peanut Special" or the "Sandfly Express". The use of the word "Pacific" must have been either a futile expression of hope or a joke. The fare was $2.00 return, which included both the ferry crossing and the train ride.

Tourism was also important elsewhere; for example, the small American private resorts of Solid Comfort and Lorraine, enjoyed the advantages of accessibility by rail to their privileged and secluded "cottage" properties. Solid Comfort was established half-a-mile west of Port Colborne in 1888, and was known officially as the Humberstone Summer Resort Company.[62] A flag station was erected on the Grand Trunk (formerly Buffalo and Lake Huron) to serve this private resort, which received American visitors from the south. The street name of Tennessee Avenue in present-day Port Colborne, and the entrance pillars to the former residential estate, provide an ongoing reminder of these former circumstances.

Lorraine was established in 1898 along the sand dunes east of Port Colborne. It was another exclusive summer resort colony and was especially favoured by businessmen from Buffalo. As described by Ernest F. Ott:

"A neat Flag station was erected by the Grand Trunk Railway Company, also called Lorraine, in 1904, and a special passenger train was in operation in the summer months, between Port Colborne and Buffalo to accommodate the summer residents. Many of them commuted daily to their offices in Buffalo. A bus, drawn by a team of horses, was operated by Edwin Davidson, between the resort and the station, a distance of one mile, to meet the 8:00 a.m. eastbound and the return train at 5:45 p.m."[63]

Railways were therefore instrumental in introducing the American summer vacationer and cottage owner to the Ontario shoreline of Lake Erie. This was an opportune and normal outcome of the conditions then prevailing, but it did pose certain problems for later resolution. A continuous line of cottages was to result from Fort Erie along Lake Erie through Welland and Haldimand Counties with consequential problems, especially pollution and restrictions over public access to the beaches.[64] The latter became an issue of deep concern in the 1960's with growing urban populations in Southern Ontario, and is more serious in Bertie and Humberstone Townships than in Wainfleet, and diminishes further in intensity (but still exists) to the West of the Grand River. The problem is compounded in the east by the high proportion of American land ownerships and their enforcement of private rights over the sandy bay-head beaches that there exist.

Small, private and exclusive recreational resorts developed along the Lake Erie shoreline in conjunction with railway access.   *John Burtniak Collection*

The Sandfly Express.   *Walter F. Parks Collection*

Lucius S. Oille, M.D., was President of the St. Catharines Street Railway and later of the St. Catharines and Niagara Central Railroad.
St. Catharines Historical Museum

Chapter V

The Introduction of Inter-Urban Railways

The late-nineteenth century witnessed the emergence of a closely integrated system of inter-urban and local street railways in the Peninsula, with the area then being in the vanguard of international progress because of its novel transportation developments. These new circumstances may be regarded as the culmination of the railway era, emerging as they did from the application of electricity to the pre-existing modes and forms of transport and serving to join more closely those urban centres which had been linked previously by the steam locomotive. These events introduced a new era of speedy, inter-urban traffic movement, of which only the foundation stages will be outlined in this chapter.

WE HANDLE THE AMERICAN EXPRESS.

St. Catharines and Niagara Central R'y.

TRAINS EAST.

STATIONS.	Miles. from St. Catharines	57 Buffalo Express.	59 Mixed.
		A. M.	P. M.
St. Catharines............... Dep	0	8.40	3.15
Merritton	3	8.53	3.26
Thorold	5	9.05	3.37
Stamford	10	9.13	3 55
Niagara Central Junction	11	9.22	4 00
Clifton ....Arrive	12	9.25	4 03
Niagara-on-the-Lake..... .Arrive			6.05
Clifton, M. C. R...............Dep.	12	9.30	5.12
Niagara Falls..........................	13	9.36	
Chippawa	16	9.46	
Black Creek..........................	22	9 56	
Fort Erie	29	10.00	
Black Rock..........................	30	10.15	
Buffalo, Exchange st .....Arrive	34	10.30	6.20

☞When you are ordering Goods from Toronto or Montreal be sure that your orders are marked "Ship via C. P. R.," M. C. R. and St. C. & N. C. R'y."

TRAINS WEST.

STATIONS.	Miles from Buffalo.	56 Mixed.	58 Buffalo Express.
		A. M.	P. M.
Buffalo..........................Dep.	0	7.07	4.35
Black Rock............................	4	7.20	4.50
Fort Erie	5	7.25	4.55
Black Creek............................	12	7.39	5.10
Chippawa	13	7.49	5.21
Niagara Falls...........................	21	7.59	5.30
Clifton........................ ... Arrive	22	8.05	5.36
Niagara-on-the-Lake..... ....Dep.		9.00	
Clifton, M. C. R .... Dep.	22	10.15	5.41
Niagara Central Junction....... ...	23	10.18	5.44
Stamford	24	10.23	5.49
Thorold..................................	29	10.38	6.00
Merritton	31	10.48	6.10
St. Catharines...............Arrive	34	11.00	6.20

Take the St. C. & N. C. R'y for Niagara Falls and Buffalo Good Coaches. No Change. Quick Time. Patronize your own Railway

When ordering Goods from New York or Great Britain, mark your order
Care of Merchants Dispatch Company at New York,
and Michigan Central Railway and St. Catharines & Niagara Central Railway.

A time table of 1894.   *John Burtniak Collection*

A Niagara Central train at its terminal on Raymond Street, St. Catharines.
John M. Mills, History of the Niagara, St. Catharines & Toronto Railway, 1967

The Niagara, St. Catharines and Toronto Railway

St. Catharines was served after the mid-1850's by two railways, the Great Western and the Welland Railway. After their amalgamation under the aegis of the Grand Trunk in 1882, only one monopolistic Company existed. Freight rates could be, and were, raised. This reduced element of competition became an argument in support of a new railway to the frontier and for a railway connection to the American system from St. Catharines. Major proponents of the scheme were Dr. Lucius S. Oille (1830-1903), who was the Mayor of St. Catharines in 1878 and who became President of the Company that was to be formed, and E. A. Smythe of Niagara Falls. The *Annual Report* of the St. Catharines Board of Trade for 1900 stated that railway amalgamation had brought about the following situation:

"The business of the city began to suffer from oppressive freight rates directly, and in selling markets where the St. Catharines manufacturers met in competition goods coming from cities and towns enjoying the advantage of competition in freight rates. Dr. Oille thereupon initiated an agitation for the construction of an independent railway extending easterly from St. Catharines to the Canada Southern Railway (operated by the Michigan Central Railway Company) and the United States Railways at the Niagara River, and westerly to a connection with the Canadian Pacific Railway. The project met general approval among the businessmen of all classes. An Act of Parliament was subsequently obtained incorporating the St. Catharines and Niagara Central Railway Company. . .The G.T.R. monopoly over St. Catharines was effectually broken".[1]

This "independent railway", the St. Catharines and Niagara Central Railway, was incorporated in 1881 to construct a steam line from St. Catharines to Smithville, Caledonia and Canfield, with branches to Hamilton and Queenston.[2] Receiving municipal support from the City of St. Catharines and the Town of Thorold, a line was opened from Niagara Falls to Thorold in 1887 and this was extended to St. Catharines in the next year. The St. Catharines terminal was located on James Street at the end of Raymond Street; in Niagara Falls, use was made of the Michigan Central's station. The line was slightly over 12 miles in length.

John Burtniak Collection

Prior to its official opening, the railway was used during 1884 to assist with the construction works on the Third Welland Canal. After completion of the line, freight grew steadily and provided competition to the Grand Trunk. In 1896, 66,000 tons and 21,000 passengers were handled. There were two passenger trains daily in each direction from St. Catharines to Niagara Falls, with through connections to Buffalo by the Michigan Central or by river steamer from Chippawa. A major customer was the Riordon Paper Mills in Merritton.

Arrangements were made to extend the line to Hamilton and Toronto in 1890, but this project was thwarted when the Toronto, Hamilton and Buffalo Railway was constructed. Consideration was then given to providing a link with the T.H. & B. at either Fenwick or Smithville, but these plans did not reach fruition. The failure of these aspirations caused consternation in the board room. Two factions arose. One group, led by Dr. Oille, wanted to electrify the line against the original plans. The other group, led by Captain Neelon (the Vice-President), wished to salvage a portion of the investment by selling out. Not unnaturally, the affairs of the Company suffered, the line fell into disuse, and the track and rolling stock decayed. The Company went into receivership and was offered for sale in 1899.

In 1899, the Niagara, St. Catharines and Toronto Railway Company, was incorporated to acquire the assets of the St. Catharines and Niagara Central Railway.[3] This new Company, known popularly and hereafter described as the "N.S. & T", was granted power to extend the line to Fort Erie, Port Dalhousie and Toronto, and to use vessels on the Niagara River and Lake Ontario. It was changed from a steam-operated line to an electric railway in 1900. The N.S. & T. began operation immediately by constructing a line from St. Catharines to Port Dalhousie, which was opened in 1901. It was authorized to acquire the Niagara Falls, Wesley Park and Clifton Tramway Company in 1901,[4] and the Port Dalhousie, St. Catharines and Thorold Electric Street Railway Company in 1902.[5] These events, and the later achievements of the N.S. & T., have been covered in an important history of the line by John M. Mills.[6] The account here is concerned only with the early years of the companies that were later absorbed into the N.S. & T., and with the other intra-urban and inter-urban systems that existed in the Peninsula towards the end of the nineteenth century.

The N. S. & T. Stations at Thorold and Humberstone.   *John Burtniak Collection*

N. St. C. & T. RAILWAY BRIDGE, OLD CANAL, ST. CATHERINES, ONT.

As with the steam railways previously, the inter-urban tracks still had to contend with crossing physical obstacles.

John Burtniak Collection

The Port Dalhousie, St. Catharines and
Thorold Electric Street Railway

The St. Catharines Street Railway Company was chartered in 1874 "to build a street railway along the streets of St. Catharines and adjoining municipalities".[7] Again, the impetus came from Dr. Oille. After considerable discussion and delays, agreement was reached in 1879 with the City of St. Catharines to construct and operate this route. It was inaugurated that same year. Service was introduced with horse-drawn cars; each car, pulled by two horses, could carry 12 persons. The line ran from the Welland House on Ontario Street, along St. Paul and Queenston Streets to the Thorold Road, a route which reflected the traditional historical elongation of St. Catharines and its growth along its major highway route of east-west travel.

In 1880, the line was extended to the Welland Railway Station on Welland Avenue, and via Thorold Road to Merritton. Further expansion took place in 1881 when track was laid along Ontario Street, and in 1882 when it was extended to Thorold. The name was changed to the St. Catharines, Merritton and Thorold Street Railway in 1882, thus reflecting in its title the close inter-linkage of these adjacent yet separate urban communities.[8] By 1887, service was provided every 40 minutes within the city and on the Welland Avenue and Geneva Street branches. The ten-foot long cars were manufactured by the firm of Patterson and Corbin, a local firm of carriage builders, who were located on the south side of Queenston Street just east of Geneva Street.

Electrification was introduced in 1887. As John M. Mills has noted:

> "It was always recognized that animal haulage was extremely inefficient in the conditions prevailing, but no really successful electric line had yet been commercially operated for more than a very short time anywhere in the world; in fact the first experimental electric line embodying even remotely modern technology had been displayed at an exhibition in Germany only a year or two before. The problems, therefore, were many and formidable. No previous electrification had been attempted anywhere in the world on a line whose operating characteristics were so severe, and the St. Catharines project received attention both on this continent and abroad."[9]

Power was obtained from a generating plant built in Merritton at Lock 12 on the Second Welland Canal system. This channel had been abandoned recently for the Third Canal and its water resource capability was, therefore, available for other purposes. This power was available at low cost, and thus gave St. Catharines an important initial advantage in pioneering the unique and innovative form of electric transportation. The Van Depoele System was used for propulsion. This made use of double overhead wires, the power from which turned the front wheels by means of a chain drive from a 15 horsepower Canadian General Electric motor mounted at the front of the car. A by-law was passed by the City of St. Catharines in 1887 which authorized the erection of poles and overhead wires; a new feature, "wirescape", therefore, was introduced into the urban street scene. These power cables extended for six miles above the central line of the street. They were supported by span wires from the opposite buildings where possible, and elsewhere from free-standing poles. Tracks were also introduced into the street width as rights of way over this public property were acquired, with the result that

The N. S. & T. Bridge over the Third Canal at Thorold. *John Burtniak Collection*

wires, poles and track became an integral and sometimes controversial aspect of the visual urban environment.

The N. S. & T. Stations at Welland, Merritton Fonthill.   *John Burtniak Collection*

N. S. & T. Electric Engine No. 1, 1905.   St. Catharines Historical Museum

Electric service began in St. Catharines in September 1887, and was extended over a distance of six miles to Thorold in October. The electric car had replaced the horse car, a prestigious event in the history of St. Catharines and the Peninsula, for this was the first inter-city electric car operation in Canada. The steam railroad had served adequately to change the concept of long distance travel, but it was unsuitable for local traffic where frequent stops for visits to shop and market, to work and for social purposes were needed. As J. F. Due has noted, "it was never a major industry, but its role in the transition of Canadian land transportation from almost sole reliance on the steam railroad to dominance of the motor vehicle should not be over-looked".[10] The electrification of the line also had an important side effect for local industry. The conversion of the old cars and the manufacture of new ones again took place in the Patterson and Corbin plant, which expanded to employ as many as 75 men and supplied cars to railway systems across Canada.

The line was well patronized by local residents. It was extended eastward to Victoria Lawn Cemetery in 1888, and to the northern city limits along Ontario Street by 1896. There were reduced evening fares, and trolley party rides between St. Catharines and Thorold were popular by 1895. Small parks were operated by the Company in Merritton and at Victoria Lawn as recreational features, while Lakeside Park at Port Dalhousie was maintained as a pleasure resort. A package freight service was also provided for premises along the track. As befitted its *modus operandi,* the name was changed in 1893 by *Letters Patent* to the Port Dalhousie, St. Catharines and Thorold Electric Street Railway. This Company took over the St. Catharines, Merritton and Thorold Street Railway Company and the Niagara and St. Catharines Street Railway Company.

Lake Steamers and the inter-urban railway system connected at Port Dalhousie.

The electric street railways and the already existing steam railways functioned as separate systems, which did not inter-connect until a much later date. Trackage along Geneva Street, constructed in 1880, was electrified. However, this line was removed before 1900, apparently because of the decline in importance of the Welland Railway Station as a street car terminus after its purchase by the Grand Trunk in 1882. More importantly, the Great Western Station on Western Hill continued to be served by horse-drawn carriages and omnibuses until a much later date, the reason being that the steep slopes of the Twelve Mile Creek Valley proved too formidable an obstacle for this important linkage to be served by street car. Even lesser slopes posed difficulties, as witness the fact that horses were used to assist the cars up the hill on the Thorold Road from Eastchester Street to Queenston Street. A street car line linking the city with its steam railway station was achieved only in 1924, when an inter-urban terminal was constructed on Geneva Street at Welland Avenue. A line was then constructed from this terminal to the Canadian National Station, but, by this time, the Burgoyne Bridge had been constructed to obviate the steep grades of the valley route.

The end of the Port Dalhousie, St. Catharines and Thorold Electric Street Railway came about in 1900 when, as its first act, the new N.S. & T. began the construction of a line from St. Catharines to Port Dalhousie. This was followed by the purchase of the line in 1901, and its seven miles of track were absorbed officially into the N.S. & T. operations in 1902. In terms of the order of occurrence, therefore, it is chronologically correct for J. M. Mills to state that "the earliest section of the N.S. & T. system was the St. Catharines local line."[11]

Horse-drawn street railway on Main Street, Niagara Falls, in the 1890's.
George A. Seibel (ed.), Niagara Falls, Canada: A History, 1967

Inter-Urban Railways at Niagara Falls

A second and less important component of the emerging N.S. & T. network was a tramway company which, in 1886, began to operate a horse-drawn street railway in Niagara Falls and Stamford Township. This line, the Niagara Falls, Wesley Park and Clifton Tramway Company, is described by J. M. Mills as "never very prosperous; in later years it suffered from being an anachronistic horse-car line in a very electricity-conscious city."[12] However, with its absorption into the N.S. & T. at the turn of the century, the line was rebuilt and electrified and so became part of a more extensive inter-urban network in the Peninsula.

A more important inter-urban system was the Niagara Falls Park and River Railway, incorporated in 1892 to build an electric railway from Queenston to Chippawa and to the Town of Niagara and to Fort Erie.[13] A 12-mile length of track was opened in 1893, running from Chippawa along the Niagara River to Niagara Falls on a right-of-way over land owned by the Niagara Parks Commission, and then on to Queenston close to the rim of the Niagara Gorge. In order to descend

TIME TABLE.

Niagara Falls, Ont.
STREET RAILWAY.

LEAVE Drummondville.			LEAVE Susp. Bridge.			Sundays.	
						Drummondville.	Susp. Bridge.
AT	6.20	A. M.	AT	7.00	A. M.	10.00	10.00
"	7.00	"	"	7.40	"	10.40	10.40
"	7.40	"	"	8.20	"	11.20	11.20
"	8.20	"	"	9.00	"	12.00	12.00
"	9.00	"	"	9.40	"	12.40	12.40
"	9.40	"	"	10.20	"	1.20	1.20
"	10.20	"	"	11.00	"	2.00	2.00
"	11.00	"	"	11.40	"	2.40	2.40
"	11.40	"	"	12.20	P. M.	3.20	3.20
"	12.20	P. M.	"	1.00	"	4.00	4.00
"	1.00	"	"	1.40	"	4.40	4.40
"	1.40	"	"	2.20	"	5.20	5.20
"	2.20	"	"	3.00	"	6.00	6.00
"	3.00	"	"	3.40	"	6.40	6.40
"	3.40	"	"	4.20	"	7.20	7.20
"	4.20	"	"	5.00	"	8.00	8.00
"	5.00	"	"	5.40	"		
"	5.40	"	"	6.20	"		
"	6.20	"	"	7.00	"		
"	7.00	"	"	7.40	"		
"	7.40	"	"	8.20	"		

J. H. BACHE,
SUPERINTENDENT.

Winter Arrangement,
OCTOBER, 15th, 1890.

The winter schedule for the inter-urban street railway between Drummondville and the Suspension Bridge in 1890. *Francis J. Petrie Collection*

from the height of the Escarpment to the level of Lake Ontario at Queenston, the track swung inland and then spiralled down by two steep and sharp 180 degree curves to the docks on the Niagara River.

Ferry connections were established at Queenston and Chippawa so that, supplemented by river navigation, the line could capture the potential of the Toronto and the Buffalo markets. At Queenston in particular, the Niagara Navigation Company (later the Canada Steamship Lines) disembarked up to 2,000 passengers at a time for onward transportation by the electric railway. Day excursions arranged by the Company became popular and important features. In 1895, half a million passengers were carried. The overwhelming success of this venture prompted the doubling of most of the track.

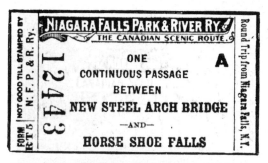

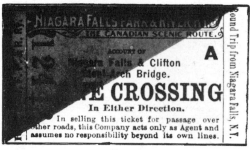

A new potential in tourism resulted with the opening of the Queenston-Lewiston Suspension Bridge in 1899 and the Upper Steel Arch Bridge below the Falls in 1897 (these bridges will be discussed in Chapter VI). They made possible a dual crossing of the Niagara River, with the first international service beginning in 1898. A route had already been constructed in the Gorge on the American side of the River. The two lines together provided an astounding international circular tour which included magnificent panoramas of the Gorge and Falls from both banks. As described graphically in 1895 when the "Great Gorge Route" was formally opened:

"There were trolley lines and trolley lines, but the one that skirted the wild gorge through which the mighty waters of Niagara tumble and pour in a mad, unending race was probably the most unique in its scenic attractions, of any in the world. The road had just been constructed in 1895 on the American side after wholesale blasting of the noble cliffs in order to carve out the roadbed. The road had its terminus at Lewiston, in the gorge below the cataract.

A long struggle with nature was necessary before the grades were established. Parts of the canyon could not be surveyed until the engineers were lowered with ropes down the side of the precipice and within a few feet of the rapids. The banks on either side of the gorge were covered to a great height with broken rocks, which had fallen from above as the result of centuries of erosion.

Some of these fragments were of enormous size. These masses sloping madly to the river, were covered with a luxuriant growth of shrubs and trees. At the base of this heap and in some cases carved out of the side wall of the canyon was the roadbed. In some instances a detour was necessary in order to avoid some of these enormous masses of limestone."[14]

The street railway next to the Niagara River at Queenston and Niagara Falls.

John Burtniak Collection

In 1899 the line was acquired by the Buffalo Railway Company, a purchase which was ratified by the Provincial Government in 1901.[15] The name was changed to the International Railway Company in 1902.[16] Under its new name, this American Company maintained a loop operation as part of Buffalo's city and inter-urban system. Passengers were able to make a circular tour along the bottom of the Niagara Gorge on the American side, across the Niagara River on the Queenston-Lewiston Bridge, and back along the edge of the cliffs on the Canadian side to the bridge at Niagara Falls. It became a unique and highly popular scenic trip billed as "the most magnificent scenic route in the world", but it had the disadvantage of only limited seasonal operations. It experienced intense peak loads from the steamer connections on the Lower Niagara River, and received virtually no freight traffic. Again, the cars were constructed in St. Catharines at the plant of Patterson and Corbin. This railway system, over the years, also provided strong encouragement to the expanding tourist industry at Niagara Falls and along the Niagara River.

The Great Gorge Route offered an unexcelled scenic panorama of the Niagara River.
John Burtniak Collection

The Great Gorge Route at the base of
the sheer slope.

John Burtniak Collection

A display of advertising brochures for the
Great Gorge Trip.   *John Burtniak Collection*

Radial Expansion from Hamilton and Grimsby

In 1902, the N.S. & T. announced an extension to Hamilton. This was to run parallel with Lake Ontario from Port Dalhousie to Twenty Mile Creek and then along the Queenston-Grimsby highway. A branch line from Beamsville to St. Anns and Smithville was also contemplated. These lines were not completed, but their consideration serves to introduce another inter-urban railway system into the Peninsula during the final years of the nineteenth century — namely the Hamilton, Grimsby and Beamsville Electric Railway Company.[17]

This line was conceived in 1892, with a charter to build an electric railway eastwards from Hamilton and Dundas through the townships of Barton, Saltfleet and North Grimsby to Beamsville.[18] Trolley lines, with overhead wires, were opened to Grimsby in 1894 and to Beamsville by 1896, thus providing a link with the Toronto, Hamilton and Buffalo Railway and the Grand Trunk. The line was built mainly along the edge of roadways, and in particular along the main road from Hamilton through Grimsby to Beamsville (No. 8 Highway). Besides providing passenger service, it handled freight from orchards and canneries as an important aspect of its service. Spurs and sidings served quarries, fruit processing plants and the recreation facilities at Grimsby Beach.

An extension from Beamsville to St. Catharines, with branches to Niagara and Niagara Falls, was approved in 1901.[19] The line was extended from Beamsville to Vineland in 1904. But the heavy cost of bridges over the creeks, change in ownership (the line was purchased in 1904 by the Hamilton Cataract Power, Light and Traction Company), and the completion of the Toronto, Hamilton and Buffalo Railway, combined to prohibit the completion of the intended expansions. This Hamilton-oriented system, though penetrating the north-west of the Peninsula, remained separate from the inter-urban system which radiated from St. Catharines.

The poles, wires and tracks of the inter-urban street system at Queenston Street/ Niagara Street in St. Catharines.

John Burtniak Collection

Street railways in the urban scene of St. Catharines: St. Paul Street and the Queenston/ Church Street Junction.

John Burtniak Collection

The Significance of the Inter-Urban Railways

The development of an inter-urban electric system introduced a new set of tracks, poles and overhead wires into the urban and rural landscapes of the Peninsula. As the lines extended out from the main centres of population, with frequent stops, the system contributed to the linear elongation of the urban centres along the routes of track. An example of this ribbon phenomenon is found in an urban renewal study of Niagara Falls:

"Within the towns the street car line became the artery along which new growth developed, and was the reason why many cities developed in a linear fashion. For instance the road [Ferry Street] joining the Town of Niagara Falls and the Village of Niagara Falls [Drummondville] was a dirt trail before 1884. In that year it was stoned and by the turn of the century it carried a horse drawn train which was electrified and linked to the international system shortly afterwards. By the first world war the route of the street car within the town was solidly built up and had almost all the residents of the two centres living within six blocks on either side of the tram line."[20]

Within the Peninsula, the new developments contributed materially to the closer inter-weaving of the urban fabric and fostered closer ties betwen separate urban communities. With more frequent communication, it was now that much easier to shop, to travel to work, or to make a social visit or recreational jaunt. The various centres of population became less isolated and more interdependent as this regional inter-play expanded. The inter-urban systems also provided competition to the freight and passenger service of the established railways. For example, in 1900, when the Michigan Central terminated their agreement with the N.S. & T. for the interchange of traffic at Niagara Falls, the St. Catharines Board of Trade resisted vigorously and successfully:

"The effect of this unjustifiable and illegal proceeding was to subject the freight traffic of St. Catharines to the Grand Trunk monopoly, to overcome which was one of the principal objects in constructing the Niagara, St. Catharines and Toronto Railway. This Board of Trade led in a vigorous effort to induce the M.C.R. management to consent for a restoration of the interchange of traffic between the two railways. The move was successful."[21]

Tourism and the Niagara Central Railway at Niagara.

John Burtniak Collection

Front Street, looking North, Thorold, Ont.

Features of the inter-urban railway scene in the Peninsula at Welland, Thorold and Niagara Falls.

John Burtniak Collection

Palace Sleeping and Drawing Room Cars

MAP SHOWING
CANADA SOUTHERN CONNECTIONS
AT
Buffalo, Suspension Bridge and Niagara.

To New York, Boston, Chicago & St. Louis

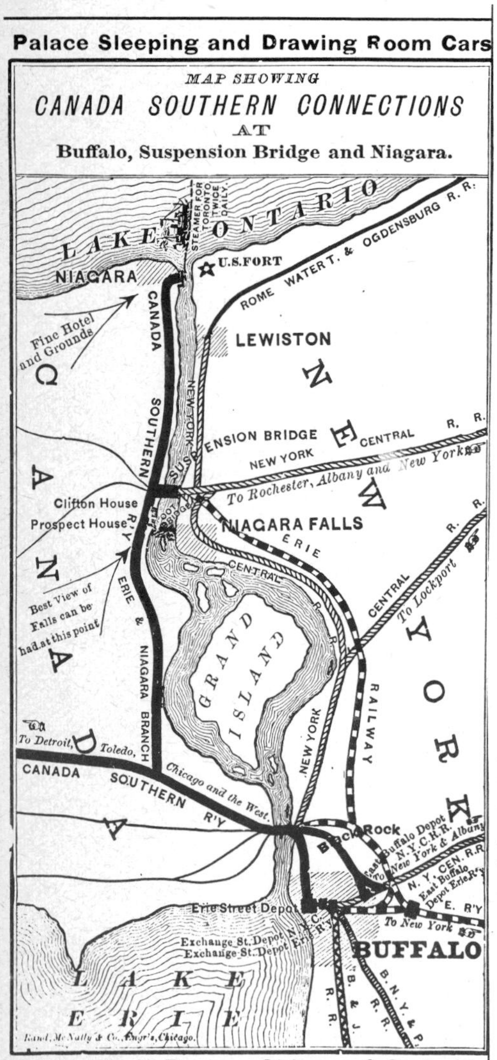

Fig. 6.1 Railway Connections Over the Niagara River: The Canada Southern, 1880.

John Burtniak Collection

Chapter VI

Railway Bridges at the International Border

The railway introduced many new features into the landscape of the Niagara Peninsula. There were the miles of track with fenced boundaries, embankments and cuttings on alignments which generally cut across the rectangular pattern of farm holdings. There were the points of direct contact with settlements and roadways, such as the passenger stations, freight yards, sidings, warehouse facilities, repair depots, roundhouses, and hotels. But, undoubtedly, the most commanding of the new features were the major bridges. These, like the locks of the canal system, exerted a most profound impact on their adjacent urban communities even though the bridges were conceived, located and designed with engineering criteria primarily in mind. The most important of the new bridges were placed on the frontier where railways crossed over the Niagara River (Fig. 6.1). They are worthy of particular examination here.[1]

The Significance of Bridge Crossings

Rail linkage to New York State, the growth of Buffalo and connections to the American railroad system were of considerable importance to the development and phasing of the railway network in the Peninsula.[2] During this era of railway expansion, the Peninsula was again fulfilling its role as a "land bridge" because of its location in North America between Lake Erie and Lake Ontario. As William J. Wilgus wrote in 1937 when he examined railway inter-relationships between the United States and Canada:

> "The *most important* traffic gateways between the two countries on the Great Lakes frontier are on the Niagara River, between Lake Erie and Lake Ontario, where three bridge crossings of the boundary, one at Black Rock, Buffalo, and two at Niagara Falls, make it possible for three American lines traversing Ontario from the west. . .to repatriate themselves; and for three Canadian roads. . .to gain entrance to the United States."[3]

The Niagara River provided a physical barrier which had to be overcome, if Canada was to be connected with the American railway system and if the expanding American interests were to be satisfied. It was an important, if not imperative, ingredient to the aspirations of both countries. The resultant bridges provide stories of great engineering achievement, but they also hold especial importance from the spatial standpoint because of their direct urban encouragement and immediate sponsorship of development. The construction of bridges provided the impetus for road and rail routes to converge on a few specific locales of incipient industrial strength, and the immediate re-direction and expansion of the previously restricted traffic flow patterns; in conjunction with the economic-political-cultural divisions which existed across an international border, a customs ports of entry, railway marshalling yards, passenger and freight stations, and their attendant urban communities were established. These changes occurred most forcibly at Niagara Falls, the railhead and terminus of the Great Western system, rather than at Fort Erie where the greatest gains were on the American side at Buffalo.

CALVERY WALKING NIAGARA GORGE ON 3/4 IN. CABLE.

Daredevil feats next to the Railway Bridges, which served as viewing platforms.

John Burtniak Collection

Niagara Falls also had the advantage of its commanding scenic attraction and the burgeoning tourist industry. The expanding railway and steamer systems enabled more people to visit the Falls and Gorge, and the bridges served as unparalleled platforms from which the river scenery could be viewed with advantage and in safety. For example, George A. Seibel, in commenting about the 60,000 visitors who were attracted to Niagara Falls in 1853, has described the advent of mass tourism as follows:

> "The Great Western had its Canadian terminus at the Bridge Street station and hotels were soon built nearby to accommodate the rail travellers arriving in increasing numbers. Since there were no sleeping cars in those days, rail travellers planned to spend the night in a hotel and get a fresh start in the morning. Even those who were travelling from Toronto to New York took time out to see the Falls before they picked up their rail connection on the U.S. side."[4]

Furthermore, the influx of engineers and construction workers during the building of the bridges and the arrival later of railway workers and bridge employees, provided an important stimulus to other urban- and service-oriented activities. In addition, the bridge structures may also be regarded as exciting aesthetic landmarks of human endeavour. They existed in stark contrast with their natural setting, yet also contributed to the scenery in terms of their form and visual appearance, the materials used, and the quality of workmanship. The bridges across the Niagara River are numbered among the great engineering works of the period. They attracted to their construction the best bridge-building talent available in the world at that time.

The bridgehead settlements became focal points in the emerging railway systems. The location of the bridge crossings greatly influenced the routes that were followed by the approaching railways. As these bridge crossing points were all situated south of the Niagara Escarpment, their emphasis counter-balanced the previous emphasis of population distribution to the north of the Escarpment. The established centres, therefore, received less of a spur and encouragement to expansion than might have been expected on the basis of their earlier population and industrial importance.

The Niagara Suspension Bridge

The Niagara Gorge was the logical location for a bridge crossing. Although the water was exceptionally turbulent in its confined chasm, the land was high and even on both banks of the River, and it was also the narrowest point along the entire length of the River. The rock formations on both banks were firm and more than adequate to support the weight and stress of a railway bridge. The gap of 800 feet could be crossed, but only if a suitable single span structure could be designed.

Previously, ferries had crossed the River where the current was relatively slow. Before 1850, these major crossing points were located at Niagara and Queenston, immediately below the Falls, at Chippawa to Fort Schlosser, and at Fort Erie to Black Rock and Buffalo. The selection of the Gorge as a crossing point for a railway bridge was a novel choice, as previously no major land route had been able to cross the perpendicular walls. This historic pattern was to be changed radically during the railway era, with important consequences for settlement.

DOUBLE BRIDGE OVER THE NIAGARA.

The Niagara Suspension Bridge is of exceptional importance as the first railway bridge over the Niagara Gorge.

John Burtniak Collection

A bridge of the suspension design proved successful, but there were early doubts about its feasibility. As stated in an American report of 1853:

> "Many minds [question] whether it will be possible to construct a bridge upon this principle sufficiently steady and firm to admit of the passage of a locomotive with a heavy train. But, be this as it may be, there will be no difficulty. . .in making the transit in single cars, by horse-power. . .Should the suspension plan, however, prove unfeasible, it is probable that the iron tubular bridge system, so triumphantly established in Great Britain on the Conway and the Menai straits, will be adopted."[5]

It was imperative that the River be crossed somewhere. The means by which this was to be accomplished was resolved by William Hamilton Merritt, who initiated and later brought to fruition the idea of a suspension bridge to span the Gorge.[6] The idea supposedly came to him from a passing comment made by his wife. According to J. P. Merritt, one day in 1844 the family went for a picnic next to the Gorge. En route to their destination, they collected a packet of letters from the post office, including one from their sons, Jedediah and William, who were completing their education at European universities. Their letter described a suspension bridge over the River Sarren in Switzerland. According to the account:

> "A full description of it followed — its length, its height, and the manner of its construction were all minutely detailed. (Mrs. M. Merritt remarked: 'I wonder if a suspension bridge could not be made to span this river.') So strongly did the remark impress the mind of our subject [W. H. Merritt] that the idea at once occurred to him of the possibility

of spanning the mighty Niagara with just such a bridge. Soon afterwards a consultation with engineers followed. Laughed at by some, and favored by others, still the idea grew. . .The author on his return, was sent up with S. Woodruff, Engineer, to ascertain the shortest line for a suspension bridge across the Niagara."[7]

Matters then moved quickly. Merritt's diary of 1845 noted:

"Mr. Slater has ascertained the width of the Niagara river to be 420 [feet] only. Obtain the right of land, and an act of the Legislature of New York State as well as Canada, to construct the same, with the right of extending railroad now or hereafter to be made. The present object is mainly to unite Manchester [Niagara Falls, N.Y.] as far up as Chippawa, reaching the town of Niagara via St. Davids, west to St. Catharines and Hamilton."[8]

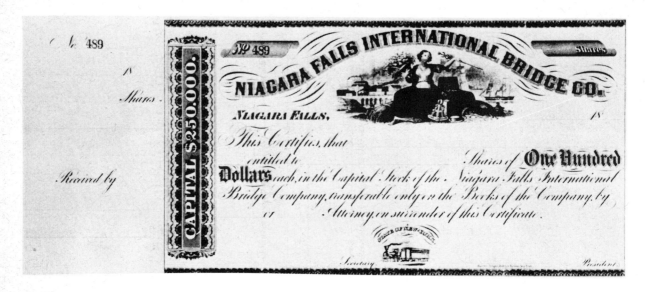

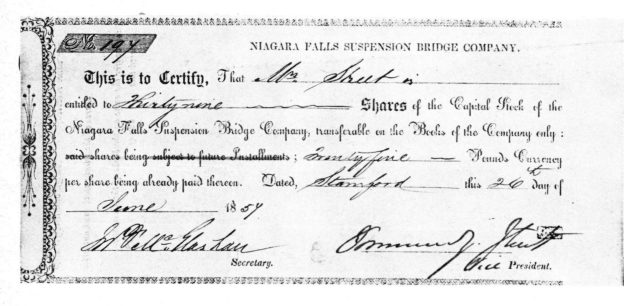

The railway bridges, like the railways, were constructed by private companies seeking a return on their investment. A confusion in names exists, because charters had to be obtained from the two governments that were involved.

John Burtniak Collection

Certainly, no monopolistic position was envisaged. The bridge would be open and accessible to all railways. Merritt's advocacy of the project is indicative of "his broad views on transportation."[9] This assessment by J. J. Talman in the *Dictionary of Canadian Biography* concluded with the statement that: "Today Merritt can be seen as one of the great figures in the history of Canadian transportation. . . Merritt's vision of an Eastern Canadian transportation system involving waterways and railways was logical, practical, and consistently pursued."[10] The great significance of the bridge lay in the fact that it was the first link between Canadian and American railway systems. It was a feat which had not been accomplished anywhere along the boundary between the two countries up to that time. For the Peninsula, it was very necessary to have a bridge to realize to the full the advantages of a railway system. A comment of 1852 expressed succinctly the necessity for this combination:

> "At this eventful era in its history, when the town was about to take a position among the manufacturing centres of the province, by its having the advantage of a new avenue by railroad *and* bridge to the outward world, the population of St. Catharines was 4,368."[11]

Charters to build a bridge across the Gorge were obtained in 1846, from the State of New York as the Niagara Falls International Bridge Company and from the Canadian Government as the Niagara Falls Suspension Bridge Company.[12] Merritt was made the President of the Canadian Company. The Canadian Act provided the Company with powers "to construct a suspension or other bridge across the Niagara River, at or near the Falls, with the necessary approaches thereto with rail, macadamized or other routes, and to connect the same with any other road now or hereafter to be made."[13]

The daunting task that faced the engineers at this formidable location has been described vividly by D. B. Steinman:

> "In all the world no place could have been found where the building of a suspension bridge would present a more spectacular accomplishment than over the Niagara Gorge, with the Falls thundering a little way upstream and the waters lashing and fuming underneath. No other setting could have provided such a dramatic and impressive background for a slender span symbolizing the genius and courage of man defying the gigantic, furious forces of nature. And to plan such a span — seemingly a frail web in contrast with the overwhelming power of the scene — to sustain the enormous loads of locomotives and freight trains was an unprecedented, breathtaking temerity of the human spirit. The idea of carrying railroad trains over that thundering turmoil of waters on a high and tenuous framework of wire and wood stunned the imagination, and the proposal evoked a storm of protest from nearly all the foremost engineers of the time."[14]

The supporting structure of Roebling's Suspension Bridge.   *John Burtniak Collection*

Charles Ellett was contracted to construct a combined railway and carriage bridge over the Niagara River. His first task was to get a line or wire across the Gorge, a feat accomplished by enlisting youngsters and awarding a prize of five dollars to the lad who could first land a kite on the opposite bank. Then, stouter wires and cables were pulled across. From these simple beginnings a light suspension bridge was completed in 1848. The bridge was 762 feet long and 8 feet wide, with wooden towers at either end, from which was suspended a heavy oak plank roadway 220 feet above the River by means of iron wire cables. It swayed and dipped considerably under a heavy load or in the wind.[15] The Gorge had been crossed and the bridge became a popular tourist feature for viewing the Falls, but a railway span had not yet been achieved. Ellett, unable to complete the bridge to accommodate railway traffic, was dismissed from his appointment in 1848.[16]

John A. Roebling (1806-1869) took over the responsibility for the contract, and it is to him that the honour of constructing the first railway bridge must, therefore, be awarded. The construction of this stronger bridge began in 1851 and occupied the next four years. The design was novel, breath-taking in appearance, and in absolute conflict with the accepted engineering tenets of the period. It was nothing less than a melding of the principles of a suspension bridge, then regarded as undulating and frail, with the demands of rigidity and strength needed for the passage of heavy locomotives and loaded freight trains. Roebling's solution was to provide stiffening by trusses, braces and stays from above, below and within the structure in order to resist any wind or swaying motion that might occur. The bridge was completed in 1855 when the first train, with 20 loaded freight cars weighing 326 tons, passed safely over the structure. Agreement had been reached in 1853, that the Bridge Company would lease the upper deck in perpetuity to the Great Western, who became its principal users.

The bridge was 821 feet in length. It consisted of two levels, a single track railway on the upper deck and an enclosed roadway below on the lower deck. The structure cost $400,000, much less than the heavier and yet no safer structures then being built in Europe. The weight of the structure was suspended from stone pylons at either end of the bridge by means of four ten-inch cables of wrought iron wire, two being connected to the upper deck and two to the lower deck.[17] It was a surprisingly strong bridge: a train of eight cars, filled with passengers, two baggage cars, a locomotive and tender — weighing about 130 tons in all — was only about one-sixtieth of the assessed capacity of the bridge.[18] Because of the confusing and conflicting gauge situation, the tracks on the bridge were laid so as to accommodate each of its approaching lines, namely 4 feet 8 inches for the New York Central, 5 feet 6 inches for the Great Western, and 6 feet for the Elmira, Canandaigua and Niagara Falls Railway.

The opening of the bridge in 1855 was an occasion of signal importance. The *Constitutional* described the event as follows:

> "The passenger engine and tender crowded with people, crossed over to the American side, and after returning, one of the mammoth English freight-engines made its appearance on the track gaily decorated with the British and American colors. . .and crowded with the novelty and excitement seeking spectators. . .The opening of this mighty and magnificent structure — well worthy of being classed with the world's wonders — really forms an epoch in the history of the world. It unites with strong iron bands two countries."[19]

This first bridge stood well the test of time, even though the volume of traffic increased and heavier trains came to be used. The wooden suspended structure was replaced by iron and steel trusses after 26 years of service, and the masonry towers by iron towers four years later. These improvements were undertaken *in situ*, without disruption in traffic. They increased the load which could be carried by several hundred tons. Roebling's Suspension Bridge remained in continuous and active service for 42 years. The increased volume, weight, and speed of rail traffic now demanded a wider and heavier structure than could have been envisaged when the first bridge was built in the 1850's.

The lower road level of the completed Niagara
Suspension Bridge. *John Burtniak Collection*

In 1896, construction of a new bridge on the site of the old one
was approved by the Privy Council. This replacement, the Niagara
Railway Steel Arch Bridge, was designed by Leiffert L. Buck. Known
technically as a "two hinged sprandel-braced arch", it was built out
from the two walls of the Gorge, completed in 1897 and modernized in
1919. The new bridge, six times stronger than its predecessor, was
itself a notable engineering achievement. It was built under the old
one, so that it rested on top of the new arch. Therefore, at the
completion of the new and before the removal of the old, two
complete bridges were built into each other.[20] The clear span
between the piers measured 550 feet, and the total length of the
bridge, with its supports, was over 1000 feet. Its two decks carried a
double railway track on the upper floor and a two-lane highway and
foot walks on the lower floor. It is interesting that, despite the change
of form, the railway crossing over the Niagara Gorge, at the site of the
Suspension Bridge, has remained in precisely the same location as it
was originally conceived, to provide a forceful and ongoing inducement for urban development in its immediate vicinity. This aspect of
the railway endeavour will be discussed in Chapter VII.

```
┌─────────────────────────────────────────┐
│           PRESIDENT'S OFFICE              │
│              ─── OF THE ───               │
│                                           │
│        Niagara  Falls  Suspension         │
│              Bridge, Co'y.                │
│              ─────••••••─────             │
│                                           │
│   ST. CATHARINES, ONT., June 1st, 1896.   │
│                                           │
│  To the Shareholders:                     │
│                                           │
│       The special shareholders meeting    │
│  held on the 12th May, was represented    │
│  by 2346 shares, out of a total of        │
│  2500 shares.  All voted in favor of      │
│  ratifying the agreement made by the      │
│  directors with the Grand Trunk Rail-     │
│  way Co. for the construction of a new    │
│  steel arch bridge in lieu of the present │
│  bridge, and for a by-law empower-        │
│  ing the directors to raise the necessary │
│  means.                                   │
│                                           │
│       The work will be carried to         │
│  completion with all reasonable dispatch, │
│  and I expect shortly to communicate      │
│  with you respecting the debentures to    │
│  be issued, and to be first offered to    │
│  the shareholders.                        │
│                                           │
│       I enclose herewith a cheque for     │
│  dividend No. 105, being three per cent.  │
│  for the half year ending thirtieth       │
│  instant on the stock standing in your    │
│  name on the books of the Company.        │
│                                           │
│            Yours truly,                   │
│                                           │
│            Thos. R. Merritt,              │
│                          President.       │
└─────────────────────────────────────────┘
```

The history of railways is the history of change. A Shareholder's notice of 1896 to replace the Suspension Bridge with a steel arch bridge.

John Burtniak Collection

A Second Railway Bridge at Niagara Falls

A second bridge was to confirm and strengthen this urban status of the Elgin-Clifton location. This was constructed across the Gorge in 1883, immediately to the south of the Suspension Bridge. This too was replaced after 40 years of service by a bridge capable of handling the heavier modern engines and freight cargoes. The first bridge, designed by C. C. Schneider, was known as the Niagara Cantilever Bridge. It provided an independent double-tracked route across the Niagara River for the Canada Southern-Michigan Central Railways. Recall that the Great Western had become part of the Grand Trunk in 1882, and the competing American interests of the Canada Southern had completed their track from Windsor to Fort Erie and from Welland to Niagara Falls. The Canada Southern had also acquired the Erie and Niagara Railway line through Clifton, so that use could be made of the Suspension Bridge until the Niagara Cantilever Bridge was constructed. The argument has also been advanced that, in order to meet the competition of its rivals, there was a desire to provide their passengers with a prime opportunity for viewing the Falls. The Canada Southern and Michigan Central both certainly used artistic licence in their advertising: their many brochures, publications and labels pictured the bridge as being next to the Falls and not downstream in its correct location!

Interior Steel Arch Bridge and Customs Office, Niagara Falls, Canada.

The Niagara Railway Steel Arch Bridge at Niagara Falls.

146

The Niagara Cantilever Bridge being tested, and an invitation to the opening
ceremony.   *John Burtniak Collection*

The bridge itself was another classic engineering design. It was
constructed with steel arms reaching out over the River from strong
steel towers anchored to the banks and to the base of the Gorge. With
a width of 495 feet over the River, it was the longest double track truss
span in the world. The speed and the capability of its construction
received immediate commendation:

"There is not on this bridge any of that wave motion noticed on a
suspension bridge as a train moves on it. Remembering that it took

three years to build the Railway Suspension Bridge for a single track, and that this bridge for a double track not only had to be finished within seven and a half months from the execution of the contract, but was actually completed with eight days to spare, it reflects great credit upon the advancement of engineering skill."[21]

The advancing skill and experience of technology certainly facilitated the crossing of the Niagara River, making it less of an obstacle than had been encountered when the first Suspension Bridge was achieved. But trains were also increasing in length and weight. The Niagara Cantilever Bridge was strengthened in 1900 and remained in operation until its successor, begun in 1923 and opened in 1925 by the Michigan Central, took over as the New York Central Bridge. This bridge was located next to, but just north of the earlier structure. This new structure, therefore, strengthened the urban position of Niagara Falls rather than initiating any new location for urban development.

The track approached the Cantilever Bridge from the south. This line descended along the outer walls of the Gorge to the level of the Bridge, passing through the urban areas of Niagara Falls. This route brought the trains close to the world-famed spectacle of the Horseshoe and Canadian Falls. It, therefore, provided an aesthetic feature of which the company could be exceptionally proud (a topic to be discussed further in Chapter VII).

Twin railway bridges crossing the Niagra Gorge at Niagra Falls.
John Burtniak Collection

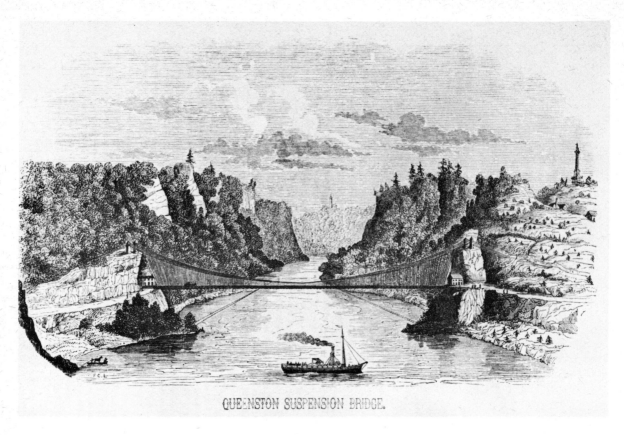

QUEENSTON SUSPENSION BRIDGE.

The Queenston-Lewiston Suspension Bridge of 1851.

Other Bridges Across the Gorge

Further downstream, at the historic Queenston-Lewiston crossing, a bridge crossing was contemplated as early as 1836. By 1849, American and Canadian charters had been secured for the Queenston Suspension Bridge Company and the Lewiston Suspension Bridge Company for the purpose of bridging the Niagara River. The Canadian Legislature empowered the Company "to construct a Suspension Bridge across the Niagara River at or near Queenston, with the necessary approaches thereto with rail, macadamized or other roads, and to connect the same with any road now or hereafter to be made, at any point within half a mile of the said town of Queenston."[22] This bill was opposed by the Niagara Falls Suspension Bridge Company, who feared that their interests were threatened.

The Queenston and Lewiston Bridge Companies exercised their sanction immediately by constructing a light-weight and swinging highway bridge. This bridge, designed by E. W. Serrell, was slung across the Niagara River by 1851. Located at the northern end of the Gorge close to the base of the Escarpment, its towers were of sufficient capacity to carry cables for railway purposes when required. The bridge, 1,040 feet in length, and 20 feet wide, carried pedestrians, horses and carriages. However, a gale damaged the bridge structure in 1855, and it was demolished in 1864 as a result of wind and ice action. The wreck of the damaged cables and their supporting towers remained for 34 years as mute testimony to both the technical problems of building over the Niagara River and of attracting railways to this location.

Roebling's success with the Suspension Bridge led to the construction of another bridge, the New Suspension Bridge, closer to the Falls. This bridge, built between 1867 and 1869, was located about 300 yards below the American Falls. It enjoyed a splendid location from which the Gorge and the Falls could be viewed. The first bridge, "a suspension bridge with timber deck and stiffening truss and timber towers supporting the cables at the Canadian and American ends,"[23] served pedestrian and carriage traffic. As its width was only ten feet, carriages could not pass each other on the bridge. It was necessary to operate a one-way system of traffic flow, thus causing long delays at each end. The bridge was owned by the Niagara Falls and Clifton Suspension Bridge Company, a combined Canadian-American venture with the Canadian company being incorporated in 1868.[24] It aided in linking the park reservations on the two sides of the river. In providing the closest view of the Falls, the bridge enhanced the tourist trade. To assist this, an elevator was installed in the bridge tower on the Canadian side in order to provide a better vantage point for viewing the scenery.

A series of changes to the bridge occurred during the next two decades. Steel replaced wood on the base of the bridge in 1872, the wooden towers were replaced by steel ones in 1884, and the bridge was widened in 1888 — a combination of improvements which resulted in virtually a new steel structure spanning 1,268 feet from bank to bank. However, it was still a flexible suspension bridge and lacked the rigidity of its downstream counterpart. In early 1889, the structure was demolished by a gale.

As the plans and patterns for the steel parts were still readily available, the bridge was replaced in 1889 with a similar steel structure. The roadway was 17 feet in width, a capacity soon deemed inadequate in the face of the rapid expansion in transportation demands. The urgency for improvement has been described by J. Morden, when commenting upon the emergence of an inter-urban transportation network, in these words:

The replacement bridge at the Queenston-Lewiston crossing of the Niagara River, as part of the Great Gorge route. *John Burtniak Collection*

> "The development of great units of electrical power at Niagara Falls was a revolutionary force in transportation. The horse-car lines of the region became electrically equipped and new electric street cars were laid down. With the construction of the electric roads on both sides of the Gorge for scenic purposes, there came a demand for international connection of the lines in order that a belt line trolley service might be operated about the gorge. The electric car was heavy and it was found that none of the bridges was sufficiently strong to furnish the required service. This led to the determination to replace the upper suspension bridge with a steel arch."[25]

The expanding needs of transportation, this time in conjunction with the growing tourist trade, demanded a new bridge. A change in the mode of transport, from horse-car lines to the much heavier electrical tramway, had taken place which, together with the expanding population and demands for inter-linking the American and Canadian systems of transportation, required a new structure. Power to erect a second bridge was granted in 1894,[26] and the new Upper Steel Arch Bridge was constructed during 1897-1898 to meet this need. Then the greatest steel arch bridge in the world, it has been described as "a two-hinged arch with latticed rib and its span was 840 feet. Trusses connected the main span to the tops of the cliffs at the Canadian and American ends. The abutments stood close to the water's edge on both sides of the river."[27]

The New Suspension Bridge next to the Falls.   *John Burtniak Collection*

151

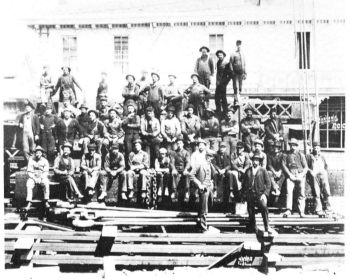

The Upper Steel Arch Bridge (known popularly as the Honeymoon Bridge)
under construction, a work-gang involved, and nearing completion, 1898.

Special Collections, Brock University Library

The bridge had a wooden deck, which provided space for two sets of electric car tracks, carriage space, and walkways in both directions. As this replacement bridge became available, the former structure was dismantled and reconstructed on the site of the ill-fated Queenston-Lewiston Bridge. As the new structure swayed somewhat in the wind and with traffic, and the wooden floor was often slippery with spray or ice, it was crossed with some trepidation by the tourist crowds. It collapsed in 1938 when the river ice piled up and wrenched the bridge supports from the abutments.

Ground was broken for yet another bridge, the present Rainbow Bridge, in 1940. This was located downstream from its predecessor. It was constructed with two 22-foot roadways and a 10-foot walkway on the main viewing side facing the Falls. A comparable highway bridge has also been constructed over the northern end of the Gorge at the Queenston-Lewiston crossing to replace the earlier, outmoded structure. This bridge, opened in 1962, was placed at a higher level and over half-a-mile south of the former bridge in order to inter-connect the modern highway system of the Queen Elizabeth Way in Ontario with the New York State Thruway system.

Bridge Construction at Fort Erie

One other major bridge-building locality emerged during the railway era. This was a crossing of the Niagara River in the vicinity of Fort Erie-Buffalo, where the waters of Lake Erie funnelled into a relatively narrow channel creating fast-flowing currents. This flow was compounded by the problem of winter ice choking the channel entrance and piling up on the banks. As early as 1849 a proposal had been placed before the Canadian Legislature to build an iron bridge at Waterloo, the name of the settlement at the Canadian lake edge at that time, but no action resulted. This was followed by an Act of 1852, which empowered the Fort Erie and Buffalo Suspension Bridge and Tunnel Company "to construct a Suspension Bridge across the Niagara River or a Tunnel under the same, at or near Waterloo Ferry."[28]

The International Bridge Company was incorporated by charters granted by the State of New York and Canada in 1857 to build a bridge across the Niagara River from Waterloo (Fort Erie) to Buffalo.[29] A letter from William A. Thomson (later involved in the Canada Southern) to William Hamilton Merritt in 1856, and headed "In the Matter of Bridging the Niagara River at Buffalo", mentioned the formation of "a Committee to co-operate with the Buffalo one and invited Merritt to act as Chairman."[30] These inaugural proceedings were delayed when the American Civil War intervened, and no progress was made until 1870 when the Grand Trunk began the construction of a bridge that would accommodate rail, carriage and pedestrian traffic.

Colonel Sir Casimir S. Gzowski (1813-1898) was the chief engineer in this undertaking.[31] He had previously obtained the contract for building the Grand Trunk line from Toronto to Sarnia. He now had to cope with the difficult task of placing the supporting piers in the deep, fast-flowing River and of counteracting the destructive force of the winter ice. At the time of its construction, this was the only bridge across the Niagara River with piers in its turbulent waters — all other bridges spanned the River from bank to bank. The piers had to be constructed in the swift current and several coffer dams were

The collapse of the Upper Steel Arch Bridge, 1938.   *John Burtniak Collection*

swept away before they were anchored by heavy stone. The bridge was opened for traffic in November 1873. It linked the Grand Trunk, which had obtained control of the Buffalo and Lake Huron Railway, with the expanding City of Buffalo and its associated network of railways. This engineering feat facilitated freight and passenger exchange between the Canadian and the American railway systems.

The International Bridge crossing the Niagara River at Fort Erie, before and after strengthening.   *John Burtniak Collection*

The site selected for the crossing was located 3.5 miles north from Buffalo harbour, where advantage could be taken of Squaw Island, situated close to the American side, to cross both the River and the Erie Canal. The completed structure, consisting of a bridge across the main River channel, an embankment across Squaw Island, and a swing span across the Erie Canal, carried a single track railway. No provision was made for carriages, as was stipulated in its enabling charter.

Its success was immediate. The heavy flow of railway traffic precluded the use of the bridge for other purposes, and it became exclusively a railway bridge. As with the other bridges across the Niagara River, the increase in the amount and size of the traffic loads necessitated a strengthening of the structure. The superstructure was replaced by steel trusses at the turn of the century, thereby doubling the weight that could be carried. In 1910-1911, the span over the Erie Canal was replaced by a double track swing bridge which permitted a wider channel into Black Rock harbour, but the bridge into Canada has remained single-tracked. This structure was the only bridge across the Niagara River at Fort Erie until the Peace Bridge, a four-lane highway arch[32] accommodating vehicular and pedestrian traffic only, was constructed in 1927.

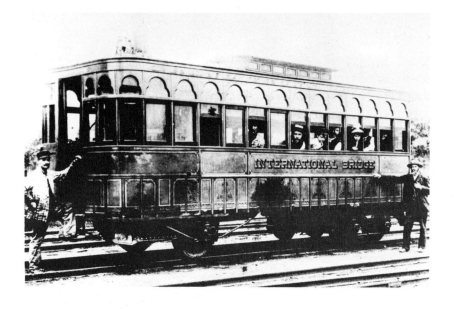

The first street car in use on the International Bridge, 1874.
St. Catharines Historical Museum, from Public Archives of Canada, C-42748

Given this sequence of bridge developments both at Fort Erie and across the Gorge, it is of more than passing interest to note the changing weight of engines and trains that were accommodated on these spans.[33] Roebling tested his Suspension Bridge with engines weighing from 20 to 34 tons, and his experimental freight train of 20 fully loaded cars had an estimated gross weight of 326 tons. When its successor, the Niagara Railway Arch Bridge, was tested in 1897, the locomotive weighed 90 tons, the cars had increased in weight from 15 to 52.5 tons, and the total test load was 1,670 tons. By 1918, when the Steel Arch Bridge was being re-tested, the locomotives ranged in weight from 177 to 221 tons, and the test load was 2,490 tons. Just as successive improvements to the locks of the Welland Canal system have been required on several occasions by the increasing size and capacity of ships, so too has technological advance required a spate of improvements to the railway system. The more remarkable and note-worthy of these changes have taken place at the major bridging points of the Niagara River.

Other Bridge Proposals

With bridges as with railways, not all schemes were approved and not all approved schemes were constructed. For example, despite many pleas, recommendations, surveys and Acts, neither a major railway bridge at Queenston-Lewiston nor a railway link from St. Catharines or Merritton to Queenston were constructed. William Hamilton Merritt, however, must have had such possibilities in mind when, in 1845, he made an informal agreement with the Directors of the Great Western that their railroad from Detroit should have one line to Buffalo and the other through Hamilton to the Niagara River at Queenston.[34] In 1847, when Clifton was being chosen as the terminus, it was seriously contemplated that this location should be abandoned and that Queenston should be made the terminus.[35] Later, in 1853, there were prospects of an American line from Lockport to Lewiston.[36] There was "a petition for a Rail Road from Queenston to St. Catharines in 1855"[37] and, in 1856, the Queenston and St. Catharines Railway Company was authorized to construct a railway between these two places in order "to intersect and unite with the Great Western or any other Railway at or near St. Catharines".[38]

In 1857, at a meeting held to consider the construction of a railroad from St. Catharines via Queenston and Lewiston to Rochester, the following resolution was recorded:

> "We the undersigned citizens of St. Catharines, Queenston, and Lewiston, do hereby associate and pledge ourselves to pay the sums set opposite our names, for the procurement of surveys. The defrayment of incidental expenses, and the negotiation of way rights, for the construction of a Rail-Road from Canada to Rochester."[39]

Later, in 1866, the Lake Ontario Shore Railroad was projected. The intention was to build a railroad from Oswego (New York) to the Niagara River at Lewiston, where the surviving towers and cables of the Queenston-Lewiston Bridge could be incorporated into a new structure. Of the Canadian terrain, it was stated that "the ground upon the west side of the river, from the proposed place of the bridge to the Great Western Railroad, along the base of the lake ridge is favourable."[40]

Surveys were also conducted by the Great Western for a route from Thorold to Queenston. A bridge was proposed at Queenston, and its costs and revenues were examined at various meetings in 1873. The discussions favoured building a double track bridge immediately. This would have cost very little more than a single track structure, and would have accommodated heavier traffic flows. The Directors of the Lewiston and Queenston Bridge Company urged "most strongly and earnestly" that the English Board of Directors of the Great Western Railway Company recognize "the absolute necessity at once of giving their assurance that they will build the branch line from Merritton to Queenston, and use the bridge when built, as a means of crossing the Niagara River in connection with the American roads connecting at that point."[41]

In fact, neither a railway bridge nor a railway route traversing the Peninsula were to reach the Queenston-Lewiston crossing. Despite many such possibilities, all schemes and aspirations came to nought. Had one of these succeeded, considerably more urban and industrial activity might well have occurred at Queenston and Lewiston. These probabilities might have been associated with harbour facilities along the Lower Niagara River, so that a major industrial complex from Queenston to Niagara could have emerged. This, in turn, might have been assisted by the construction of either the Welland Canal, or a lateral cut from this waterway, to the Lower Niagara River.

Mather's daring concept of a spectacular bridge at Fort Erie to climax the technological advances of the nineteenth century.

Alonzo C. Mather, Buffalo . . . , 1893

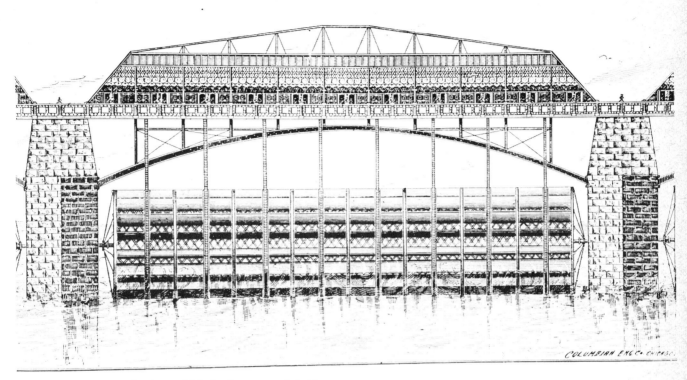

The power mechanism of Mather's proposed bridge.

Atonzo C. Mather, Buffalo . . ., 1893

Another interesting possibility was to cross the Niagara River by tunnel, as had been done at Windsor under the Detroit River. This concept, "to tunnel the Niagara River, so as to have an underground passage to Canada",[42] was noted in Buffalo in 1880, since the International Bridge was said to be inadequate. It was thought that this scheme, the cost of which was estimated at $2,000,000, would increase local trade. There were also more sinister motivations. Judge Clinton stated "that with a tunnel under Niagara and Detroit Rivers, the annexation of our neighbour the Dominion, cannot long be deferred."[43] A border location promoted argument for commerce and communications to cross the frontier; it also fostered rivalry and innate hostility between the two countries as each side jostled for trading and business advantages.

The hazards of international construction schemes involved much more than just bridge-building skills. Legislation had to be steered through complicated procedures in both Canada and the United States, with the usual conflicting sets of interests and pressure groups. Within this context, mention should be made of an astounding scheme proposed by Alonzo C. Mather in the 1890's. He visualized a great international harbour on both sides of the River at Buffalo and Fort Erie, with a bridge linking the two countries. This concept, taken to the extend of constructing a working model at the scale of one-half inch to the foot, envisaged a massive steel wheel (weighing 460,000 pounds) slung beneath the bridge. This power-producing wheel would be turned by the regular and continuing flow of the current in the Niagara River. Mather described the design of this structure: "I have planned the ornamentation. . .so elaborately it can be made as attractive in steel as point lace in thread. . .and though it may take generations to complete the ornamentations of this structure, it can be made something beautiful, and work continued only as revenue is derived for that purpose.[44] The bridge itself would be "a Memorial Bridge in this wonderful location that shall be a perpetual monument to the works that have been accomplished by them [the inventors] during the 19th century."[45] It would have carried two sets of railway and street car tracks.

Mather's grandiose plans also envisaged, on the Canadian side, a major protected harbour, grain elevators, extensive wharves and factories. To this end, he acquired a large block of real estate with river frontage in Fort Erie. The proposal, though favourably received in Canada, was thwarted when legislative approval was not obtained in Albany and Washington. If constructed, the proposal would have provided a remarkable, culminating monument to the nineteenth century railway and bridge achievements in the Peninsula. As it was, it became but one of the many ideas which are now largely forgotten because it was not constructed.

Another unfulfilled scheme was contained in an American report of 1853 which declared that, if the Suspension Bridge then under construction could not be completed, a permanent arched bridge with stone piers and arched spans could be built across the Niagara River near the mouth of the Chippawa Creek.[46] Another bridge was proposed by the Niagara Grand Island Bridge Company, which was incorporated in 1874 for the purpose of constructing a railway bridge across the Niagara River at or near Black Creek to Grand Island,[47] but no bridge was built.

The Niagara River was the supreme obstacle that had to be overcome during the evolutionary stages of the railway era. The acute dilemmas faced by the engineers and builders at the various points of crossing along the River were eventually resolved by the developing technology of the period. But there were also as many improbable and unsuccessful proposals as there were successful attempts to bridge the Niagara River. It should be realized that the urban endowments of the present can reflect only the reality of successful projects, but the others should not be forgotten as the successes and the failures of the period are evaluated.

Chapter VII

The Urban Impact of Railways

Railways were much more than political squabbles or economic bargaining in their achievement, or constructional features in the landscape when they were opened. They became, almost immediately, a vital force for change in the urban and regional setting in which they were located. They created railway towns such as Bridgeburg and Fort Erie, affected existing centres, and exerted a differential effect on the growth and status of settlements. Some communities prospered and others waned because of their railway characteristics. These effects on the urban environment of selected communities will be described in this chapter.

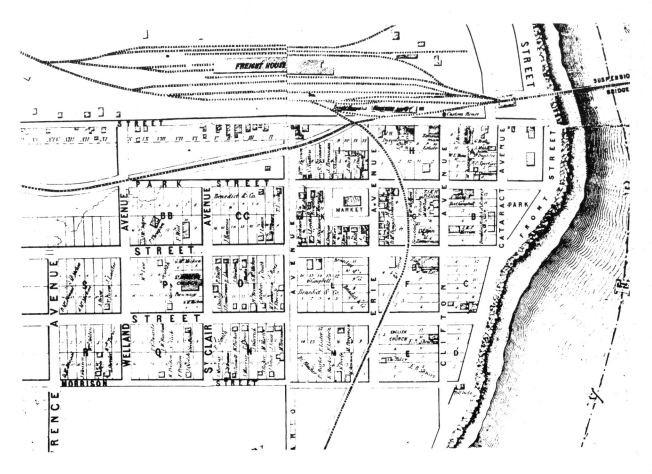

Fig. 7.1 Clifton and the Suspension Bridge, 1857.

J. H. French, Corporations of Niagara Falls and Niagara City, N.Y., and Clifton, C.W., 1857

Railway Towns on the Niagara River

Two towns in the Peninsula, Clifton-Niagara Falls and Bridgeburg-Fort Erie, owe a special debt to the influence that the railways exerted on their foundation, growth and urban evolution. An immediate effect of the lines and the bridge crossings at the frontier was to render obsolete those ferries which had previously crossed the Niagara River. The steam-boat crossings of Lake Ontario were also affected. As stated by B. Cumberland, with the opening of the Great Western from Niagara Falls to Hamilton and to Toronto and the Grand Trunk to Montreal:

> "The steamboating interests suffered still further and great decay. In the financial crisis of 1857 many steamers were laid up. In 1858 all the American Line steamers were in bankruptcy, and in 1860 the *Zimmerman* abandoned the Niagara River to the *Peerless*, the one steamer being sufficient."[1]

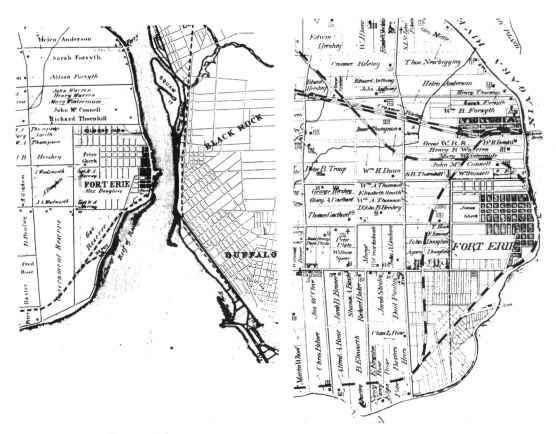

Fig. 7.2   Fort Erie: A Study of Urban Transition, 1862 and 1876.
Tremaines' Map of the Counties of Lincoln and Welland, 1862,
and H. R. Page, Illustrated Historical Atlas of the Counties of Lincoln and Welland, 1876

A longer term repercussion was the funnelling of the heavier traffic loads to selected river crossing points. Nodal points of railway significance and attention emerged at Clifton-Niagara Falls and to a lesser extent at Bridgeburg-Fort Erie. By the same token, those frontier centres which did not obtain international trans-river railway connections (Niagara, Queenston and Chippawa) dwindled in relative importance. Characteristics of the railway era in the Peninsula included both decay at some of the earlier portage settlements and growth at the new river crossing points, a re-invigoration at Fort Erie in contrast with the waning importance of Niagara, and the unprecedented boost of Niagara Falls compared to the much slower advance and promotion of St. Catharines, the major city within the Peninsula.

The impact of the Great Western Railway and the Suspension Bridge on urbanization was immediate and considerable as railway promoters, shareholders and landowners sought to reap substantial financial returns. For example, an advertisement in 1855 drew attention to the sale of:

"280 eligible building lots lying immediately North and adjoining the Depot Ground of the Great Western Railway in the most promising village in Canada West. The Lots vary in size, and price from $150 to $300. Persons intending to build at once can have any time short of 10 years to make their payments in."[2]

The railway did, in fact, nurture Niagara Falls into effective existence as an important centre within the Peninsula. Previously, these were three small villages — Drummondville at the junction of the Portage Road with Lundy's Lane and Ferry Street, Clifton in the present central area of Niagara Falls, and the area immediately adjacent to the Suspension Bridge where the workers had built their homes when the bridge was under construction. This bridgehead settlement and railway terminus soon attained village status, being incorporated as the Village of Elgin in 1853. It was named after Lord Elgin, the Governor General of the period who resided at nearby Drummondville. An account, some three years later, stated:

"Perhaps no place in Canada has made such progress in so short a period of time. . .Before another year passes away we will, it is expected, be able to boast of our places of worship, our market hall, now in course of erection, our school houses, and other public buildings. Thus, from a place of obscurity, it has become an enterprising, brisk, busy and lively town, with upwards of one thousand inhabitants. A year or two past, we had one grocery store, — now about fourteen or fifteen, with upwards of twenty saloons and hotels, some of these equal to any kept in large cities."[3]

Elgin became a place of importance; in 1856, it amalgamated with the Village of Clifton to form the Town of Clifton (Fig. 7.1). In turn, with further growth, Clifton at its own request was renamed the Town of Niagara Falls by Act of Parliament in 1881. Drummondville also wished to change its name to Niagara Falls, a request which was approved in 1882 when it was incorporated under a by-law of Welland County Council as the Village of Niagara Falls. The Town of Niagara Falls became the City of Niagara Falls by proclamation in 1903, and the Village of Niagara Falls was incorporated into this unit as one City in 1904.

In terms of population size, the Town of Clifton grew from a few residents in 1851 to 1,610 in 1871 (when St. Catharines had 7,864

Customs facilities developed at the international border in conjunction with the Great Western and other railways.

Buchanan Papers, Public Archives of Canada

people), to 2,347 in 1881 and to 5,702 by 1901 (when the population of St. Catharines was 9,946 persons). The difference in population between the two centres continued to diminish and was even less by 1911 — 9,248 people in Niagara Falls compared with 12,484 in St. Catharines. A new centre had been born in the Peninsula, primarily because of its direct railway accessibility and the new opportunities which it sponsored.

G. T. R. Station, Bridgeburg, Ontario.

A contrast in the styles of railway architecture, the Michigan Central and Grand Trunk Stations at Bridgeburg.   *John Burtniak Collection*

The new border crossing established at the Suspension Bridge required a customs house and, in 1851, a proclamation did "declare, constitute and appoint the Suspension Bridge across the Niagara river, in the township of Stamford, by the name of *Port Stamford, a Port or place of entry*."[4] This name was retained until 1856 when it was renamed the Port of Clifton; it became the Port of Niagara Falls in 1893. As the number of railways and their traffic increased, so too did the volume of customs' work. Trains also had to be organized to new points of destination, a requirement which resulted in two sets of railway yards in the Niagara Falls area, each possessing their own repair, service, industrial and commercial facilities. The Great Western yards were situated to the north-east of the main urban area, strongly influencing its structural form and the patterns of growth. The Montrose Yards were located to the south-west and, though in a more remote position, they nevertheless provided a spur to industrial growth in the direction of the Welland River.

At the entrance to the Niagara River, the settlement in the vicinity of old Fort Erie enjoyed various names — including Waterloo, and before that Fort Erie Mills or Fort Erie Rapids. Its early importance was as a military post, which commanded a ferry crossing to Buffalo. It was also a trading centre, exporting merchandise and supplies and receiving furs and other local produce.[5] Waterloo suffered with the transfer of trade inland to the Welland Canal in 1833, but the construction of the Erie and Niagara Railway helped to redeem the situation for a time. Then, in 1854, the Buffalo and Lake Huron Railway came into the settlement from the west past the fort. The population increased to about 900, and it was incorporated as the Village of Fort Erie in 1857.

At this time, the village extended two and a half miles along the River front, and had four taverns, ten stores, four churches, a blacksmith shop and a drill shed.[6] To these service facilities the railway added its yard, station and repair shops. But Fort Erie's growth was short-lived. With the construction of the International Bridge its hopes as a railway centre were eclipsed by the development of rail facilities on the American side and by Buffalo becoming the terminal. As noted by E. W. Johnson:

"Construction of the International Bridge and abandonment of the car ferries to Buffalo spelt the end of Fort Erie's importance as a railway centre. But it wound up in the creation of the village, later the town, of Bridgeburg, which soon outstripped the up-river community in population and commerce."[7]

Here, indeed, is a fascinating story of urban transfer that resulted directly from the development of railways and their associated features (Fig. 7.2). The emergence of a new centre began when the construction gangs and workers established boarding houses, stores, taverns, a school and a church:

"Almost overnight there mushroomed up all those accompanying enterprises that follow any great undertaking. . .Skilled workmen, laborers, executives, inspectors, merchants and hangers-on, all poured in to reap whatever benefit they could from 'the bridge'. Station, sheds, machine and work shops were erected and employment given to hundreds; customs and immigration staffs were needed, and all paths led to that fair hill 'just down the river' to form the nucleus of Victoria. . .And so Fort Erie's rival sister was born."[8]

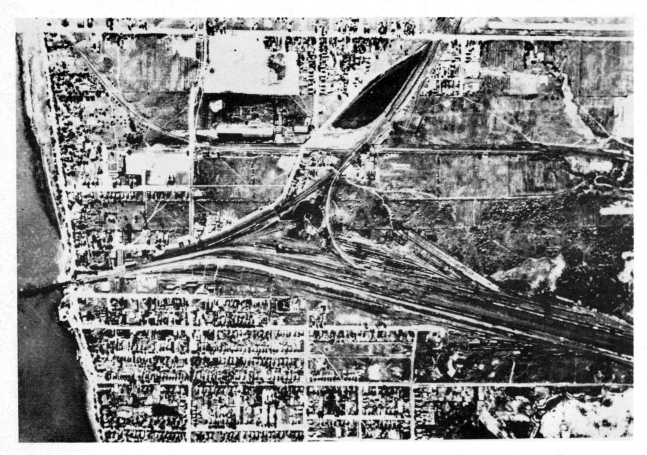

The International Bridge and its associated railway yards, 1934.

National Air Photo Library, Ottawa

The railway was re-routed to the International Bridge in 1873, thereby avoiding Fort Erie. The Canada Southern also sent its trains to this bridge. The new community that sprang up at the entrance was named Victoria after the reigning monarch, but it was also called International Bridge.[9] It became the Village of Bridgeburg in 1894 when its territory was increased, the Town of Bridgeburg in 1915, and remained as a separate unit from Fort Erie until the two communities were united under the older historic name of Fort Erie in 1932.

The various railway-oriented facilities included freight yards inland and coal docks on the Niagara River, and a round-house, shops, and customs and immigration buildings. The original Grand Trunk station of Victoria was built west of the bridge entrance, and was replaced by a turreted building at the beginning of the twentieth century. The original board and batten station of the Michigan Central line, named Fort Erie, has succumbed to a modern brick depot.[10]

H. R. Page has offered this extended description of the railway involvement at Fort Erie in 1876 and the expectations at that time for the future:

"Victoria, the name of the new Town claiming public attention is situated at the west end of the International Iron Bridge. . .[It] has its west end station on a portion of the town plot of Victoria, which is likewise the terminus of the Grand Trunk, Great Western Air Line, and Canada Southern Railways, whose stations are upon and adjoin it. It has a large frontage on the Niagara River, and possesses all the advantages of the unlimited water power of that noble river, as well as its harbor and dock accommodation. It is comtemplated that Victoria will, by means of this bridge become a suburb of Buffalo. . .The extensive works connected with these railway stations and necessary machine and works shops, will afford constant employment for numbers of men, who will likewise have the advantage of work in the large iron and other factories on the opposite (American side) of the river. The centre of the City of Buffalo can be reached in a few minutes by regular trains and street cars. Victoria has already good hotels, stores and neat cottages. A glance at its situation, railway and water shipping accommodation, demonstrates it as a point possessing unsurpassed facilities for all classes of manufacturing and mercantile business."[11]

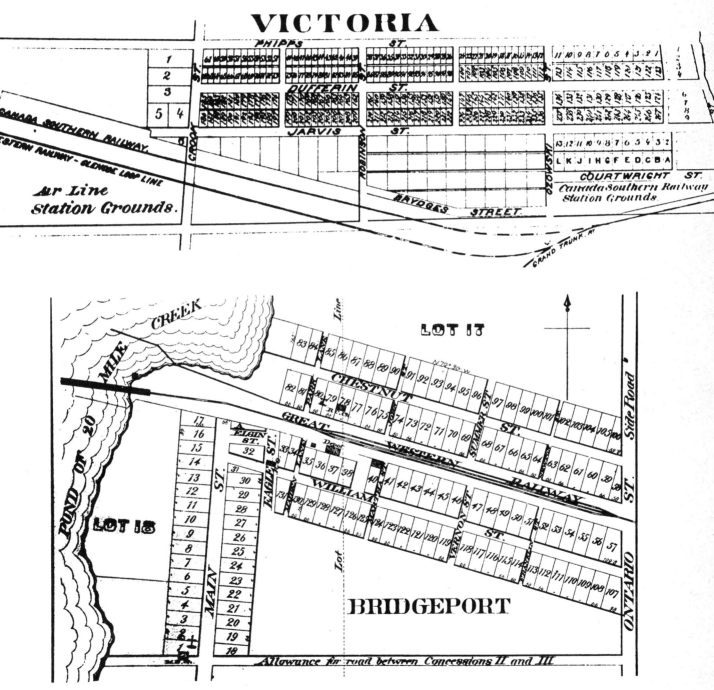

Fig. 7.3 Victoria (Bridgeburg) and Bridgeport (Jordan Station): Two Linear Railway Communities, 1876.

H. R. Page, Illustrated Historical Atlas of the Counties of Lincoln and Welland, 1876

"Rivers of Steel" in the urban environment of Niagara Falls, 1934.   *National Air Photo Library, Ottawa*

Bridgeburg and Clifton, as the two prime examples of railway towns in the Peninsula, took on a comparable urban form. In each instance, a town centre developed along a main street (Jarvis Street and Bridge Street, respectively), which closely paralleled the track and its associated railway-oriented facilities. This linear urban characteristic may be compared, in its originating force and in its physical expression, with the main street of Thorold (Front Street) with the evolution of St. Paul Street in St. Catharines in conjunction with the First and the Second Welland Canals, or with the railway village of Bridgeport (now Jordan Station) that developed where the Great Western crossed Twenty Mile Creek (Fig. 7.3).

Another characteristic feature at Bridgeburg and Clifton was the pronounced division of the urban area into two separate parts on either side of the track. In addition, there were the broad "rivers of steel" in the railway marshalling yards. These wide barriers with their interchanging lines, trucks, shunting locomotives and concentrated activity presented severe limitations on road connections, inter-communication and service linkages. The towns were compartmentalized to the detriment of social provision and community inter-action between their component units. The swathes which segmented the growing towns physically and socially were also evident on land owned and developed by the railways. As major land owners and employers of labour, they exerted a considerable (and generally unwitting) control over the processes of urban evolution.

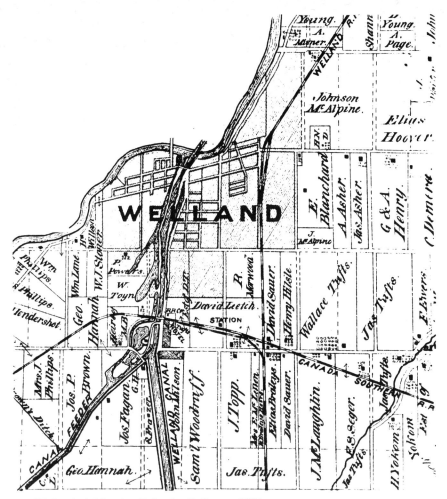

Fig. 7.4   Welland: A Meeting Point for Railways, 1876.

H. R. Page, Illustrated Historical Atlas of the Counties of Lincoln and Welland, 1876

One illustration of this fact is that in Bridgeburg, the property owned by the International Bridge was assessed at $175,000 annually by 1895, which compared with $21,000 for the property of the Grand Trunk Railway and $13,000 for the property of the Canada Southern.[12] Further north, at the Suspension Bridge crossing, the Canada Southern properties in Niagara Falls were assessed at $150,000 in 1899.[13]

The routes and the locations of the railway lines also exerted a tremendous effect upon the direction and forms of urban growth. The towns grew discontinuously and sporadically, rather than progressively outward from a core nucleus. A major factor was that the houses built for the railway employees and industries next to the line of track had to be within walking distance of the major centres of employment. There could be little control or direction by the municipal authority. The town had to grow around, along and between the various railway lines that existed and this railway-dominated process, to a large extent, established the character and personality of the whole urban area. Industries, warehouses and distribution centres followed along the railways. They were located by the dictates of railway access, often to the detriment of their immediate neighbourhoods, and poorer housing was relegated to unwanted sites between the arms of the railway. As it was not possible to introduce a more rational division of land into railway-industrial and residential areas, acute problems were presented for later resolution by the municipal planning process.

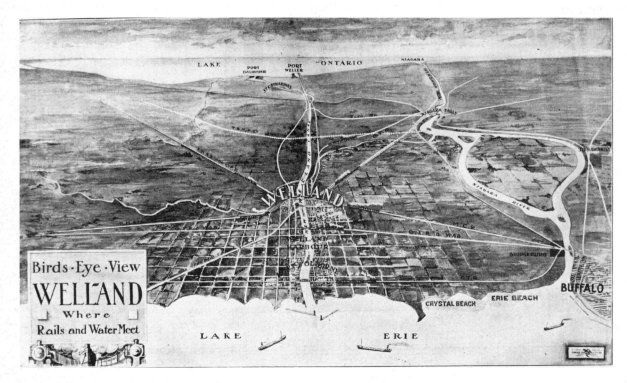

Fig. 7.5   Welland: The Railway Hub of the Peninsula, 1924.
Special Collections, Brock University Library

Interestingly enough, as the automobile era dawned and railway passenger traffic gradually declined, the new main roads did not pass through these railway-oriented centres. The Niagara River Parkway along the River frontage and the modern highways serving the road bridges by-passed the downtown centres of Niagara Falls and Fort Erie, so that they are not seen by many visitors, to the detriment and disadvantage of their full service capability. As throughout this text, changing fortunes and new circumstances have amended continually the railway scene as it was first established in a particular location.

Welland: "Where Rails and Water Meet"

Welland was initiated by the Welland Canal and has been responsive to this waterway throughout its urban history.[14] Nevertheless, it reveals many railway traits in its urban format. Specifically, it was transformed in its regional accessibility and potential by the railways which traversed the southern part of the Peninsula. The town and its vicinity received a series of stimuli — first, the Welland Railway to the east of the town in 1859, then the Canada Southern and the Canada Air Line to the south in 1873 (Fig. 7.4) and, most significantly, the Toronto, Hamilton and Buffalo Railway about 20 years later. Welland became the railway centre for the inner areas of the Peninsula by these developments and could offer, in its railway connections and facilities, a range greater than most other locations in Ontario and equalled by few places in Canada. Previously, it had no direct access to important nearby places such as Toronto, Hamilton or Buffalo.

Welland's urban motto, "Where Rails and Water Meet", is, therefore, much more than mere symbolism. It reflected the geographical advantages of the town's urban setting from the late-nineteenth century onwards (Fig. 7.5). Industry was now able to use either canal or railway facilities and could compare their respective rates, convenience and facilities for the shipment of goods. In its turn, the Toronto, Hamilton and Buffalo Railway must have been attracted to Welland because the construction of the Third Welland Canal had upgraded the channel to higher standards and provided a greater navigational capacity. More trade could be expected as a result of these improvements.

The advantages of possessing both the Welland Canal and railway modes of transport at its doorstep, and their combined impact on the personality of Welland, were clearly expressed by H. R. Page in 1876:

> "The Village of Welland. . .has a population of about 1900 people, and is the County Town of the County of Welland. . .Like most of the villages situated on the Welland Ship Canal, it owes a great deal of its growth to that work; and with the Welland Railway. . .and the Canada Southern Railway. . .it has ample facilities for travellers and shippers. The village has a grammar and two common schools, and the County Agricultural Society hold their annual meeting here. . .A swing bridge across the canal connects the village, which is situated on either side of the canal. The place has several churches belonging to different denominations, and a number of fine brick stores and some large mills and manufacturers of various kinds."[15]

The railways were located on the periphery of the developed area — the Welland Railway to the east and the later east-west routes further to the south. As a result, many extensive sites were available for future expansion and these offered the dual advantage of access to the railway and to the Canal. Industrial sites were, therefore, generally close to the line of the Canal, often using its water for industrial processes such as forging and cooling; and they could capitalize on its transportational advantages for the import and export of raw materials and products. The factories also had connecting links to one or more of the Canadian or American railway systems. The town, in turn, expanded from its core nucleus next to the Canal up to and beyond these industrial plants. The railway tracks, at grade in the landscape, broke up the new urban developments into distinctive areas. It was not an orderly pattern of growth, but segmented.

The railway network, in conjunction with the development of heavy industry, therefore encouraged growth. It also produced a built-in blighting effect on the quality of the resultant urban form. To this composite picture was soon added the attraction of the new and cheap power source of hydro-electricity, which spurred the expansion of established industries and induced others to locate here. The population then expanded rapidly, from 1,863 persons in 1901 to 5,318 in 1911. The consequences for Welland of combining the Canal with railways and power advantages were substantial and contributed markedly to the rapid progress of its urban evolution.

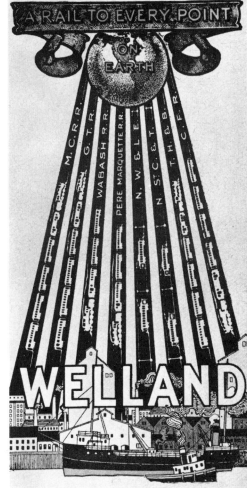

WHERE RAILS AND WATER MEET

An industrial brochure highlights Welland's focal position on the railway network.

Special Collections, Brock University Library

T. R. Depot, Welland, Ont.

Main Street, Welland, Ont., Canada

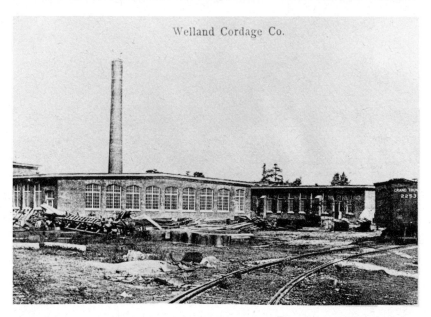

Welland Cordage Co.

Urbanization at Welland was enhanced by the railway endeavour.

Canada Forge Co. Limited, Welland. Ont. Canada.

Shipyards, Beatty & Co. Works, Welland, Ontario.

AQUEDUCT AND LOCK, WELLAND, ONT.

Welland's advance in urban-industrial status owed much to the advantages
created by its railways.   *John Burtniak Collection*

Niagara, Queenston and Chippawa

Whilst the railway centres were booming, Niagara (Fig. 7.6) was by-passed. As the former capital of Upper Canada and the district centre of the region, it had diminished in importance before the dawn of the railway era. Niagara began to fight this changing shift in its influence and importance as early as 1836, when St. Catharines was expanding as a result of the Welland Canal. The struggle reached a higher pitch in the early railway era when Niagara received only the Erie and Ontario Railway, while St. Catharines obtained both the Welland Railway and the Great Western Railway. A disparate emphasis emerged and, in the acute period of rivalry between the two communities in the 1850's and 1860's, even petitions for a lateral cut from the Welland Canal to the Niagara River were of no avail. Nor could the town sustain its status as the County seat.[16] St. Catharines increased its regional supremacy and Niagara dwindled considerably in local and regional importance.

An account by W. H. Smith, in 1851, recorded this adverse change in the fortunes of Niagara as follows:

"Niagara, lately the district town of the Niagara District, and now the county town of the united counties of Lincoln and Welland, was formerly called Newark. It is one of the oldest settlements in Upper Canada, and was for a short time the capital of the country. It was once a place of considerable business, but since the formation of the Welland Canal, St. Catharines, being more centrically situated, has absorbed its trade and thrown it completely in the shade. The town, however, is airily and healthily situated, and is a pleasant summer residence, and will remain a quiet country town, frequented during the summer season by families having spare time and spare money, by health-seekers and hypochondriacs. Many schemes are projected by parties having property in the town to endeavour to resuscitate it, and bring back the trade of the olden times, but none of them promise sufficiently well to temp those who must furnish the means to run the risk."[17]

Fig. 7.6 Niagara: Its Railway Routes, 1876.

H.R. Page, Illustrated Historical Atlas of the Counties of Lincoln and Welland, 1876

Niagara declined in absolute and relative terms. It had a population of 3,340 at 1851, 2,004 by 1881 and only 1,258 by 1901. Nevertheless, the Erie and Niagara Railway was of particular importance to the Town and Township. As Francis Petrie has observed: "It was its sole railway connection with the rest of the country and was its chief hope for regaining the loss of trade sustained by the opening of the Welland Canal."[18] The railway was strongly supported locally, with the Township purchasing its shares, lending money to the company to ensure its continued operation, and even commuting its taxes in 1890 for a five-year period. As Petrie has continued:

> "The balmy days of this rail line were from the 1880's through to the 1920's when three steamers, and later two, operated between Niagara and Toronto. Six passenger trains a day used this line to carry passengers and freight to the docks at Niagara.
>
> The government of Canada was the largest source of revenue to the line. The Federal government maintained the large army training camp at Niagara and this railroad was the only line to it. Consequently thousands of men, long trains of horses, guns, and equipment came and went by rail.
>
> During the summer camp time with its many special military tattoos, extra trains were needed to carry civilian visitors to the town and camp as well. At about this time the Canadian Chatauqua movement was in full swing at Niagara-on-the-Lake and its participants used the Michigan Central railway service to get there."[19]

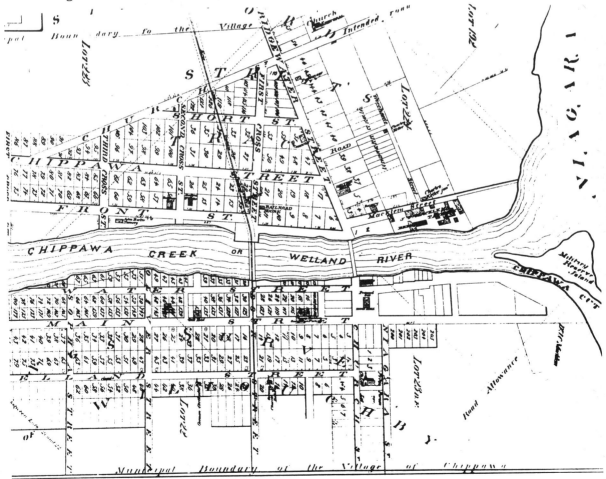

Fig. 7.7   Chippawa: The Erie and Ontario Railway crossing the Welland River, 1876.

H. R. Page, Illustrated Historical Atlas of the Counties of Lincoln and Welland, 1876

Niagara, the oldest centre in the Peninsula and the former Capital of Upper Canada, developed harbour facilities in conjunction with its railway.

John Burtniak Collection

Within Niagara, an interesting conflict of purpose that developed between its Railway and the historic assets of the town is recorded in 1898. A letter to the Secretary of State from Janet Carnochan, long-time President of the Niagara Historical Society, presented a worried appeal for his intervention:

"The Members of the Historical Society. . .have just heard with great pain and regret that a lease is being given to the Michigan Central Railway of 81 acres of the river front — including part of Fort George enclosure. A lease had been granted them before which has now expired. They however only occupy one part of what is called the Paradise Grove for picnic parties, but these have been very few lately. It is believed their only reason for asking this is to prevent any other Company [such] as an Electric railway from obtaining a right of way. It is felt that this would be an injury to the town as an Electric RR from Queenston continued to St. Catharines and Niagara Falls would benefit the town but not benefit the M.C.R."[20]

The response of government was immediate: "The lease to the Railway Company has been cancelled permitting them to occupy only such portions of the reserve as may be necessary for the purposes of the Railway."[21]

In a like manner to Niagara, Queenston and Chippawa (Fig. 7.7) lost some of their earlier transportation advantages as the modes of travel changed. Both centres were at heads of navigation on the Niagara River, both were terminal points on the Niagara Portage, and both had a fort, warehouses and small attendant service facilities. Both were affected by the transfer of navigation inland to the Welland Canal. Neither obtained a bridge crossing of the Niagara River and, when the Suspension Bridge opened, railways converged on this point rather than on either Queenston or Chippawa. The strong stimuli of railway-sponsored growth did not occur and for Chippawa, as Ray Corry Bond has stated:

"The new [Second] Welland Canal, the Great Western railroad and the Railway Suspension Bridge all proved to be stumbling blocks in the way of Chippawa's future development. In 1881 her population had dropped to six hundred and forty-four and four years later her assessment had fallen to seventy-three thousand."[22]

A similar remark could be made with equal validity for Queenston.

Areas Not Served by Railways

The routes selected by the Railway Companies did not serve all the areas of established settlement in the Peninsula (Fig. 7.8). Many hamlets and villages retained their previous degree of isolation and independence as the railways fostered growth elsewhere. This fact of life applied with particular force to an extensive tract of land south from the Escarpment in the west of the Peninsula, bounded in the east by the Welland Canal and in the south by the Welland River. Communities such as Smithville, Glen Elgin, Campden, Tintern, Rockway, Wellandport, and Effingham and St. Johns in the Short Hills, did not receive railways. This area of isolation was diminished with the construction of the Toronto, Hamilton and Buffalo Railway at the end of the nineteenth century but, even so, most of these places did not obtain either railway tracks or a station — Smithville being the notable exception. Three other "excluded areas" existed — between St. Catharines and Niagara-Queenston centred on Virgil, between Welland-Port Robinson and Chippawa-Fort Erie in Crowland and

Willoughby Townships, and the shoreline communities west of the Grand River in Haldimand County (South Cayuga, Rainham, Selkirk, and Nanticoke).

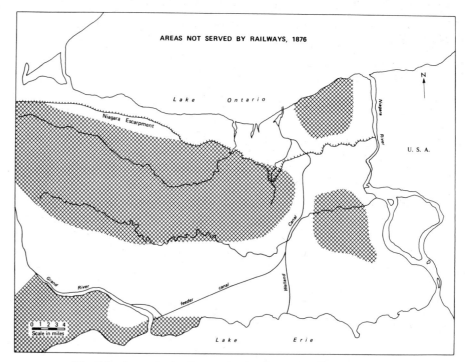

Fig. 7.8   Areas in the Peninsula Not Served by Railways, 1876.

The nature of the contrast between communities attached to a railway line and those which were omitted has been expressed by William F. Rannie as follows:

"The railway era had arrived in Lincoln. It signalled a change in travel habits. . .The route chosen by the railway builders also ended hopes of pioneer hamlets like the Thirty, Glen Elgin and Tintern that their best days of growth and prosperity still lay ahead. In the years that followed, some small centres withered for lack of connections with the world beyond; others like Beamsville, the Vineland area and Jordan [Station] saw the arrival of the railways as bringing bright promise for outdistancing their rivals."[23]

Writing about St. Johns in 1926, J. F. Gross referred to it as:

"'The Deserted Village'. There is one grist-mill still standing, but it has been dead for about thirty years. The last carding mill, later known as the Pitts mill. . .has not been running for a good many years, and was torn down this summer. . .The population has dwindled to about twenty or thirty people. Both churches have been torn down or removed. The cemeteries are uncared for. The old Zenas Fell homestead . . . is being torn down this summer. This gentleman's residence. . .has not been occupied for the last ten or twelve years."[24]

The sad decline of this village, described in this account, is attributed to the railway. By contrast, in 1850, St. Johns had been described by W. H. Smith as a:

"picturesque looking village. . .It contains about one hundred and fifty inhabitants, who have a handsome brick church, Wesleyan Methodist; and about a mile from the village is an Episcopal Church — There are in St. Johns, five grist and three saw mills, a cloth factory, founding and machine shop, carding machine, and tannery."[25]

Jordan was another place to suffer, though not so seriously as the settlements in the Short Hills. In 1851, "it contains two hundred inhabitants; a carding machine and fulling mill, tannery, ashery, saw mill, and four churches, Episcopal, Methodist, Disciple's and Menonist."[26] It was obviously a self-sufficient village community. But then, change and transition occurred:

"Arrival of the Great Western a mile north of Jordan in 1853 and the development of a small village centred around the station, decline of the Ball enterprises through loss of easy access to shipping [caused by the railway] and changes in the grain trade. . .saw a halt to the growth of Jordan by mid-century."[27]

It is interesting to note that Jordan Station, the new community, became a police village in 1915. The older centre did not obtain this status until 1924, nine years later than its junior partner.

Campden (formerly Moyers Corners) provides another case illustration of desuetude. In 1850, a number of self-sufficient trades and crafts could be described — the potter making crocks and other vessels, the two cabinet-makers, the village undertaker who also made household furniture, two blacksmiths, a corner store, the pressing of apples for cider, a tinsmith making pans and pails, and his brother who dried apples and made cigars.[28] The railway disrupted this independence. As A. E. Coombs noted with tolerant forbearance: "The village has not increased in size nor in business importance for a good many years, but this is due to its location. No railway nor main highway passes through it. It is just a pretty and properous rural hamlet."[29]

More recently, many of these smaller communities — from Niagara to the smallest hamlet — have been "re-discovered" as attractive localities for settlement in the changing life style and new mobility of the 1960's and 1970's. Residence in rural areas has taken on a nuance which represents a new set of values and appreciation of the rural background. Decline must not be taken to mean despondence about the future and, indeed, has many positive features of value.

St. Catharines and Merritton

The curious anomaly or enigma of St. Catharines may now be introduced. It was undoubtedly the major centre by 1851 and of robust vitality with the Welland Canal, a hydraulic raceway, mills and industries. Considering the tenets of T. C. Keefer that were presented in Chapter I, nothing but further growth could have been expected for St. Catharines. The town anticipated a great leap forward in its fortunes, as first the Great Western Railway and then the Welland Railway were added to its already commanding repertoire of transportation facilities. But its aspirations were not to be fulfilled. The town certainly grew, but this was in absolute and physical terms only. Relatively, it declined against greater growth elsewhere. This was not the expected consequence, which must now be explained with the hindsight wisdom of experience.

St. Catharines received two sets of railway tracks, and two stations at opposite ends of the town. The urban area was, therefore, almost encircled by railways at 1862 (Fig. 7.9), but they were both at a distance from the centres of activity and did not penetrate nor directly serve the urban area. The Great Western Station was located west of the town off the main Queenston-Ancaster highway, and the Welland Railway station was located east of the town at the north-eastern corner of the Welland Avenue-Geneva Street junction (Fig. 7.10). With the two stations situated in opposite directions from the urban core, the town was pulled towards two conflicting centres of activity and, as a result, became extended and elongated in its form.

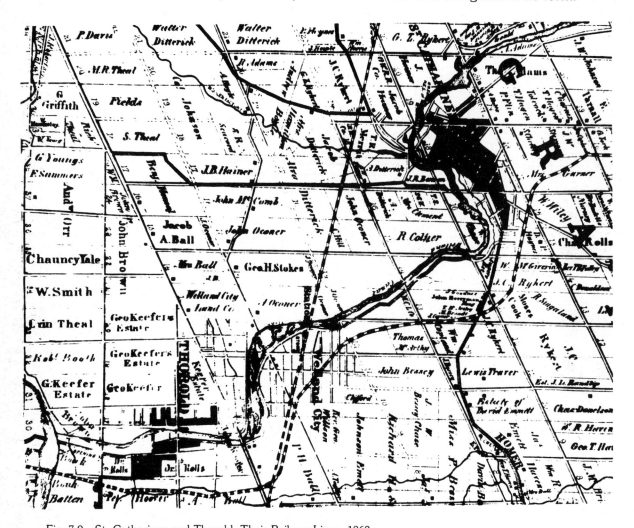

Fig. 7.9   St. Catharines and Thorold: Their Railway Lines, 1862.

Tremaines' Map of the Counties of Lincoln and Welland, 1862

Real estate advertisements soon appeared, and attractive lots were offered for sale in the vicinity of the Great Western Station. An editorial in the *Constitutional* in 1855 pointed out that "proximity to the business part of the town where lots are held at extravagant figures, to the G.W. Railway depot. . .[make these] the most favorable presented for many years. . .The lots are well laid out, mostly at right angles, of easy access, streets running all through them, excellent water privileges."[30] An advertisement for the sale of a large number of lots on the Hainer property noted that "this property is very pleasantly situated in a very healthy locality, and is rendered valuable by its proximity to the Railway Depot, Ship Yard, Mills and other places of business."[31]

Attention was drawn to these lavish opportunities in editorial comment, which pointed out that lucrative business could be expected to arise near the Station. The role of the railway in this trend was described. The lots were regarded as a profitable investment. They attracted purchasers from nearby communities such as Merritton. The editorial stated that:

These street scenes at Port Robinson and Smithville suggest that not all communities were transformed by the railway.   *John Burtniak Collection*

"Without the aid of a Railway, this flourishing town would in the natural operation of things, spread itself over many broad acres now occupied for agricultural purposes. . .But it is one of the almost certain effects of Railways to change the centre of business in neighbourhoods where they establish a depot, or, perhaps, more frequently, to build up new and other centres of local and general traffic, thereby giving a value and saleability to property that never would have existed to the same extent but for the Railway; a value nevertheless which will be permanent and increasing, in proportion as business upon the thoroughfare enlarges, and enterprising men — mechanics or tradesmen — carry on their operations in this vicinity."[32]

Undoubtedly, the development of St. Catharines and its urban future would have taken on a different form if either railway route had been placed closer to the town, and/or if the railways had pooled their resources to build one integrated set of station and freight facilities in a "union depot." This idea might have required a bridge over Twelve Mile Creek, an alignment of the Great Western line route close to the developed area (possibly on a route broadly parallel to Welland Avenue), and one station situated where the Great Western and the Welland Railway crossed. It is indeed probable that William Hamilton Merritt may have contemplated such an overall scheme in his early discussions with the Great Western.[33] That a route closer to St. Catharines was at least a possibility in 1851 is shown in Fig. 7.11.[34]

Fig. 7.10   St. Catharines: Railways in Relation to the Urban Core, 1872.
*T. Munro, Topographical Plan Showing Proposed Line
for Enlarged Welland Canal, 1872*

These substantial possibilities were rejected when the main line effectively by-passed St. Catharines on its route from Hamilton to the Niagara River. The Directors had no desire either to serve or to promote its interests, and the town became little more than an incidental way stop on the main line of track. It was not destined to become a major railway centre. Had some of these other possibilities become a reality, then growth northward to and beyond the combined station and in the only direction without adverse relief features, would doubtless have occurred. Industrial development along the line of track, near the station, and on the eastern bank of Twelve Mile Creek in association with the Welland Canal and extended hydraulic facilities, can also be envisaged.

THE GREAT WESTERN RAILWAY: EXPECTATION AND ACHIEVEMENT

————— Line of the Great Western Railway as indicated in W.H. Smith, *Canada, Past, Present and Future*, Maclear (Toronto), 1851.

•••••••• As achieved by 1855.

Fig. 7.11   St. Catharines and East Lincoln County: The Great Western Railway as Proposed and as Achieved, 1851 and 1855.

The Town Council perhaps recognized this potential when, in 1847, it requested that the Great Western bring its line into the centre of the town. The Council's resolution stated "that the line surveyed through this place be adopted".[35] The operative word is *through*, rather than near, close or next to. Somewhat later, in 1853, the Council appointed a committee to discuss with the Great Western whether a subscription of £25,000 for stock would induce them to bring their line through the town. Local editorial comment in the *St. Catharines Mail* praised Council for the prudence of its move: "We would rejoice to see it succeed. St. Catharines might bear *all the cost* of bringing the Great Western Line into the Town, if practicable, rather than be left on one side as it now is."[36]

Unfortunately, it is not known what arguments were advanced by this civic delegation, or what response was made by the Company. Perhaps an engineering preference for a straight railway route prevailed. Perhaps shipping interests insisted that the Canal be crossed by some form of swing bridge which would allow the free and uninterrupted passage of sailing vessels with their tall masts. Perhaps this swing bridge would have been too costly a proposition for a railway that was exceeding its financial resources, or perhaps it presented too many technical difficulties. Perhaps a fixed railway bridge on high stone arches would have disrupted shipping and been too costly to construct, given the height and width of the valley.

Certainly, analogous situations of a severe clash between railway and shipping interests existed elsewhere, and the Great Western might have wished to avoid a contentious Canal crossing. For example, at Jordan Harbour where the Great Western crossed over Twenty Mile Creek, the first temporary bridge (completed in 1852-1853) apparently did not inconvenience vessels. But the permanent stone bridge completed in 1855 hindered navigation and the Great Western was sued successfully by two local businessmen, John Wismer and Jacob Snure.[37] A similar set of physical circumstances occurred where the railway from Hamilton to Toronto crossed the Humber River to the west of Toronto; the company wished to be relieved from the obligation of having to erect a swing bridge even though the former design of a fixed structure would have effectively curtailed commercial navigation on the river.[38]

In St. Catharines, an awkward conflict between railway and canal requirements was avoided, but at the expense of a poor railway location for an important, established and growing settlement. As a visitor to the town noted in 1872, "the view of the town from the station *(which bye the bye is as inconveniently situated as can be),* is very pretty."[39] This "inconvenient station" was located about a mile to the west of the urban core, and at a greater distance from most of the residential areas and industrial sites. Its "inconvenient" approach from the town required a sharp descent into the valley of Twelve Mile Creek, across the Canal with possible delays at a narrow swing bridge, and then a steep ascent up to the Station. These grades militated against the extensive movement of heavy goods by wagon, and were not overcome until the construction of the Burgoyne Bridge in the second decade of the twentieth century.

In contrast to the distinct separation and inconvenience of the Great Western and the Welland Railway facilities at St. Catharines, the coveted and ardently desired distinction of a railway junction town was awarded to Merritton. This railway-sponsored centre was incorporated as a village in 1874, having grown over the previous decades because of its attractive rail and water communications. The formation of the Welland Canal Loan Company and their purchase of land at Merritton also provided an important stimulus. Water power was obtained from the succession of locks and basins from Locks 14 to 23 on the Welland Canal, and upwards of 500 acres of land were purchased on either side of the Canal for industrial purposes. The *Journal,* in 1855, carried the following notice:

"The Great Western Railroad Crosses the canal at this point, and has a station on a portion of the above lands, thus affording uninterrupted communication from the seaboard to the Western States and Canada, by land or water, throughout the year, altogether forming a combination of advantages to the Manufacturer, Miller, Mechanic or man-of-business, not exceeded, if equalled in any other locality."[40]

The advertisement then presented a special invitation, intended to attract particular types of industry and to encourage certain manufacturers:

"Any company who will invest not less than $100,000 in erecting durable stone buildings, and, machinery for the purpose of manufacturing Iron, Cotton or Woolen Goods — to be in operation by the 1st January, 1857 — may have the choice of the best site, with all the water power, and grounds for the erection of buildings required for the establishment, free of rent or any other charge."[41]

Fig. 7.12   St. Catharines: A Canal-Oriented Community, 1875.
H. Brosius, St. Catharines, 1875

Merritton received the railway and grew steadily on the basis of its canal and railway connections. St. Catharines, the more important centre, failed in its attempts to attract a railway within its urban boundaries, despite the sincere efforts of civic officials and local businessmen to secure this advantageous element for their town. Its two railways provided useful and important additional assets, but the real urban strength was still considered to be the Welland Canal (Fig. 7.12). For example, manufacturers and businessmen were especially excited by the prospects of renewed vigour that the construction of the Third Welland Canal system could bring to the city. As H. R. Page noted in 1876:

184

"When the new canal is open, a variety of new industries will spring up, the old manufactories will be enlarged, and an immense impetus will be given to ship building of larger tonnage. While the Canal, the largest public work of the Dominion, costing nearly fifteen million dollars, is in progress, the spending of so vast a sum of money in the vicinity is making the city prosperous, and on its completion the rise and extension of manufacturing and shipbuilding will cause that prosperity to be permanent and increasing. . .Situated as the city is on the great highway of the world's commerce at a sufficient distance from other competing points, it cannot fail to receive great benefit from the commercial marine traffic; and being the chief city of the Niagara Peninsula, which already approaches a population of one hundred thousand, it will absorb the local traffic and continue as the wholesale mart of the district."[42]

The railway, in conjunction with the Welland Canal, fostered industrial development at Merritton. *John Burtniak Collection*

This theme was endorsed by the local newspapers. The *St. Catharines Weekly News* noted with enthusiasm that, "with Welland Canal enlargement, St. Catharines cannot fail to become the Manchester of America".[43] It even had the audacity to suggest that American centres would be displaced, and stated that it would pay Buffalo, Albany and New York to spend millions to forestall this enlargement.[44] It also warned strongly against bringing the Welland Canal to the outlet of the Niagara River, which would "place our great national thoroughfare to the seaboard under the guns of American forts."[45] In reality, the Third Canal was routed to the east of St. Catharines, the City was deprived of its immediate advantages in association with the waterway, and the population did not expand between 1881 to 1901. Prognostication and reality are often very different creatures. The Canal was undoubtedly important to St. Catharines — but it should not have been regarded either as the prime or the only *métier* to its growth.

St. Catharines: A Story of Relative Decline

A process of relative change has been identified thus far in this chapter. As G. P. de T. Glazebrook has written:

"Probably every town and village in southern Ontario made some effort to have a railway (more than one if its ambition soared) run past its door, believing that its future success would thus be ensured. Many of the calculated results were in the realm of day-dreams but there is no doubt that some urban communities grew larger and others fell into decay depending on whether or not they lay on the line of the railway. It did not follow, of course, that all towns or railways made notable progress, indeed to some extent the opposite was true since the railway made possible concentration of industry in a few places like Toronto and Hamilton. Raw materials could be collected and finished products distributed by rail over distances and to a degree that had hitherto been impossible."[46]

St. Catharines provided a full exemplification of such arguments. It lost out on a relative basis to the stronger external forces of industrial and service expansion. It grew in population from 4,368 in 1851 to 9,946 a half century later (Table 7.1), but this growth, in absolute terms, was substantially less than that which occurred in centres outside the region, such as Hamilton or Toronto. While St. Catharines added 5,500 people to its residential role, Hamilton expanded by almost 40,000 persons and Toronto to over 200,000 persons by 1901.

The workshops of the Great Western Railway at Hamilton, 1863. St. Catharines could not compete with its superior facilities and progress of development.   *Canadian Illustrated News, 14 February, 1863*

St. Catharines could not cope with the superior railway and port facilities which had been developed at both Hamilton and Toronto. At Hamilton, the Desjardins Canal was usurped by the railway, Dundas declined, and Hamilton bounded to commercial prominence with mills, grain elevators, machine shops, and foundries. It obtained the Great Western railway shops for the manufacture of passenger cars, a mill for rolling rails, and contracts for producing heavy railway equipment.[47] The significance of railways in this urban evolution is stated as follows by R. W. Camm:

"Hamilton benefitted from its position on the main line of the Great Western. Before the railway's construction all goods shipped out to markets from the Hamilton district had been sent to Dundas, and from there conveyed through the Desjardins Canal by boat. This did not benefit Hamilton, and its citizens were quick to support the building of the Great Western. Not long after the construction of the railway, the Central Market was established to extend the city's facilities and to handle the new business that was coming to it. Hamilton was also given her first impetus towards industrialization. The foundry of Fisher and McQuesten made threshing mills, while stoves were the product of Gurney's Foundry. When the advent of the Great Western Railway brought the need for engines, the D. C. Gunn machine shop came into existence. The firm of Williams and Cooper saw the future for a freight and passenger car factory. They secured quarters near the railway yards and built the first rolling stock ever made in Canada. In addition, the Great Western Railway established a mill in Hamilton for re-rolling rails. Its cost was $107,000 which seemed like an enormous sum at the time."[48]

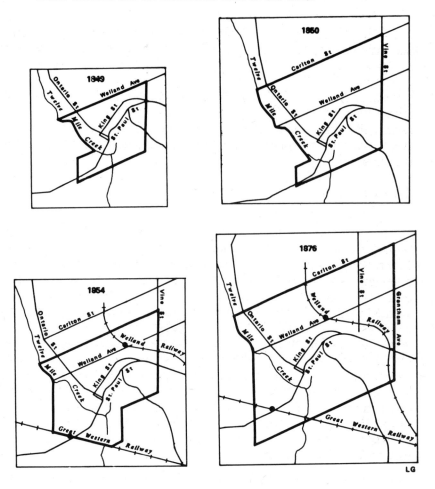

Fig. 7.13 Boundary change at St. Catharines, 1849-1876.

Table 7.1
Population Change at St. Catharines, Hamilton and Toronto,
1851-1911

	St. Catharines	Hamilton	Toronto
	(Percentage Change in Parentheses)		
1851	4,368	14,112	30,775
1861	6,284 (43.9)	19,096 (35.3)	44,821 (45.6)
1871	7,864 (25.1)	26,880 (39.9)	59,000 (25.1)
1881	9,631 (22.5)	36,661 (34.6)	96,196 (54.0)
1891	9,170 (-4.7)	48,959 (36.2)	181,215 (88.4)
1901	9,946 (8.5)	52,634 (7.5)	208,040 (14.8)
1911	12,484 (25.5)	81,969 (55.7)	376,538 (81.0)

Source: *Census Canada,* 1851-1911

Toronto, as the provincial capital, likewise encouraged and fostered a series of railway developments. As stated by C. Pelham Mulvany in 1882:

> "Despite a little grumbling that is occasionally indulged in it is generally admitted that no other one thing has contributed so materially in building up the city. It has made it really the metropolis, the mother city, the mart of Ontario. . .A study of the map will show how the whole railway system of the Province converges on this one favoured spot. Indeed, the figure it presents on a railway map reminds one of a black-bodied spider with legs of very irregular formation and extent, spreading out into the adjacent country."[49]

In 1851, St. Catharines was the seventh largest centre according to its population size in Canada West, being surpassed only by Belleville, Bytown (Ottawa), Hamilton, Kingston, London and Toronto. By 1891, six more towns — Brantford, Guelph, Peterborough, St. Thomas, Stratford and Windsor — were ranked above St. Catharines, dropping it to thirteenth place in Ontario and twenty-fifth in Canada. Both expansion and relative diminution in status have to be explained when the railway geography of the period is examined.

The Legal Boundaries of St. Catharines

Within St. Catharines, as the tracks and the stations were ·located beyond the then developed extent of the town, the legal boundaries of the settlement were extended to incorporate the new railway facilities into its administrative milieu. A sequence of boundary changes were promulgated in 1849, 1850 and 1854.[50] The northern boundry, Welland Avenue in 1849 and Carlton Street in 1850, was located centrally between these east-west concession roads in 1854. The western boundary in 1849 and 1850 followed the outer edge of the Welland Canal lands along Twelve Mile Creek; it also included a significant western projection along the main road to Hamilton, and was extended beyond the Creek to include more land around the Great Western Station in 1854. In the south, the boundary in 1849 and 1850 crossed the present Glenridge area; in 1854, it was extended to the Great Western Railway and followed the line of track across the southern parts of St. Catharines. The eastern boundary was extended to Vine Street in 1850.

The achievement of City status in 1876, coupled with the population increase and urban expansion since 1854, created the need for further territorial expansion. These extensions went beyond the Great Western Station in a south-west direction, from Vine Street to Grantham Avenue in the east, and to Carlton Street in the north. The City, therefore, now incorporated the two railway systems within its legal boundaries. St. Catharines had now become more than a town on the Welland Canal. It was growing to a degree of maturity in its urban form and expression.

It should also be mentioned that the distance, inconvenience and inaccessibility of the town from the Great Western Station soon gave rise to citizen protests for improved conditions. The need for a bridge over the canal was suggested as early as 1855 when Jacob Hainer offered land for sale in this vicinity. His advertisement read: "As there is no doubt a bridge will be thrown across the canal near the Stephenson House, so as to open a more direct route to the above station. . .an excellent opportunity is thus thrown open to cash purchasers to secure the above property, comprising nearly eighty acres."[51]

In 1861, a petition was signed by about 80 rate-payers, requesting that the Town Council "take the necessary measures to have a road opened from the Great Western Railway to Salina Street, and construct a bridge over the Canal near the Stephenson House."[52] The *Constitutional* commented that "the boldness of this idea at the present time alarmed the people generally, and caused a good deal of out-door discussion, of which the large expenditure necessary to complete such a work formed a prominent element."[53] However, the idea proved acceptable to the Town Council, who passed a motion as follows:

> "That in the opinion of this Council, owing to the increasing population and trade of the town, an additional Bridge is required across the Welland Canal, at some point between the present bridge at Lock No. 2, and that below Lock No. 3, and the Mayor is hereby authorized to communicate with the Board of Works upon the subject."[54]

G. T. R. Station, St. Catharines, Ont., Canada

The Great Western (Grand Trunk) Station at St. Catharines.
John Burtniak Collection

In 1867, the Commissioner of Public Works recommended that the Town Council should petition Parliament for the erection of an elevated bridge to cross the Canal near the Stephenson House. It was also reported that Mr. Page, the Canal Engineer:

> "was opposed to the construction of a double track bridge, as on account of its great weight, it would be necessary to swing it by machinery, thereby impeding traffic both on the canal and road. . . . [He was] in favour of constructing a high level bridge near the Stephenson House — the town to pay the cost of the approaches."[55]

Eventually, a high-level steel bridge (the Burgoyne Bridge) was constructed over Twelve Mile Creek to connect the main part of the town with the Great Western Station. But debate was sharp and serious before the right-of-way was purchased and the bridge constructed and opened in 1915. Several important points were at issue: a high level design versus low level, several different routes, various costs and opposing interest groups. A low-level crossing on the existing route would have avoided the cost of purchasing the approach routes, but the improvement to a two-lane swing bridge was opposed by the canal authorities. A high-level bridge was much more costly because of the breadth and the height to be spanned, and because land would have to be acquired for the approaches to the bridge. There were the ever-important questions of who would pay for the bridge and for its approaches; would this be the Town, or a senior level of government, or both, and in what proportion?

Three high level routes were considered over the years. These included a straightened extension to St. Paul Street (the route that was finally adopted), another to connect with King Street, and a third past the Stephenson House to Salina Street. This question became a *cause célèbre* over several decades and inspired much heated and often acute and virulent discussion. The final structure resulted only after many years of persuasive newspaper columns by W. B. Burgoyne, after whom the bridge was named. However, the real foundations of the problem stem back to the inappropriate location of the Great Western Railway and its Station away from the developed parts of the town.

Burgoyne Bridge crossing the valley of Twelve Mile Creek in St. Catharines.   *St. Catharines Historical Museum, from Public Archives of Canada, PA-72608*

Canal-Oriented Settlements

Two communities grew to prominence in the Peninsula from the 1830's onwards, because of their location at the northern and southern entrances to the Welland Canal system, Port Dalhousie on Lake Ontario and Port Colborne on Lake Erie. Each received a further boost to its fortunes, as successive improvements were made to the Canal and as the depth and capacity of the Canal was reconstructed as the Second and Third Canals. The ports remained, though their urban structure was affected somewhat by the Canal works.

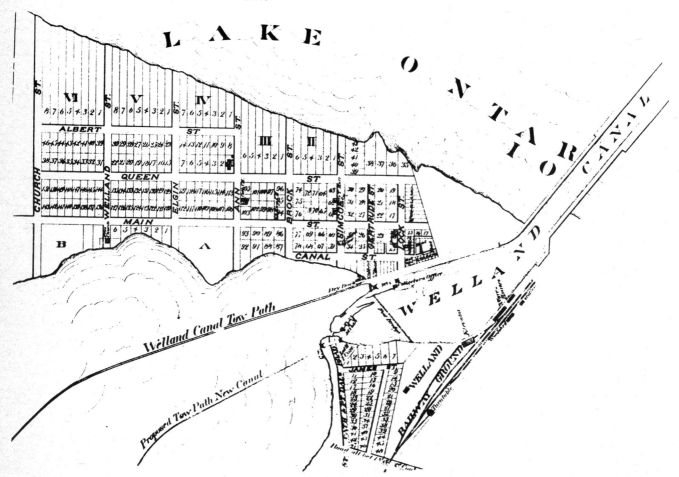

Fig. 7.14   Port Dalhousie: The Northern Entrance to the Welland Canal, 1876.

H. R. Page, Illustrated Historical Atlas of the Counties of Lincoln and Welland, 1876

Interestingly enough, each Canal community also received the Welland Railway, became the terminus of this short-distance route across the Peninsula, and attracted comparable features such as a station, grain storage facilities, repair services, wood and coal depots on their railway-owned grounds. Another similarity is that, as the Railway was routed to the *east* of the Canal system and as each community had developed on the *west* bank of the Canal, a striking feature about their urban structures (Figs. 7.14 and 7.15) is that the main streets with shops, hotel and other service buildings are quite separate from the railway facilities. There is the wide intervening gulf of the Canal between the two parts of the community, a quite different type of situation from that which has been described for Bridgeburg and Jordan Station.

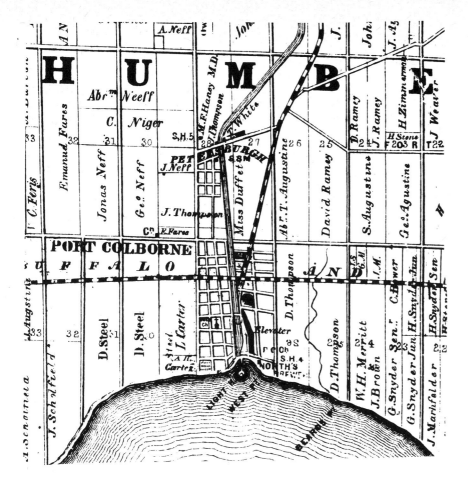

Fig. 7.15   Port Colborne: The Southern Entrance to the Welland Canal,
1876.   *H. R. Page, Illustrated Historical Atlas of the Counties of Lincoln and Welland, 1876*

However, the regional associations of the two communities were different, so that the urban characteristics gradually diverged and became more distinctive. Port Dalhousie faced Toronto over Lake Ontario, and soon established steamer connections to the Provincial Capital. This involved industrial and passenger traffic, including a significant seasonal passenger flow from across the lake to Port Dalhousie, either en route to the scenic attractions at the Falls or to enjoy a day of rest and fun on the beach facilities that existed at Port Dalhousie. Likewise, the beach was also convenient of access for an outing for the communities situated nearby along the line of the Welland Railway. Several such visits have been described, with this potential as a local recreational site being increased with the development of the inter-urban street railways.

Port Colborne also had its beaches and, indeed, the summer attraction of warmer waters next to the shallower depths of Lake Erie — but it was more distant from the principal communities in the Peninsula. Residents from Buffalo dispersed to a variety of points along the Lake Erie shoreline, with Crystal Beach and Erie Beach emerging as the major centre of recreational activity rather than Port Colborne. Instead, as it possessed the Canal, the east-west route of the Buffalo and Lake Huron Railway, the Welland Railway and more superior railway links than Port Dalhousie with railway expansion and amalgamations, marine services were combined with industrial activity. Gradually, the industrial landscape expanded to include flour milling, primary metals and the quarrying of local limestone resources for cement production, with the railways being important to each but not necessarily the prime instrumental factor.

Port Colborne, with its two railways and the Welland Canal, attracted industry and harbour-related facilities, including grain elevators.

John Burtniak Collection

Port Dalhousie, at the northern entrance to the Welland Canal, advanced considerably because of the railway endeavour and because of its railway-steamer connections.

John Burtniak Collection

Two other communities on the line of the Canal may also be noted, namely Allanburg and Port Robinson. Both had the advantage of Canal and railway affiliations, but neither prospered relative to the growth of other centres in the Peninsula. As vessels became larger and steam-propelled, no need existed for stopping or servicing within the canal system. And likewise with the railway, the stations were used as a local asset by the community (some recreational visits have been indicated), but the majority of the traffic involved a through flow to other destinations.

It may indeed be concluded that the railway only provided an important mechanism for industrial location and urban growth when other extraneous factors also existed; for example, the frontier at Niagara and Fort Erie, an abundance of local water power especially at Thorold and Merritton across the brow of the Escarpment, a nodal situation in the Peninsula as at Welland, extensive railway facilities as at Hamilton, or the growth propensity of Toronto as the Provincial Capital. The railway did not provide a universal panacea for growth as had been anticipated by T. C. Keefer, but only a selective variable, a point which will be discussed further in the following chapter. Many "Sleepy Hollows" remained, without any very great transition to their urban structure by the nearby presence of railways.

The Queenston Quarries, 1876. The active production of stone blocks was encouraged by spur lines.

H. R. Page, Illustrated Historical Atlas of the Counties of Lincoln and Welland, 1876

Chapter VIII

The Overall Impact and Significance of Railways

Railways accomplished many things. Movement and travel no longer depended upon the pace of the horse and buggy. There was a new pattern of inter-association between adjacent centres and more distant communities. The concept of spatial distance was changed. Raw materials and finished products could be moved more easily. People could travel for leisure and pleasure. Railways provided employment, during construction and as an operating system. They promoted employment in ancillary and railway-oriented industries that located next to the line of track. The railways, in contrast with the stage coach on poor roads, personified speed and comfort. They were also personal, with the local station becoming a meeting place, its staff were known as individuals, the arrival and departure of trains were events not routine procedures, and the traffic which it generated reflected the commercial, business and industrial activities of the community. The railway changed radically the regional scene within the Peninsula.

The Use of Local Resources: Stone and Timber

The initial construction of the railways and subsequent improvements made use of local resources, such as stone and timber wherever and whenever possible. For example, in 1854 when the Great Western was ballasting its line, gravel trains were working from local pits, including one that had been opened recently at St. Davids and another at St. Catharines.[1] Likewise, during the preliminary phases of construction of the Welland Railway, the Engineer mentioned "laying out the siding to the gravel pit at St. Catharines."[2]

The Queenston Stone Quarries, which were first opened to provide stone for the locks of the Welland Canal, expanded substantially through the impetus of railways. They were described as being "used extensively on the Grand Trunk and Great Western Railways, in making culverts, foundations for bridges, etc."[3] The availability of transport by railway also facilitated the export of stone to a broad market. In 1876, for example, H. R. Page noted:

"The above named stone quarries. . .are without doubt the most extensive stone quarries in Ontario, if not in the Dominion of Canada. . . .The quarries now cover about eighty or ninety acres, and more are being opened every month. The facilities for shipping are excellent, a branch track of the Great Western Railway running directly to the quarries, and the Niagara River being navigatable [sic] up as far as Queenston, and the Welland ship canal but a few miles off — these give ample means for shipping the stone, and at the present time it is sent to all parts of the Dominion, and is largely used in government and private buildings. Besides the stone mentioned, there is any amount of rubble stone, which is extensively used for cellars, window casings, etc."[4]

Other stone quarries along the edge of the Escarpment also gained some advantage. For example, the *Thorold Post* in 1880 recorded:

"Mr. John Battle has secured the contract for supplying broken stone to the G. W. Railway, and a large quantity of broken stone has already been shipped to various depots. This industry will give employment to quite a large number of men during the winter months, as a great part of the stone required by the contract has still to be broken."[5]

Another major quarry was located on the Escarpment edge at Beamsville. William F. Rannie has this to say about its operation:

"At the former station there was much additional tonnage for the line. Tremendous amounts of cut stone, much of it used for bridge and culvert building on Grand Trunk lines, arrived by tramway from the Gibson quarry atop the Escarpment, to be loaded on railway cars. The days of quarrying grew to a close in the early 1900's as the railway and industry began substituting the cheaper Portland cement. At Beamsville station in 1904 the greatest activity was provided by two large stone crushers that created materials for bridges and for ballasting of the road bed."[6]

Contracts for cut stone included bridges along the Grand Trunk Railway from Toronto to Sarnia, masonry for the portals and approaches on both sides of the St. Clair tunnel, stone for the Victoria Jubilee Bridge at Montreal, and coping stones for the Welland Canal locks.[7]

Timber, an abundant local product, was required in vast amounts for buildings, bridges, cross-ties (sleepers) and fencing. It was also required in large quantities as fuel for locomotives until superceded by coal in the mid-1870's. The purchase of this basic necessity is recorded by every railway. For example, the Port Dalhousie and Thorold Railway advertised in 1856 for "the furnishing and delivery of about *forty thousand cross-ties,* on the line of the Railway between Thorold Station and Port Colborne, and the furnishing material and completion of the fencing of the line between the same points."[8]

This demand continued. As William Pay noted when serving with the Welland Railway:

"From 1870 to 1874 I was authorized by the directors to purchase all the wood ties for the use of the road, money being placed to my credit in the bank for that purpose as I required it. . . .[There] was a total of 16,520 cords of wood, cost at $39,648; average cost, $2.50 per cord. The total number of ties were 15,130, costing $5,295.50; average, 35¢. Total cost, $44,942.50".[9]

Another example is provided by the Erie and Ontario Railroad which, in 1852, advertised a contract for lumber requiring 198,000 feet of white oak scantling, 6" x 6"; 210,000' of white oak plank, 3" thick; 130,000 of fine plank, 3" thick; and 1,000 feet of 1" white oak. This timber was to be delivered at the opening of the navigation season, either to the line of the railroad or to Queenston or Chippawa.

Related to this was the wood trade and fuel business, with Elkanah Rogers being the principal supplier in St. Catharines. By 1856, he was bringing "into this market annually 8,000 cords, 4,000 of which the Great Western Railway takes of him, and the other 4,000 cords he sells to his customers".[10] Apparently, St. Catharines became a fuelling stop on the Great Western in 1861 for, as suggested by an entry in Hugh Neilson's diary, "engines commenced Wooding here today. They moved from Thorold yesterday. John Hogan is Headman".[11] Cords of fuel wood for the Welland Railway were obtained primarily from Humberstone and Crowland Townships, which contributed materially to the removal of the forest cover from these two areas.

The railway also encouraged brick-making. Where the clay was suitable, then its transportation facilities could be used to make possible the manufacture and distribution of this bulky product. One such factory was established near the junction of the tracks of the Great Western and the Welland Railway at Merritton. D. W. Corbin advertised in 1858 that he had commenced this business at this location.[12]

An interesting example of a small local mineral line is the one which crossed Pt. Abino in 1876. This is described as a horse railway by H. R. Page.[13] Sand was dug from the sand hills to the west of the Point, and transported to the lee shore where there was a sand dock. The sand was then carried by boat to Buffalo, Cleveland and other American ports on Lake Erie.

The Impact on Business

Secondary production in manufacturing industry was also promoted by the railway. In 1856, a furnace and machine shop on St. Paul Street in St. Catharines, belonging to George N. Oille, produced mowing machines and other agricultural machinery; it also made "two horse rail powers, car wheels and axle trees, and all kinds of railroad work, steam engines and boilers, &c., and turns off [out] some $15,000 worth of work yearly."[14] The railway brought another direct benefit to this town when, in 1858, it was agreed that the Welland Railway would rent from Mrs. Louisa Towers:

> "the premises known as the 'Novelty Iron Works', together with all tools and machinery contained on or about the premises (including the Blacksmith's Shop but excluding the Foundry and Moulding Shop) for the purpose of repairing the Locomotive Engines and other rolling stock — the property of the said Railway Company, or such other purposes as they may require them in connection with their works."[15]

A spur line was laid to the plant for this purpose. The account books of the Great Western have recorded a small number of miscellaneous purchases made from companies located in St. Catharines. These items, in 1897, included a capstan bottom from Yale and Coy and circular saws from R. H. Smith. Regular payments to the gas company and for the carriage of mails are also recorded.[16] In 1855, Friesman the Great described "his work on the Great Western Railway buildings, between Grimsby and the Falls, as fair specimens of plain Painting".[17] However, payments to companies in St. Catharines are rare. The area was not important for purchase of supplies and equipment by the Great Western, and only small miscellaneous contracts are indicated in the revenue ledgers and cash books.

The Welland Railway exerted a greater impact. For instance, ships for this Company were constructed in St. Catharines at the

Shickluna Yards on the Welland Canal below the present Burgoyne Bridge.[18] The *Constitutional* in 1864 announced the launch of "another splendid propeller for the Welland Railway Company".[19] This was the *Enterprise,* which had a keel length of 177 feet, a breadth of 31 feet, and a capacity of 750 tons — sufficient for about 37,000 bushels of wheat. The *Perseverance* had also been commissioned there a few weeks earlier for the same Railway.[20] Both were intended for the run from Port Dalhousie to Oswego.

The nature of the work on this ship construction, the division of work between different specialist trades, the spin-off into ancillary production and the benefit thereby accruing to the economy of the Peninsula because of railway requirements, are suggested in the memoirs of William Pay:

> "The contract was given to Louis Shickluna to build and finish the boats up to the main decks, put in the stanchions all round for the bulwarks and put the mast in, for $36,000. The company decided that I should build the cabins and finish the boats from the main decks upwards and to furnish the boats with everything required, this included all lines of tackling of all kinds, and including the compasses and stoves, carpets, bedding, glass and crockery, curtains, lamps and everything required for the boats, also painting from main decks upwards. Money was placed to my credit in the bank to do the work. . . .Gartshore, of Dundas, put in the engine and boilers".[21]

In 1864, the *Constitutional* recorded a commitment to local industry with pride, as follows:

> "The Welland Railway Company have placed another very handsome and commodious passenger car upon their road, but the chief reason why it deserves notice is the fact that it was built here for the company by Mr. Pay, and received the finishing touches from the magical paint brush of Mr. Friesman. . . .Whilst such cars can be manufactured at home, there will be no necessity to look for them elsewhere."[22]

Rolling stock for the Welland Railway was also purchased from Niagara. A contract in 1857 called for the construction of 25 eight-wheeled platform cars, to be made of seasoned wood, at $650 each.[23] Next year, a second contract was awarded for 75 freight box cars.[24] The first car wheels were cast in Niagara in 1856, an event which the *Niagara Mail* reported with enthusiasm:

> "This foundry is capable we should think of supplying a large portion of the iron wheels used in the Province; there is no longer any necessity for importing these articles. Such establishments. . .with all its various benefits accruing from them to society, are the consequence of the extension of Railways in Canada, combined, will Mr. Merritt please note in his next pamphlet, with the fact of our levying a duty on the imported article."[25]

Niagara also shared in ship construction; the *America* and the *Canada* were built there for the Great Western in 1854. As stated by H. A. Musham:

> "These two vessels were intended to extend the road's service across the lake to Oswego connecting there with a branch of the New York Central. They went into service between Hamilton, Toronto and Oswego on 16 July, 1855. The next year the Great Western connected with the Grand Trunk at Toronto and the *America* and the *Canada* became redundant. They were sister ships 298 feet long, 30 feet wide and drew 9 feet of water."[26]

The *Zimmerman* was also constructed at Niagara; it ran in conjunction with the Erie and Niagara Railway, and was described as "certainly the finest and reputed to be the fastest steamer which up to that time sailed the river".[27] Its companion vessel, the *Peerless*, was constructed in Scotland, then dismantled for shipping and reassembled at Niagara.

The tenders by local businesses for railway contracts were not always successful. For example, in 1857, the Welland Railway invited estimates for the construction of the Port Dalhousie freight and passenger depot and for the enlargement of the St. Catharines freight house. Henry Burgoyne quoted $2,500 and $781 respectively, and William Pay bid $2,850 and $680 respectively, but neither was successful.[28] When tenders were called for constructing and equipping the grain warehouses and elevators at Port Dalhousie and Port Colborne, there were 15 bids; five came from St. Catharines; two each from Thorold and Dundas; and one from each of Niagara Falls, Port Maitland, Ogdensburg, Oswego, Ingersoll and Chicago.[29] The bids on both buildings ranged from $50,350 to $61,900, and on both sets of machinery from $11,800 to $26,000. The building contract was awarded to Nathaniel Taggart of Ogdensburg and Norman Booth of Preston, while the elevator machinery was supplied by a Dundas contractor.

The construction of these early railway buildings was no easy task. As Pay, an unsuccessful bidder for the elevator at Port Dalhousie, has described:

"The railway company advertised for tenders for the Port Dalhousie elevator, station and freight houses on the line. There was four feet of water all over where the elevator was to be built. A coffer dam had to be made and the water pumped out. Two thousand piles had to be driven and cut off, and covered with long 12 x 12 pine timber for the heavy stone walls that had to be built. Upon this my estimate was $38,000, not including the boiler and engine and the engine house. Mr. Shanly, the engineer, told me I had made a good bid but Mr. Tyrgot of Oswego, was somewhat less and got the job, although I got all the stations and freight houses to be built and the workshops at St. Catharines".[30]

William Pay carried out work for the Welland Railway. He has stated that, when the cargoes of wheat began to arrive at Port Colborne, "it cost too much to load and unload the box cars, so...[he built] fifty four-wheeled hopper cars to convey 200 bushels each. These cars cost 5 cents to load and 10 cents to unload at Port Dalhousie".[31] Later, it was found that these hopper cars were too light when empty to run at high speed. He rectified the situation by building "25 eight-wheeled double hopper cars carrying 400 bushels each", which "were much better"; he "also made 25 box cars into double hoppers".[32]

From such beginnings, Pay advanced to the construction and fitting out of cars. In 1873, when the Welland Railway purchased a new passenger car from Rhode Island for $5,000, Pay built two new baggage and mail cars for $950 each.[33] He informed the Board that he could construct a passenger car at less than $5,000, as related in this interesting story:

"James R. Benson, a member of the board, said he thought we had not mechanics that could build one. At a subsequent meeting it was spoken of again. I told them I had commenced to build one. I kept a strict account of everything, and it amounted to $4,035. In May, 1875,

Mr. Merritt told me that Sir Charles Tupper was going to Welland and Port Colborne to inspect the works on the new canal, and he and James R. Benson would go with him and would require an engine and special car, and wanted me to go with them. My new car being finished, I took it. In going up Sir Charles Tupper, pointing at the special car, said to Mr. Merritt:

'You have a nice car.'

'Yes, Sir Charles,' said Mr. Merritt, 'and it was built in our shops in St. Catharines'.

James R. Benson said nothing."[34]

During his extended involvement with the Welland Railway, Pay received $70 a month beginning in 1864 as a master craftsman, which was increased to $80 a month in 1870 when he became Superintendent. His salary was raised to $100 a month in 1874, and to $120 in 1876 until his retirement in 1883. He first lived in a brick cottage on Ann Street in St. Catharines. In 1853 he sold this, bought six acres of land for $625, and built a house and barn for $1,300. Before retiring, in 1881, he purchased 22 acres of land for $3,800, on which "land there was a dwelling house, a large barn and twelve acres of apple orchard."[35] The railway provided a not uncomfortable living for its senior employees.

Pay was, of course, only one of many railway employees. The railways employed a galaxy of personnel directly in a range of operative positions. For example, at the Census of 1860-1861, persons classified as "Rail Road Employees" included within the Peninsula: 9 in Haldimand County, 15 in Lincoln County and, with its bridge-head activities, 50 in Welland County. These totals may appear somewhat small, but they are out of 855 for the whole of Upper Canada at that time. Moving on to the Census of 1881, the then definition of "Railway Employees" included 71 for Haldimand County, 49 for Lincoln County and 282 for Welland County, or 402 persons for the Peninsula as a whole. These numbers are impressive, though somewhat higher figures are recorded at the prime railway centres; for example, the City of Toronto had 597 railway employees and the City of Hamilton had 183 workers in this category.

One business, that had hoped to expand with the coming of railways, did not fulfill its expectations. It had been anticipated that railways (especially the Welland Railway) would encourage the wheat trade. Flour mills had been constructed along the lower length of the Welland Canal and, by the early 1850's, these were concentrated mainly in Thorold and St. Catharines. The local supplies of wheat which were brought to the mills at that time proved inadequate but, with the enlarged capacity of the Second Welland Canal, the catchment area for incoming supplies was greatly extended as the West opened up. But only a small proportion of this western grain was ever brought to the local mills. Much more grain passed across the Peninsula for more distant destinations either by way of the Welland Canal or the Welland Railway to Port Dalhousie. The grain was then transferred to ships for passage either to Toronto or to Europe along the St. Lawrence-Montreal route. Flour milling declined in St. Catharines during the railway era despite considerable previous argument that railway facilities would enhance the wheat trade and thereby boost the economy of the town. In this respect, the railways unexpectedly exercised an adverse influence on the local industrial structure.

The Area of Business Influence

The enthusiasm for railways at their infancy, which was described in the introduction to this book, was persuasive at the time. It was founded on the somewhat simplistic and naive assumption that, for any one urban locality, its market, business and service opportunities could be equated broadly with the number of families living in its market area multiplied by the wealth of these customers. Growth was possible if the catchment area was expanded by the building of railways, or if incomes were increased (for example, by higher agricultural production engendered by the railway), or if the population could be increased (with the railway again playing a significant role as it improved the factor of accessibility to those places which it served).

However, the cause-effect relationship of railway development was much more complicated. The important element of staunch competition between communities had not been taken into account. Adjacent centres were critical rivals of each other's progress. Railways introduced not only the possibility of growth, but also the possibility of differential growth — and the devil take the hindmost in the battle for commercial supremacy. Pride and "boosterism" for the railways was more effective in some places than in others, all centres were not equal starters in the race for supremacy, and some towns received more advantages than others from their railways.

Specifically, when a railway was routed into or close to a town, then its potential hinterland areas were extended in the directions served by the track. This, in turn, also introduced the possibility that all or a part of the existing trade could be absorbed or taken over from other centres along the routes of track. It was a two-sided and competitive situation, but one in which the larger centres might reasonably be expected to reap the advantage at the expense of the smaller communities.

However, the early railway era was also a period of road improvement, with these improvements being supported by the local communities. For example, in 1850, the *Journal* referred to the St. Catharines and Pelham Turnpike Road. The editorial observed: "It is now an excellent one. . .no improvement was more required in the way of road-building. . . .We are pleased to find, that while other parts of the Province are occupied in promoting railroad enterprise, that we in this part are doing something towards the advancement of the highways of travel and commerce".[36] A week later, it was noted that a company had been formed to construct a plank and macadamized road from Merrittville (Welland) to St. Catharines: "We are persuaded that our fellow citizens will at once see the importance of sustaining this Company by an immediate purchase of stock, and, in all other ways possible. By the construction of this road, a large tract of country will be enabled to send its produce to this market."[37]

It became obvious that local roads should be improved, both to facilitate the movement of passengers and goods to and from the railway stations and to prevent the town's trading sphere of influence being captured from some other centre. This dual situation, with its potential for either advancement or loss, was recognized by the St. Catharines and Merrittville Turnpike Commission:

"The result of the opening of the Great Western Railway past this town, will be to divert the country trade, on both sides of St. Catharines, to the larger markets of Hamilton and Buffalo, an advantage admitted to equalize prices on the whole extent of country; that is, that the farmer living near any railway station can always take advantage of the highest market, which is invariably in the larger towns. If this be the case, unless we open up to our merchants and mechanics the country trade of the townships lying back of us, our scope of population will be very limited indeed; and if the progress and advancement of the town become checked by any such cause, we shall find those smaller communities which interfere very little with our present limited radius of country become formidable rivals".[38]

The close relationships between communities which the railways fostered also exacerbated the rivalry between nearby centres of service importance. Two examples of this feature will suffice. The *Annual Report* of the St. Catharines Board of Trade for 1900 noted the opening of the N.S.&T. between Niagara Falls and St. Catharines, and then stated that this transportation facility "brought hundreds of new customers to the mercantile establishments of this city. Under the stimulus of this influx of new and profitable business, the merchants are making it their aim to carry the best quality and the largest variety of styles of goods".[39]

Likewise, when a company was formed to build an electric street railway from St. Catharines to Grimsby with a branch through Campden to Smithville, the *St. Catharines Evening Star* "confidently expected that the extension of this electric railway westward...will be the means of restoring to St. Catharines the extensive traffic of the western portion of the County of Lincoln, of which it was deprived when the Hamilton, Grimsby and Beamsville Electric Railway commenced operations in 1895".[40] The Hamilton business interests were not slow to perceive this threat to their catchment area. They responded with alacrity, and severely criticized the Hamilton, Grimsby and Beamsville Company for not extending their line to Beamsville. They argued that the proposed transit system would secure "for St. Catharines the trade that would inevitably have gone to Hamilton....St. Catharines evidently sees the golden opportunity, and is not slow to grasp it. . .[and] if that projected electric railway between St. Catharines and Grimsby is built, it will divert a good deal of trade from Hamilton".[41]

Evidence of this inter-urban rivalry may be gleaned from newspaper advertisements of the period. In the 1850's, as compared with the 1840's, advertisements were placed in the St. Catharines newspapers by business interests in Hamilton and Toronto. For instance, an 1855 issue carried insertions from Hamilton: Buchanan Harris & Co. advertising spring and summer fabrics, hardware, dry goods and groceries; Whan, MacLean & Co. advertising dry goods; and Gordon McKay advertising staple dry goods and clothing; and from Toronto, Ross, Mitchell & Co. advertising their "Grand Show of Spring Importations".[42] This was a sign of the whole broadening of urban horizons that had been introduced by the railways.

Incidentally, with the advent of railways, the seasonal distribution of goods and the structural pattern of the retail trade was changed markedly. Previously, with dependence primarily on roads and canals which were closed by winter ice from mid-December to April, goods arrived in the shops seasonally and on irregular schedules. With the railway, the movement of goods no longer had to await the spring thaw and the opening of the canals for navigation. External products became not only more plentiful, but more evenly distributed throughout the year. In this respect, the Peninsula gained from its trading associations with Buffalo, its American rail connections, and the advantages of year-round access to the ice-free ports of Boston and New York. By contrast, the Grand Trunk route along the north shore of Lake Ontario led to the frozen winter ports of Montreal and Quebec, while the extended journey to Halifax and Portland, Maine (where ice-free conditions prevailed), was both lengthy and costly.

Travel and Special Occasions

The railway changed travel habits, which took on a particular importance for special occasions. For example, railways receive considerable mention in 1866 at the time of the Fenian Invasion of Canada West.[43] When these Irish soldiers and American sympathizers crossed the Niagara River from Black Rock and landed two miles below (north of) Fort Erie, the railway yards of the Buffalo and Lake Huron Railway in Fort Erie Village were their first objective. As described by E. A. Cruickshank:

"O'Neill soon after landing ordered Colonel Starr, with his regiment to take possession of the railway yard. . . .This was done about sunrise, but the railway officials had taken the alarm and hastily made up all their rolling stock into one huge train drawn by four locomotives, which moved slowly off when the invaders came in sight of it. Captain Geary of the 17th Kentucky with a few men went in pursuit on a hand-car, but gave up the chase on arriving at Sauerwein's bridge over the Six Mile Creek, which he burned and then tore up some of the track nearby."[44]

Forces to repel the invasion were moved to the area by rail:

"Colonel George Peacocke of the 16th Regiment, arrived at Niagara Falls by a special train [on the Great Western line] with a battery of the Royal Artillery having six guns and wagons, fully horsed, three companies of his own regiment and three of the 47th. . .He went forward with his infantry by rail to secure the bridges over the creek at Chippawa, instructing his artillery to follow by road, as he stated, from want of proper cars to convey the guns."[45]

Another group advanced by train along the Buffalo and Lake Huron tracks from Port Colborne to Ridgeway:

"At 5 a.m., half an hour ahead of the time fixed, an order was given for the train to start. The force on board, nominally 840 of all ranks, probably did not exceed 800 effective combatants. . . .Shortly before six o'clock the train arrived at Ridgeway and the men were quickly detrained at the platform. . . .Much time was necessarily consumed in forming up, inspecting arms, and distributing ammunition."[46]

The Battle of Ridgeway followed, the Fenians gained the upper hand, and the humiliated troops retreated — again by rail:

"The retreat was continued from Ridgeway station along the railway track towards Port Colborne. When about half way to that place, Mr. Larmour met them with a locomotive and two flat cars bringing back the reserve ammunition. By noon the discomfitted force was again at Port Colborne utterly exhausted and dispirited."[47]

Another special occasion in which the railway provided yeoman service occurred at the inauguration of the Monument to General Brock on Queenston Heights in 1859. For this occasion:

"Every vehicle [in St. Catharines] that could by any means be rendered available was put in requisition, and those who had none or preferred going by Railroad and Steamer [*Peerless*], began to move long before the appointed hour towards the Welland Railway station.

...The Rifle Company..., preceded by a brass band, arrived at the Railway Station....

After waiting some time at the station, the train came thundering along and rushed by without stopping, leaving the expectant crowd astonished and a little irritated by this unlooked-for delay. In a short time, however, the train returned....A rush now occurred to get into the cars, which were soon filled, leaving more than half the people still standing on the platform; and the train again moved on to Port Dalhousie, and after disgorging, returned to St. Catharines for the remainder."[48]

The street railway used for the embarkation of troops at Thorold in 1914.
John Burtniak Collection

The Royal Train carrying the Duke and Duchess of Cornwall and York at Niagara Falls, 1901.
St. Catharines Historical Museum, from Public Archives of Canada, C-46987

A third special event was the visit of H.R.H. The Prince of Wales, later King Edward VII, in 1860 when he passed through Dunnville on the Buffalo and Lake Huron line en route from Brantford to Fort Erie. The visit was described as follows:

"The loyal inhabitants of Haldimand were invited to be present, and they responded generously. They came in thousands; there was a stream of carriages to be seen on every road leading to the town, and long before two o'clock, the hour at which the Prince was expected to arrive, the streets around the railway station were thronged. . . .

The 'Tigers', as our first citizen soldiers were called, were on the ground. . . . The town possessed a strong, brass cannon, too, and that was there, 'ready to roar' at the proper moment. . . .

Ere long, a shrill whistle was heard, the pilot engine hove in sight and steamed into the station. Another whistle, and a minute afterwards, the throng caught sight of the royal car, — Bang! went that brass piece of artillery! Cheer after cheer rose from the assembled multitude, and before the echoes had died away, the Prince of Wales was there, standing on the platform of the car, lifting his hat and duly acknowledging the warm welcome. . . .

After a stay of not more than fifteen minutes, the train steamed out of the station, and the royal visitor departed amid the cheers of the assembled multitude and the roaring of the corporation cannon."[49]

The race course at Fort Erie was promoted by railways.

John Burtniak Collection

The opportunities and possibilities for personal travel, and the extent, ease and freedom of movement, were greatly enhanced by the advent of railways. This is indicated by a railway time table for the Great Western Railway and its connecting lines for 1879, which revealed the extent to which the travel situation had changed, a mere 25 years after the introduction of the first railway into the Peninsula.[50] The time table itself is interesting. Its cover shows the Suspension Bridge, backed by the Falls of Niagara. Inside, there is a descriptive statement, presented in English, French and German, about the Great Niagara Falls Route between New York, Boston, Philadelphia and Chicago. It states that:

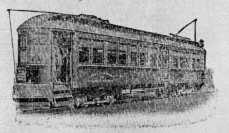
Many forms of recreation were promoted by the new factor of accessibility introduced by the railway. *John Burtniak Collection*

John Burtniak Collection

"This Railway, with the New York Central, Boston and Albany, and Michigan Central Railways, forms the shortest route between New York and Boston and Chicago, and is the only route between these cities on which Palace Sleeping and Drawing Room Cars are run via Niagara Falls without charge. It is a link in the great chain of railways stretching across the American Continent from the Atlantic to the Pacific. It is laid throughout with steel rails, and has running over it the magnificent Parlor, Drawing-Room, Dining and Palace Sleeping Cars for which this continent is so famous. All the stock is of the best description, fitted with Westinghouse Air Brake, Miller Platform and Coupling, and every other requisite for the safety and comfort of travellers. . . .The Line passes the Garden of Canada."[51]

Such, then, was a major railway's expression of pride in its facilities, conveniences and importance in the developing network of the time. Certainly, the potentials for travel to or from this "Garden of Canada" had been changed radically by the railway. By way of the Welland Railway, one could reach within 15 minutes either the docks at Port Dalhousie or connect with the main line at Merritton. Across the Peninsula, the times from St. Catharines were Thorold, 25 minutes; Allanburg, 34 minutes; Port Robinson, 43 minutes; Welland, 54 minutes; Welland Junction, 64 minutes; Humberstone, 72 minutes; and Port Colborne, 77 minutes.

On the main line, it took just over one hour to reach Hamilton, about two hours to Oakville, and about three hours to Toronto. London was four hours away and Detroit some eight hours distant by the Chicago express. Times varied according to the type of train — express, mixed, sleeping accommodation and mail — and the number of stops. On the loop line, St. Thomas was four hours from Welland Junction. Even New York, about 400 miles away from the Suspension Bridge, was only 15 hours away. Certainly, the external relationships of the urban centres had been changed radically by the presence of railways and the greater ease and convenience of travel that they represented.

Some of the rules for passengers from the same time table also make interesting reading. Station ticket offices were stated to be open only 20 minutes before the departure of each train. Passengers were requested "to be at the station at least five minutes before the advertised time of leaving. Those with excess baggage over one hundred pounds weight must be at the Station fifteen minutes before train time".[52] Tickets could be purchased on the train, but these were valid only for a single trip in one direction to a station on the Great Western; all other tickets had to be purchased at the station or downtown ticket offices. Transfer points for baggage were indicated for connections to the New York Central Railroad, the Erie Railway and the Great Western Loop Line. Black Rock, Windsor, Detroit and Toronto (Union Station) were noted as major transfer points.

Under the heading of summer resorts, the places that were mentioned included Niagara Falls, St. Catharines and the Grimsby Camp Ground. Of St. Catharines, it was written: "This pleasant little city is one favorite summer residence of many visitors from the United States."[53] Mention was then made of the Mineral Springs and, as objects of interest, "the great works now in progress on the Welland Canal [the Third Welland Canal]", the town of Niagara, Port Dalhousie, and "the extensive paper mills and other manufactories at Welland".[54] It also stated that in St. Catharines: "The hotel accommodation is unrivalled in Canada, including the Stephenson

House, Welland House [and] Grand Central Hotel. All trains on the
Great Western stop at St. Catharines."[55]

Grimsby Beach became an important recreational centre because of the
railway.   *John Burtniak Collection*

The programme of a Grand Lodge convention in St. Catharines listing
available hotels, 1894.
John Burtniak Collection

With these new facilities available for movement, as the St. Catharines newspaper columnist, "Junius", recorded in 1856, "many of our citizens. . .have become no inconsiderable travellers".[56] His list included many residents of the City who had visited England, Europe and the continent, the United States, California (including an unfortunate Capt. Taylor who was murdered in Mexico by bandits), and a group of citizens who had been to Australia. Ideas were greatly broadened in direct consequence of these visits; for example, Merritt's inspiration for a Suspension Bridge over the Niagara Gorge has been attributed to the mention of a Swiss design by his sons. As "Junius" commented: "A trip now to Europe, or in fact to almost any part of the world in these days of lightning [sic] and steam is considered less by our citizens, than it was a few years ago to Montreal or New York."[57]

Emigration was also facilitated. "Junius" noted that: "On Thursday we saw Elkanah Rogers taking J. E. Ryerson's baggage to the G.W.R. Depot, which was marked Augusta, Ga., whither, we learn, Mr. R. has gone to reside."[58] Some people were even tendered special send-offs from the Station, as in this instance: "The Brass Band was at the Station this morning playing. Mrs. A. C. Rykert is going to Ireland and to get married to some one in Dublin or Belfast. There was a good many folks up with her."[59] Funerals, too, sometimes received the last call at the Station.

Nor was long distance travel necessarily limited to the well-to-do and socially conscious upper echelons of society. It extended to many groups. For example, the *Thorold Post* in 1877 recorded with a tinge of distaste that:

"There not being any prospect of much stone cutting being done on the new canal this winter, several of the stone cutters employed here, intend 'spending the winter in Europe.' Rather high tones. . .They intend leaving here for Liverpool on Monday".[60]

The beach and Lakeside Park at Port Dalhousie became a summer recreational resort because of its railway and steamer links. *John Burtniak Collection*

This growing interest in travel began with the accessibility of railways by steamer across Lake Ontario. An example of this is shown by the following incident:

"The *Mazeppa* steamer [was] making regular trips to Toronto for a short time, the boat coming up the Canal to Lock No. 1; but the construction of the Grand Trunk R.R. caused such an increase in the freight and passengers, the latter averaging 100 per day, that the detention at the port [Port Dalhousie], or lower dock, caused them to be carried down in omnibuses."[61]

Short, daily, weekend and evening excursions also became common and were encouraged by the offer of cheap fares from the railway companies. Two such excursions in 1856 were described as follows: "About six o'clock P.M. we saw the mass move depot-ward — tall women and little maidens, beardless youths and bright eyed beaux, short men and tall boys, some 300 in all, took passage on the Port Dalhousie and Thorold Railway to the Port, and there on board the cracked [sic] steamer *Welland*";[62] and somewhat later: "on Wednesday last, a fishing party of ladies and gentlemen went down to the Port, which by the by is a favorite resort, in one of Forbes' busses, amused themselves in fishing, sailing, &c., and returned by the Railway having spent the afternoon very pleasantly."[63]

Still another excursion was reported as follows: "We had a ride, in company with a lady California friend on Wednesday last on the Port Dalhousie and Thorold Railway to and from the Port and were much pleased with the able Conductor, Capt. Hamilton, and the new passenger car, and the road itself, about which so much has been said."[64] The description continued: "On Thursday evening last, the advertised Moonlight Excursion came off, as usual, with great pleasure and regalement to some 150 of our citizens, who enjoyed themselves much. Osborne's band discoursed sweet music and enlivened the hilarity of the Railway and *Welland* trip and tour."[65] Obviously, closer links were forged between several communities in the Peninsula, and those with railway connections became less isolated from their neighbours than previously. Short-term travel became possible, as shown by the following comment in 1861: "As today was Good Friday all the stores in town were shut and the clerks had a holiday. Some of them went away on the trains."[66] Grimsby Beach, Port Dalhousie and Niagara Falls each expanded as popular excursion localities because of the railway.

The mutual glee and thrill of shared enthusiasm on such trips are well portrayed by a Sunday School excursion and picnic to Port Dalhousie in 1867. Between 2,300 and 2,400 tickets were issued from Allanburg, Port Robinson, Welland and Port Colborne on the Welland Railway for the great day, which was described as follows:

"We arrived on the ground at 1:20 in somewhat of a jam everywhere, but especially in the cars. One locomotive brought down the 21 cars filled within and on top. The crowd was large and made of great and small. On arriving at the grounds water was in great demand. Very soon, the cloths were spread all around, and from personal observation I am confident in saying that a great many baskets were very quickly emptied of their contents, to the great comfort of all.

. . .[After addresses and choir singing], the excursionists amused themselves in one way and another until 7:30 p.m. when the engines Chippawa, Amazon and Ontario were attached to the immense train of 23 cars, whistles, off brakes, and we started on our beautiful moonlight excursion homeward bound."[67]

Many summer day excursion trains also passed through the Peninsula en route to the Suspension Bridge to take in the sights at the Falls. Hugh Neilson recorded, in 1861, special tourist trains on the Great Western from places such as Chatham, Detroit, Guelph, Hamilton, Milwaukee, Paris, Princeton, and a "great excursion from Sarnia to view the Niagara Falls and other objects of interest in this vicinity. Fare was only $2.00, so there was a good lot of persons — 2 car loads altogether — they are coming back tonight."[68]

Special tourist fares often had to be negotiated between the organizer of an occasion and the railway companies. For example, when the centennial celebrations of the landing of the United Empire Loyalists in Upper Canada were being held in Niagara in 1884, special fares were provided by the Michigan Central. This is shown by the following statement of the passenger agent:

"I do not think there will be a very large number attending from points on our line, and I think a rate of one and one third fare for the round trip would be sufficiently low to allow all desiring to take part to attend. I will instruct our agents to sell tickets accordingly."[69]

Neilson also described an outing that was being planned from St. Catharines: "A great excursion from here to the Niagara Falls on the 16th inst., the fare is only 25 cts. The Poster came out today. There is also going to be one from London, Guelph, Toronto, and Hamilton. All the fares are very cheap."[70] The tickets for this recreational frolic arrived on the 14th and on the great day (a Friday):

"Excursion day folks commenced to crowd in about 9 o'clock. At 11 they stopped coming in and at that time Father had sold 276 tickets. There were two trains, one from Hamilton and one from Toronto. First one had 26 cars, the other 27; 53 altogether. They sold in Hamilton 1450 tickets."[71]

Much less frequent were the trips by rail, or by a combination of lake steamer and railway, to St. Catharines, though some of these jaunts did take place. Hugh Neilson reported two such trips: "Evangelists came today from Montreal,"[72] and "there is an excursion today from Toronto of the Toronto Field battery and the other soldiers in that City to this place. They came over on the 'Zimmerman' to Port Dalhousie, thence by Welland R.R. to here."[73]

Within all towns, horse-drawn buses met the major trains. These conveyances provided transport for passengers and baggage to the principal hotels, and stage coaches furnished a feeder service to nearby communities. For example, an advertisement of 1857 announced public conveyance from St. Catharines to Niagara for 50 cents: "Leaving St. Catharines daily on the arrival of the train from the west at 10.50 a.m. Returning leaves the principal hotels in Niagara in time for the 4.17 train going West."[74] As G. P. de T. Glazebrook has noted and as many of the illustrations indicate: "Lines of buggies and waggons formed a background to what was essentially a community scene."[75]

The Mail and Telegraph Service

The railway improved communication by facilitating the movement of people and goods. It also played a significant role in expediting messages. For instance, mail was carried on trains almost from the beginning, thus taking this service away from the stage coach lines. One consequence was that many small hamlets along the line of track received railway stations and post offices were then established nearby. Some examples of these post offices are Silverdale Station, Brookfield Station, Perry Station and Attercliffe Station, whose post-marks now provide an interesting facet of Canadian postal history. The railway played a vital role in hastening the despatch of mail across the Peninsula, and indeed across the country. With the several lines and frequent trains in the Peninsula, mail often reached its destination the next day and sometimes even the same day, a feat that is much envied in this modern age. Outgoing mail from the post offices was delivered to the stations and incoming mail picked up regularly, sometimes several times a day, so that new mail could be expected at least daily.

There was also the introduction of an electric telegraph service, which was inaugurated in the Peninsula in 1846 as part of a line from Queenston to Toronto, with stations at St. Catharines and Hamilton.[76] As Ernest Green has noted: "It became possible, for the first time in the world's history, to convey intelligence from place to place without sending the substance upon which it was written and regardless of conditions of light and weather."[77] The Company bore the name "The Toronto, Hamilton & Niagara Electro-Magnetic Telegraph Company", with St. Catharines frequently being added to this title. It was sponsored by railway promoters, and had one director (J. L. Ranney) from St. Catharines. The line spanned the Niagara River at the Queenston-Lewiston crossing, and a connection was added from Queenston to Niagara in 1847.

This pioneer system was augmented considerably when the Great Western installed its own system along the line of track. The telegraph assisted in lessening isolation from the outside world, with the railway stations playing their role in this regard. Hugh Neilson described one busy day at St. Catharines in 1861 very tersely: "sent and received over 60 messages."[78] Business and commercial trans-actions were aided greatly as information could now be relayed rapidly over previously inaccessible distances. The telegraph, with its overhead wires, also added the new visual feature of poles and wires to the landscape along the line of track as the railway traversed the countryside.

Tourism

The contribution of the railways to the development of the tourist industry at Niagara Falls was substantial. This is indicated by a description in the *Red Book of Niagara,* published at the turn of the century:

> "On the Canadian side, Grand Trunk passengers alight at Niagara Falls North and take carriage or trolley to other points. Trains by the Michigan Central and Canadian Southern Railroads stop, if flagged, at Niagara Falls Central, Ont., five minutes' walk from Upper Arch Bridge, or at Clifton, Niagara Falls North. Boats from Buffalo by the International Navigation Company's line, land passengers at Slater's point [located above Chippawa], where they connect with the Niagara Falls Park & River Electric Railway for the Falls, Queenston and intermediate points. The steamers of the Niagara Navigation Company land passengers at Queenston or Lewiston, whence the Falls are reached by trolley, or from Lewiston if desired, by New York Central Railroad."[79]

An important Station, known first as Victoria Park and later as Clifton Hill, had been constructed at the top of Clifton Hill by the

Canada Southern-Michigan Central Railway. This Railway had also built the Wesley Park and Falls View Stations. These stations each served and promoted tourism. The Wesley Park Station served two camp meeting grounds; these sites are now occupied by the Niagara Falls Collegiate and Vocational Institute and an unusual double circle of streets. The Clifton Hill station, being the closest stop to the Falls, provided easy access to Queen Victoria Park. The Falls View, or "Inspiration Point" Station, was the most important and was stressed in the railway guides of the periods. Its advantageous situation is described by Francis Petrie as follows:

> "The Michigan Central built a special station in front of Loretto Academy with a large viewing platform in a pleasant parklike atmosphere at which all day trains stopped for five minutes to give the passengers an unexpected view of Niagara Falls....In fact this stop at Falls View was the one great advertising slogan of the Michigan Central for many years and thousands rode the Michigan Central just because of this attraction."[80]

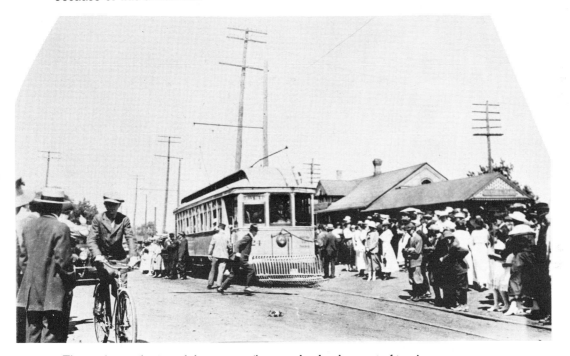

The vital contribution of the street railway to the development of tourism is indicated by this scene at Victoria Park Station on Clifton Hill.
Francis J. Petrie Collection

The same author has written elsewhere that: "This Falls View Station was remembered by many thousands of railroad passengers as the place where they obtained their finest view of the Falls."[81] An advertisement by the Michigan Central stated that their line was the only real Niagara Falls route in the country:

> "Every train stops from five to ten minutes at Falls View — which as the name indicates, is a splendid point from which to view the great cataract. It is right on the brink of the grand canyon, at the end of the Horseshoe, and every part of the Falls is in plain sight. Even if he is too ill, or too lazy, to get out of his car, every passenger can see this liquid wonder of the world from the window or the platform. . .
>
> Thousands of beauty lovers and grandeur-worshippers will journey over the only railroad from which it can be seen. There is but one Niagara Falls on earth and but one great railway to it."[82]

The Falls View Station at Niagara Falls.   *Francis J. Petrie Collection*

The station itself was small in size, resembling a six-sided summer house in a landscaped setting. As such, it was a popular landmark from the 1870's to the 1920's but, when the stop-over was no longer required, the building was demolished.

Niagara Falls was extremely popular as a vacation spot and the railway greatly encouraged its growth as a tourist resort but it also, somewhat ironically, encouraged industrial development which became an anathema to the tourist industry. For example, the Canadian Southern-Michigan Central line brought in the Montrose yards with its associated facilities such as a roundhouse and shops, and a double-tracked line was constructed from Welland to the bridge crossing at Niagara Falls. It carved up the urban landscape and encouraged industrial location along the line of track. The railway, therefore, exerted an adverse influence on the very tourist industry that it was seeking to foster. It was an instrument in urban and industrial change, whereas tourists arrived to view a natural spectacle. This acute conflict of purpose in Niagara Falls remains unresolved to this day. Reports from the mid-1960's onwards, have made recommendations for the removal of trackage from the city.[83] With changed concepts in the tourist industry, different attitudes in society, and the advent of the ubiquitous automobile, railways in Niagara Falls have become a topic of concern to the city whose very growth they encouraged.

Reverting to the past, railway companies were certainly aware of the fantastic tourist merit and aesthetic quality of their lines as they passed either near to or close by the magnificent scenery of the Niagara River. The Niagara Gorge, the Horseshoe Falls, the American Falls and the swirling rapids above the Falls were each used in railway advertisements to provide impressive and prestigious views of the remarkable scenery for their patrons. This deserving quality of the railway has been captured in a realistic painting by the artist, Robert Whale, which now hangs in the National Art Gallery at Ottawa. It depicts a Canada Southern engine and coaches stopped at the Falls so that the passengers could view the inspiring environment.

On a smaller scale, but nevertheless important for the local community, the railway promoted trips to the lake shores at Grimsby Beach and at Port Dalhousie on Lake Ontario and to Crystal Beach and Erie Beach on Lake Erie. It also sponsored the growth of St. Catharines as a health spa resort, as visitors could now travel from a distance with relative ease and speed to imbibe or bathe in the curative waters at one of the several mineral springs. That this was a popular attraction by 1861 is shown by Hugh Neilson's comment: "Went downtown in the Bus to the Stephenson House; great lot of Yankees there, about 125 there now. House can accommodate 200."[84]

The establishment of spa hotels, which depended on railways for their business, has been described by J. P. Merritt in these words:

A selection of excursion tags, worn on the lapel for purpose of identification.

John Burtniak Collection

"Another important local event was the opening of the Stephenson House and mineral baths, followed soon by the Welland House. Great exertions were made to complete those buildings, as, since the railways were finished, a great many travellers stopped at St. Catharines. The mineral waters of this town owe their celebrity to the fact that numerous cures of long standing diseases have been effected by their use".[85]

STEPHENSON HOUSE.

ST. CATHARINES.

CANADA WEST.

CANADA MINERAL SPRINGS.

The railways promoted the development of spa hotels in St. Catharines.

John Burtniak Collection

The Stephenson House, a four-storey building, stood at the corner of Yates and Salina Streets. The Welland House, five storeys high, was situated on the corner of Ontario and King Streets. As "Junius" remarked:

"In consequence of the great rush of people from all parts of Canada and the United States to the St. Catharines Mineral Springs this season, and of the limited accommodations of the Stephenson House, the worthy proprietor has entered into an arrangement. . .whereby said House is to be greatly enlarged, the grounds beautified and the whole enchanting spot made still more enticing and bewitching to travellers and invalids seeking health, comfort and a summer seclusion from a melting sun".[86]

These facilities earned St. Catharines the descriptive epithet, "The Saratoga of Canada." As H. R. Page observed in 1876:

"St. Catharines is noted far and wide for its Mineral Springs. . . .

"The Artesian Wells, which are now widely known, much resemble the Spas, of Germany, but their curative properties are of a far higher order. . . .

"The Stephenson house, erected in 1842, and now under the direction of Messrs. Stinson & May, is furnished in such a manner, with regard to elegance and comfort, as will make it compare favorably with any first-class hotel on this continent. . . .

"The Springbank Hotel and Bathing Establishment, another famous resort for tourists and invalids, was erected at great expense by Dr. Theophilus Mack, whose reputation as a surgeon and physician is not confined to this country alone. . . .

"The Welland House, is also a first class commercial house, and is a large and elegant white brick structure.

"The Murray House and Cairns House have also a good reputation as commercial hotels."[87]

The New Murray Hotel, St. Catharines.   *John Burtniak Collection*

The attractiveness of the town, with many visitors coming from the United States by train, is indicated by the numbers staying at the Stephenson House in 1859. This was estimated to be 2,004 from 1 April to 15 October. The *Journal,* in calculating the total for the whole town, concluded that:

"We do not have the means of ascertaining correctly the number of arrivals at the other houses in town: but assuming that they were at least three times as many as above — (which, when we take into account their number, is a low estimate), the number of persons who have sought relief from the St. Catharines Mineral Waters during the year 1859, up to the present time, could not have been less than between 6,000 and 7,000."[88]

The new look of the Welland Hotel, St. Catharines, after renovation.
John Burtniak Collection

Helderleigh nurseries, Winona.   *John Burtniak Collection*

Agricultural Change: The Fruit Industry

The pattern of land use in the north of the Peninsula changed radically over the last decades of the nineteenth century, with the major transition being from mixed and primarily subsistence farming to the more specialized production of fruit crops. Railways were one element in this positive and expressive change. They opened up new and extensive areas in the West for wheat production and enabled local crops to be transported easily to nearby urban markets. A history of Niagara Township, published in 1967, has summarized this transition in farming practice:

> "The railroad opened new vistas in agriculture. Agriculture had previously been limited to the raising of cattle, sheep and hogs, and the production of wheat, oats and hay. But everyone knew that the soil was perfectly suited for various kinds of fruits. The only problem was a market. When the railroads were built, and 'fruit cars' introduced, the markets of southern Ontario opened up for farmers in Niagara Township. They developed the new opportunity quickly. There was very little fruit sold commercially in 1861. But, by the early 1880s, the township was a full-blown fruit-oriented community. Peach orchards with 2,000 trees were common by 1880. Niagara probably had about 500 acres planted to peaches — most of them Crawfords — with about 125,000 trees. This township produced about 350,000 bushels of peaches annually in the early 1880s. . . .Baskets of carefully picked peaches were taken to a shed, where the damaged ones were removed. The best of the fruit was put in baskets and covered with a heavy pink gauze. The baskets were loaded onto a wagon, and taken to a 'peach car' at the railway station."[89]

A comparable situation prevailed in the west of Lincoln County where, during the first half of the nineteenth century, wheat was the prime crop and apples the most valuable fruit crop. Wheat production decreased as other areas expanded, but apple production thrived. As William F. Rannie has noted: "By 1875 about 80 per cent of the apples grown were shipped to Britain in barrels and the volume of apples shipped from Jordan Station in 1896 was estimated at 50,000 barrels".[90] To augment this export, "at the height of the trade, apples by the carload were imported from the West to supplement the local supply".[91]

The soft fruit industry also expanded with the railway. The Great Western was especially instrumental in fostering this new set of rural circumstances. In 1880, "70,000 baskets of peaches were shipped from Grimsby station. Grimsby Beach, Beamsville and Jordan added to the total, with Beamsville rivalling its western shipping point."[92] Small fruits were also added as export crops to the growing Canadian urban market. As noted by Rannie:

> "Large shipments of berries were made from the platform at the station, and in two days at the height of the season in 1896, 1,500 crates of strawberries left Jordan Station by train for the Montreal market. . . .There were blackberries, too. . . .In 1896 over 6,000 crates of Lawton berries left Jordan Station."[93]

To accommodate this burgeoning business, the Great Western lengthened its platforms at Beamsville and Jordan Station, and later added a station at Vineland. But freight rates were high, and the fruit growers complained bitterly at the monopolistic situation which prevailed. The Jordan Harbour Shipping Company was formed in 1897 to provide an alternative means of transport, at lower cost, to the Toronto market. Even so, the railway continued to play an important role in the shipping of fruit. By 1901, railways were still exporting fruit to distant places with apparent efficiency and speed, as shown by the fact that "fruit graded by shippers anywhere along the line, up to as late as six p.m." could be "shipped to Ottawa or Montreal, arriving at their destination by six a.m. next morning without transhipment."[94]

Charles Lamont Collection

John Burtniak Collection

John Burtniak Collection

The railway helped in the introduction of the soft fruit industry across the Peninsula and encouraged the marketing of its produce.

St. Catharines was probably the most important fruit shipping point. By 1900, it exported by water to the Montreal and Toronto markets and by railway to all parts of Canada, an aggregate total amounting to almost 13 million pounds.[95] The fruit and vegetable canning industry also expanded greatly, from one factory in 1891 to six by the turn of the century. The wine industry was also becoming firmly established by this time.

By 1913, Lincoln County had approximately 14,600 acres under fruit production, including 5,496 of peaches, 3,627 of grapes and 1,601 of apples. Other crops, in their descending sequence of acreage, included plums, pears, blackberries, raspberries, strawberries, cherries, currants and gooseberries. A considerable revolution in agricultural production had been achieved. Intensive and specialized farming was not practical, and large holdings were being divided into economical and more productive smaller holdings ranging from five to 25 acres in size. Many factors were involved in this transition, including the development of a railway network which changed the potential of agricultural land by making available new markets for its products.

Canning Factory, Fonthill, Canada.

"Helderleigh" Jam Factory and Fruit House.
Winona, Ontario

Jam and canning factories were served by railway access.

John Burtniak Collection

The Railways: A Foundation for the Future

The railways connected the larger existing centres and enhanced their growth potential. They were especially important to Welland, which was not on a major east-west road, and to St. Catharines, Merritton and Thorold. They gave a marked impetus to the development of frontier or border towns which became rail bridge-crossings of the Niagara River and termini for Canadian railways. Thus, Niagara Falls and Fort Erie grew rather than Chippawa, Queenston or Niagara. At the same time, the railways had some negative effects on settlement: some existing centres such as Jordan, St. Johns, Balls Falls (Elgin) and Wellandport were by-passed and went into decline, and Jordan Harbour was closed to shipping by the railway bridge across Twenty Mile Creek.

The railways, therefore, strengthened the focus for industrial development along the Canal and at border crossings along the Niagara River, and flour milling came to be concentrated at the Canal-rail transhipment point of Port Colborne rather than in St. Catharines or Thorold. Generally, the railways rendered the Peninsula more favourable for industrial development on a large scale by facilitating access to more widely distributed sources of raw materials, by which the industries were enabled to serve national, and even continental, markets.

As for changes in urban status, by the turn of the century, Hamilton had improved its relative position and emerged at the head of the urban hierarchy far outstripping the smaller centres in the Peninsula, Chippawa and Niagara shifted down, while Dunnville and Welland moved up. But the most spectacular change in scale during the last half of the nineteenth century was undoubtedly the growth of Niagara Falls, from about 130 inhabitants in 1850 to 4,500 by 1900. This was due to the advent of the railway and the growing popularity of the Falls as a tourist attraction. The railway made the Falls more accessible to the expanding Canadian and American populations, and indeed for visitors from abroad. They also improved the relative location of the town for large-scale industrial development. The hierarchy of settlement had been broadened by the addition of a large number of small settlements and by a new centre of regional status. St. Catharines remained the principal centre within the Peninsula, but not to the extent that might have been expected from a reading of the Keefer doctrine.

The railways also provided a platform from which the Peninsula could be launched into the future. As the pages of historical momentum turn onwards into the twentieth century, new forces, new technological capacities and new opportunities became apparent. However, the old was not displaced. It continued to play a forceful, active and critical role, with the railway system still providing one considerable inducement for industrial location and urban growth. The complete story of industrial development is beyond the compass of this book, but it will suffice to note that, when John N. Jackson and Carole White in 1971 assessed the industrial characteristics of the Peninsula from the attitudes and viewpoints expressed by industrialists, their conclusions for St. Catharines and Thorold were that:

> "The availability of rail access was mentioned by 12 firms, although none of these were established immediately after the railways were built. Apparently one of the earliest firms to regard access as an

important factor was McKinnons, when building their first large plant in 1901 and this was followed by two firms requiring good rail connections with their American parent companies, a greenhouse manufacturing firm which moved into St. Catharines in 1914, a zip fastener manufacturer in 1924, and another auto parts manufacturer in 1931. Four of the paper companies required rail access so that they could bring in their timber and pulp from the north by railcar; two more recently established large companies required rail access in order to move large quantities of materials and parts; and this factor is still important for certain firms to-day, the most recently established firm to mention it being set up in 1962."[96]

Such details are not isolated examples. They can be repeated from elsewhere in the Peninsula. For Welland, the same authors concluded that: "eleven of the twenty-seven firms interviewed stated that access to rail transport and Welland's nodal point on the railway network of Canada and the U.S. was one of the original location factors which led them to choose the city for their plants."[97] In Niagara Falls and Chippawa, rail access was used "to bring in heavy raw materials such as wheat, bauxite, sand, coke, glass, chemicals and iron and steel, and to distribute products, especially abrasives, and also chemicals, windshields and machinery."[98]

In these towns, and at other centres, the railway remained an important asset for industrial development. Sites could now be developed in conjunction with new locational factors, as these became available during the twentieth century. The most notable new element was the development of cheap and abundant hydro-electric power, using water diverted from the Niagara River and from the Welland Canal for this purpose. The Niagara Peninsula was enabled to harvest a dormant potential and thereby capitalize considerably in the use of its railway resources. These later opportunities, however, relied heavily upon the facilities whose foundations had been laid during the nineteenth century and which have been described over the previous pages. The period under review may be regarded as but a prelude to the further expansion and later use of the railway system.

At the turn of the century railways, in conjunction with the development of hydro-electric power, provided a new and forceful role for urban and industrial growth.

John Burtniak Collection

NOTES AND REFERENCES
CHAPTER I

1 The potential of disused railway rights-of-way is examined in *Alternative Uses for Abandoned Railway Rights of Way in Regional Niagara*, by Len Laba [et al], Institute of Urban and Environmental Studies, Brock University (St. Catharines), 1977.

2 T. C. Keefer, Travel and Transportation, in H. Y. Hind [et al], *Eighty Years' Progress of British North America . . .*, Nicholas (Toronto), 1864, p. 221.

3 Quoted in Asa Briggs, *Victorian Cities*, Penguin (Harmondsworth, England), 1968, p. 13.

4 T. C. Keefer, *Philosophy of Railroads and Other Essays*, edited by H. V. Nelles, University of Toronto Press (Toronto), 1972, p. xx. Keefer was the son of George Keefer, the first President of the Welland Canal Company.

5 *Ibid.*, p. xxxi.

6 *Ibid.*, p. 6.

7 *Ibid.*, pp. 8-9.

8 12 Vic., Cap. 29, 1849.

9 L. J. Chapman and D. F. Putnam, *The Physiography of Southern Ontario*, 2d ed., University of Toronto Press (Toronto), 1973, p. 173.

10 Lloyd G. Reeds, The Environment, in Louis Gentilcore (ed.), *Studies in Canadian Geography: Ontario*, University of Toronto Press (Toronto), 1972. See also Walter M. Tovell, *The Niagara Escarpment*, Royal Ontario Museum (Toronto), 1965; and Thomas E. Bolton, *Silurian Stratigraphy of the Niagara Escarpment in Ontario*, Geological Survey of Canada (Ottawa), 1957 (Memoir, no. 289).

11 Walter M. Tovell, *Niagara Falls: Story of a River*, Royal Ontario Museum (Toronto), 1966.

12 Hugh G. J. Aitken, *The Welland Canal Company: A Study in Canadian Enterprise*, Harvard University Press (Cambridge, Mass.). 1954. See also J. P. Merritt, *Biography of the Hon. W. H. Merritt, M. P. . . .*, E. S. Leavenworth (St. Catharines), 1875; J. J. Talman, William Hamilton Merritt, in *Dictionary of Canadian Biography*, v. 9, University of Toronto Press (Toronto), 1976, pp. 544-548; the *Merritt Papers*, PAC and PAO; and John M. Bassett and A. R. Petrie, *William Hamilton Merritt, Canada's Father of Transportation*, Fitzhenry and Whiteside (Don Mills), 1975.

13 The emergence of this settlement pattern is discussed in John N. Jackson, *St. Catharines, Ontario: Its Early Years*, Mika (Belleville), 1976, which book may be regarded as the predecessor to this text.

14 The town at the mouth of the Niagara River is referred to as Niagara throughout this text.

15 Andrew F. Burghardt, The Origin and Development of the Road Network in the Niagara Peninsula, 1770-1851, *AAG.*, v. 59, 1969, pp. 417-440.

16 L. Rodwell Jones and P. W. Bryan, *North America: An Historical, Economic and Regional Geography*, 8th Ed., Methuen (London), 1946, pp. 440-442.

17 John P. Heisler, *The Canals of Canada*, Department of Indian and Northern Affairs (Ottawa), 1973, (Canadian Historic Sites: Occasional Papers in Archaeology and History, no. 8).

18 See, for example, Robert W. Bingham, *The Cradle of the Queen City: A History of Buffalo to the Incorporation of the City*, Buffalo Historical Society (Buffalo), 1931, and other volumes of the Buffalo Historical Society, now Buffalo and Erie County Historical Society.

19 A recent assessment is Jacob Spelt, *Toronto*, Collier-Macmillan (Toronto), 1973. See also D. C. Masters, *The Rise of Toronto, 1850-1890*, University of Toronto Press (Toronto), 1947, and Jacob Spelt, *Urban Development in South-Central Ontario*, Van Gorcum (Assen, The Netherlands), 1955, reprinted by McClelland and Stewart (Toronto), 1972.

20 Ernest Alexander Cruikshank, The Inception of the Welland Canal, *OHS*, v. 22, 1925, p. 68.

21 *Ibid.*, p. 72, quoted from the *Niagara Gleaner*.

22 *Ibid.*

23 Robert Nichols, The Erie and Ontario Rail Road, *CRHA News Report*, No. 118, January 1861, p. 4.

24 5 Wm. IV, Cap. 19, 1835.

25 *St. C. J.*, 8 June 1842.

26 See Ernest Green, The Niagara Portage Road, *OHS*, v. 23, 1926, pp. 298-301, and James C. Morden, *Historic Niagara Falls*, Lundy's Lane Historical Society (Niagara Falls), 1932, pp. 28-33.

27 Major background material includes: C. A. Andreae, *A Historical Railway Atlas of Southwestern Ontario*, (London), 1972; A. W. Currie, *The Grand Trunk Railway of Canada*, University of Toronto Press (Toronto), 1957; W. T. Easterbrook and Hugh G. J. Aitken, *Canadian Economic History*, Macmillan (Toronto), 1956; G. P. de T. Glazebrook, *A History of Transportation in Canada*, McClelland and Stewart (Toronto), 1964; Nick and Helma Mika, *Railways of Canada: A Pictorial History*, McGraw-Hill Ryerson (Toronto), 1972; Myles Pennington, *Railways and Other Ways*, Williamson (Toronto), 1894; Robert F. Leggett, *Railroads of Canada*, Douglas, David & Charles (Vancouver), 1973; G. R. Stevens, *Canadian National Railways*, v. 1, Clarke and Irwin (Toronto), 1966; Norman Thompson and J. H. Edgar, *Canadian Railway Development*, Macmillan (Toronto), 1933; and J. M. and Edw. Trout, *The Railways of Canada*, 1870-1 . . ., Monetary Times (Toronto), 1871. For legal enactments see Robert Dorman (comp.), *A Statutory History of the Steam and Electric Railways of Canada, 1836-1937*, King's Printer (Ottawa), 1938. An important historical journal is *Canadian Rail*, published by the Canadian Railroad Historical Association. Some further introductory sources include W. H. Breithaupt, The Railways of Ontario, *OHS*, v. 25, 1929, pp. 12-25; Terry Ferris, Railways of British North America, *OHS*, v. 38, 1946, pp. 31-42; and Russell D. Smith, The Early Years of the Great Western Railway, 1833-1857, *OHS*, v. 60, 1968, pp. 205-227.

28 *Communication from the Secretary of the Treasury . . . on the Trade and Commerce of the British North American Colonies . . .*, Robert Armstrong (Washington), 1853, p. 53.

29 *St. C. J.*, 17 August 1843.

30 J. M. & Edw. Trout, *op. cit.*, p. 62.

31 Leget, *op. cit.*, p. 48.

32 The spelling of names on this map series presents many problems. Railway companies have changed their names, or different companies may have operating rights over the same length of line, or a former name may be used at a later period because of its earlier associations and meanings. Place names have different spellings, such as Chippawa, or Chippewa, DeCew or DeCou, Queenston or Queenstown, St. Catharines or St. Catherines, St. Johns or St. John's. Some places have changed their name over time, Bridgeburg to Fort Erie, Bridgeport to Jordan Station, Clifton to Niagara Falls, Welland City to Merritton, and Merrittsville to Welland. In other instances, the railway station and the community served have different names, such as the Suspension Bridge at Clifton, Sherks at Sherkston, International Bridge at Bridgeburg. Inconsistencies exist, therefore, between the text and either quotations or the names on original maps.

33 12 Vic., Cap. 196, 1849.

34 *The Canada Directory*, John Lovell (Montreal), 1851, p. 574.

35 *The Canada Directory*, John Lovell (Montreal), 1857, p. 1146.

CHAPTER II

1 4 Wm. IV, Cap. 29, 1834. See Russell D. Smith, The Early Years of the Great Western Railway, 1833-1857, *OHS*, v. 60, 1968, pp. 205-227, and J. J. Talman, The Great Western Railway, *WOHN*, v. 6, 1948, pp. 1-9.

2 8 Vic., Cap. 86, 1845, and 16 Vic., Cap. 99, 1853.

3 8 Vic., Cap. 86, 1845.

4 Report of the Directors of the Great Western Railway Company, 24 September 1854, *JLA*, v. 13, 1855, Appendix YY, p. 154.

5 *St. C. J.*, 22 May 1845, as quoted from the *H. G.*, 19 May 1845.

6 For example, in 1846, the *St. C. J.* discussed aspects of the Great Western Railway on 15 January, 22 January, 12 February, 5 March, 16 July, 15 October, and 3 December, *inter alia*. The complex question of the gauge to be adopted was discussed in *St. C. J.*, 23 October 1845.

7 *St. C. J.*, 15 October 1846.

8 *St. C. J.*, 25 March 1847.

9 See Augusta Gilkinson, The Great Western Railway, *LMHS*, v. 2, 1909, pp. 31-52.

10 *St. C. J.*, 21 October 1847.

11 William F. Rannie, *Lincoln: The Story of an Ontario Town*, (Lincoln), 1974, p. 95.

12 *St. C. J.*, 15 June 1848.

13 For example, *St. C. J.*, 6 September 1849, quotes from *H. S.*: "Our St. Catharines neighbours will, during the ensuing week, have an opportunity of subscribing for stock in the company."

14 14 and 15 Vic., Cap. 74, 1851.

15 *St. C. J.*, 1 July 1852.

16 *Ibid.*

17 G. R. Stevens, *Canadian National Railways*, Macmillan (Toronto), 1933, p. 105.

18 Report of the Directors of the Great Western Railway of Canada, 29 September 1854, *JLA*, v. 13, 1855, Appendix YY, p. 154.

19 *Ibid.*

20 *Ibid.*, p. 155.

21 *Ibid.*

22 G. M. Found, *Winona Centennial, 1867-1967*, (Winona), 1967, p. 1.

23 Letter from Samuel Keefer, Chief Engineer, Public Works, to the Secretary, Public Works, 22nd December, 1852, *JLA*, 1852, Appendix YYY, p. 32.

24 Letter from John T. Clark, Chief Engineer, to C. J. Bridges, Managing Director, 17 October 1853, *JLA*, v. 13, 1855, Appendix YY.

25 *St. C. J.*, 3 November 1853.

26 *N. M.*, 9 November 1853. The *N. C.*, 27 January 1853, mentions that the first private run on the Great Western from Hamilton to the Suspension Bridge was on 31 October 1853.

27 J. Sheridan Hogan, *Canada. An Essay: To Which Was Awarded the First Prize by the Paris Exhibition Committee of Canada*, Lovell (Montreal), 1855, p. 100.

28 *Ibid.*, p. 99.

29 *Ibid.*, p. 100.

30 James R. Benson to his son, 11 November 1853 in the Alex W. Ormston Collection.

31 Nick and Helma Mika, *Railways of Canada: A Pictorial History*, McGraw-Hill Ryerson (Toronto), 1972, p. 39.

32 Deposition of William Bowman, Superintendent, Mechanical Department, Great Western Railway, Canada West, Montreal, 5th January 1854, *JLA*, v. 13, 1855, Appendix YY, pp. 140-141.

33 Accident reports are found in *JLA*, v. 13, 1855, Appendix YY.

34 *St. C. C.*, 5 March 1858.

35 G. Lowe Reid, Report of the Engineer to the President and Directors of the Great Western Company, 14 September 1854, *JLA*, v. 13, 1855, Appendix YY, p. 161.

36 George A. Seibel, The Iron Horse, in George A. Seibel (ed.), *Niagara Falls, Canada*, Kiwanis Club of Stamford (Niagara Falls), 1967, p. 62.

37 Francis Petrie, 95-Year-Old Station, *N. F. R.*, 31 August 1974.

38 Reid, *op. cit.*, p. 160.

39 Samuel Keefer, *op. cit.*, p. 29.

40 *Ibid.*

41 *Ibid.*

42 Reid, *op. cit.*, p. 160.

43 Great Western Timetable, October 23 1854, *JLA*, v. 13, 1855, Appendix YY, pp. 146-149.

44 *Diary of Hugh Neilson, St. Catharines Station*, 1861, PAO.

45 *Ibid.*, 9 February 1861.

46 *Ibid.*, 5 August 1861.

47 *Ibid.*, 19 November 1861.

48 *Ibid.*

49 *Ibid.*, 26 December 1861.

50 *Ibid.*, 25 April 1861.

51 *St. C. J.*, 14 February 1856.

52 *Report of the Chief Engineer of Canals*, Department of Railways and Canals (Ottawa), 1880, p. 35.

53 *Th. P.*, 4 March 1881.

54 Michelle Greenwald [et al], *The Welland Canals: Historical Resource Analysis and Preservation Alternatives*, Rev. Ed., Historical Planning and Research Branch, Ministry of Culture and Recreation (Toronto), 1977, pp. 58-59, 101-104.

55 47 Vic., Cap. 52, 1884.

56 33 Vic., Cap. 49, 1870.

57 47 Vic., Cap. 53, 1884.

58 16 Vic., Cap. 37, 1852. See A. W. Currie, *The Grand Trunk Railway of Canada*, University of Toronto Press (Toronto), 1957.

59 Elizabeth A. Willmot, *Meet Me at the Station*, Gage (Toronto), 1976, p. 84.

60 Kevin Lynch, *What Time is This Place*, M. I. T. Press (Cambridge, Mass.), 1972, p. 49.

CHAPTER III

1 16 Vic., Cap. 50, 1852.

2 *St. C. J.*, 4 May 1854, as quoted from the *N. M.*

3 Arthur W. Roebeck, *The Macklems of Chippawa*, Best (Don Mills), 1969, p. 24.

4 Barlow Cumberland, *A Century of Sail and Steam on the Niagara River*, Musson (Toronto), 1913, pp. 40-41.

5 *St. C. C.*, 19 September 1855, quoting *N. M.*

6 20 Vic., Cap. 151, 1857.

7 27 Vic., Cap. 59, 1863.

8 38 Vic., Cap. 66, 1875; 41 Vic., Cap. 27, 1878; 57-58 Vic., Cap. 34, 1894; *Order of the Privy Council,* 9 October 1903; 4 Edw. VII, Cap. 55, 1904; and *Order of the Privy Council,* 21 August 1929.

9 W. Shanly, *Report of W. Shanly: Survey of a Branch Canal to Connect the Welland Canal with the Mouth of the Niagara River,* (Toronto), 1854.

10 See *St. C. C.,* 28 September 1855.

11 R. W. Geary, Samuel Zimmerman, 1815-1857, *WCHS, v. 3, 1927, pp. 47-57.*

12 *St. C. J.,* 16 April 1857.

13 Francis J. Petrie, A City Grows, in George A. Seibel (ed.), *Niagara Falls, Canada,* Kiwanis Club of Stamford (Niagara Falls), 1967, p. 39.

14 Francis Petrie, The Paddy Miles Road, *N. F. R.,* 5 October 1964.

15 George V. Taylor, *Historical Writings of Willoughby Township,* Evening Review (Niagara Falls), 1967, p. 10.

16 16 Vic., Cap. 136, 1853.

17 *Ibid.*

18 *Ibid.*

19 George Keefer to W. H. Merritt, *Merritt Papers,* 22 April 1853, PAC.

20 19-20 Vic., Cap. 23, 1856.

21 20 Vic., Cap. 141, 1857.

22 J. M. and Edw. Trout, *The Railways of Canada for 1870-1. . .,* Monetary Times (Toronto), 1871, p. 146.

23 Donald C. Masters, W. H. Merritt and the Expansion of Canadian Railways, *CHR,* v. 12, 1931, p. 168.

24 W. H. Merritt to Frederick Widder, 23 June 1845, in *Merritt Papers,* PAC.

25 Prospectus of the Welland Railway, June 1856, *St. C. J.,* 6 August 1857.

26 Prospectus of the Welland Railway, September 1856, *ibid.*

27 Robert Stephenson to W. H. Merritt, 27 August 1856, *St. C. J.,* 6 August 1857.

28 Prospectus of the Welland Railway, July 1857, *ibid.*

29 J. P. Merritt, *Biography of the Hon. W. H. Merritt, M. P. . . .,* E. S. Leavenworth (St. Catharines), 1875, p. 419.

30 Prospectus of the Welland Railway, July 1857, *op. cit.*

31 *Ibid.*

32 *Ibid.*

33 *Ibid.*

34 *Ibid.*

35 *Ibid.*

36 *N. M.,* 2 February 1853.

37 *Ibid.*

38 *N. M.,* 28 December 1853.

39 *Ibid.*

40 *N. M.,* 22 March 1854. See also 8 March 1856 and 19 August 1857, and *St. C. C.,* 14 March 1855.

41 The Cities of Canada: St. Catherines, *Anglo-American Magazine,* v. 3, 1853, p. 131. In early documents, the spelling is either St. Catharines or St. Catherines. The former became the approved spelling by decision of the Geographical Board of Canada on 25 June 1906. For a discussion of this issue see John N. Jackson, *St. Catharines, Ontario: Its Early Years,* Mika (Belleville), 1976, pp. 134-138.

42 *St. C. J.,* 30 June 1853.

43 *St. C. J.,* 5 January 1854.

44 *St. C. J.,* 19 January 1854.

45 *St. C. J.,* 16 March 1854.

46 *Ibid.*

47 Report of the Port Dalhousie and Thorold Railway Company, *St. C. J.,* 22 November 1855.

48 *St. C. J.,* 31 August 1854.

49 *St. C. J.,* 7 September 1854.

50 *St. C. J.,* 24 August 1854, and *St. C. C.,* 11 April 1855.

51 *St. C. C.,* 11 April 1855.

52 *St. C. C.,* 25 April and 2 May 1855.

53 *St. C. J.,* 22 November 1855.

54 *St. C. J.,* 9 May 1855.

55 *St. C. J.,* 6 December 1855.

56 Welland Railway Company, *Engineer's Report,* 22 November 1855, in J. P. Merritt, *op. cit.,* p. 416.

57 *St. C. J.,* 22 May 1856.

58 *Ibid.*

59 *Ibid.*

60 *Ibid.*

61 *St. C. J.,* 12 June 1856.

62 22 Vic., Cap. 92, 1859.

63 *St. C. J.,* 1 July 1858.

64 *St. C. J.,* 14 October 1858, and *N. M.,* 29 September 1858.

65 *St. C. J.,* 28 October 1858.

66 *Ibid.*

67 *St. C. J.,* 7 April 1859.

68 *St. C. J.,* 16 June 1859.

69 *St. C. J.,* 30 June 1859. Timetables are included frequently in the *St. C. J.:* see, for example, the issues of 16 February 1860; 19 April 1860; 16 May 1861; and 20 June 1861.

70 Welland Railway Passenger Time Table, No. 2, *St. C. J.,* 14 July 1859.

71 *St. C. J.,* 16 May 1861.

72 *St. C. J.,* 3 November 1859.

73 T. C. Keefer, Travel and Transportation in H. Y. Hind [et al], *Eighty Years Progress of British North America . . .,* Nichols (Toronto), 1864, pp. 236-237.

74 A. W. Currie, *The Grand Trunk Railway of Canada,* University of Toronto Press (Toronto), 1957, p. 255.

75 *Th. P.,* 7 May 1880.

76 *Shanly Papers,* Boxes 74-79, PAO. For an account of the engineering career of the Shanly brothers, especially in the Canadian West, see Walter and Francis Shanly, *Daylight Through the Mountain,* edited by Frank Norman Walker, Engineering Institute of Canada (Montreal), 1957.

77 *St. C. J.,* 22 October 1855.

78 *St. C. C.,* 11 April 1855.

79 J. P. Merritt, *op. cit.,* p. 406.

80 *St. C. J.,* 13 October 1853.

81 Articles of Agreement Made Between the Great Western Railway Company and the Port Dalhousie and Thorold Railway Company, 8 February 1855, *St. C. C.,* 11 April 1855.

82 Engineer's Department, Great Western Railway to F. Shanly, 27 March 1858, *Shanly Papers,* PAO.

83 *Contract — Boston Locomotive Works,* 19 June 1857, Shanly Papers, PAO.

84 *Specification For Combined Station Buildings at Port Dalhousie,* 24 June 1857, Shanly Papers, PAO.

85 *Ibid.*

86 *Specification for the Enlargement of the St. Catharines Station Building,* 11 July 1857, Shanly Papers, PAO.

87 William Pay, *Struggles and Triumphs,* (St. Catharines), 1902, p. 10.

88 *Ibid.*

89 *Ibid.,* p. 11.

90 *Ibid.*

91 J. A. Blyth, The Development of the Paper Industry in Old Ontario, 1824-1867, *OHS,* v. 62, 1970, p. 131.

92 The history of the paper industry in the Niagara Peninsula is outlined in John N. Jackson and Carole White, *The Industrial Structure of the Niagara Peninsula,* Department of Geography, Brock University (St. Catharines), 1971, pp. 136-142.

93 Carl Wiegman, *Trees to News: A Chronicle of the Ontario Paper Company's Origin and Development,* McClelland & Stewart (Toronto), 1953, p. 12.

94 P. J. Cowan, *The Welland Ship Canal,* Department of Railways and Canals (Ottawa) 1935, Introduction.

95 *Th. P.,* 28 July 1876.

96 *Th. P.,* 24 August 1877.

97 47 Vic., Cap. 53, 1884.

98 Currie, *op. cit.,* p. 255.

CHAPTER IV

1 16 Vic., Cap. 45, 1852. The rights of this company were recognized in 14-15 Vic., Cap. 121, 1851.

2 T. C. Keefer, Travel and Transportation, in H. Y. Hind [et al], *Eighty Years' Progress of British North America . . .,* Nichols (Toronto), 1864, p. 234.

3 Frank N. Walker, Birth of the Buffalo and Brantford Railway, *OHS,* v. 47, 1955, p. 81.

4 *Brantford Expositor,* 13 January 1854, quoted in *ibid.,* p. 85.

5 *St. C. C.,* 24 January 1855.

6 19 Vic., Cap. 21, 1856.

7 Eric Heyl, Railroad Ferry Boats on the Niagara River, *IS,* v. 17, 1961, p. 98.

8 *Ibid.*

9 Keefer, *op. cit.,* p. 235.

228

10 33 Vic., Cap. 49, 1870. The working agreements appear in 29-30 Vic., Cap. 92, 1866 and 31 Vic., Cap. 19, 1867.

11 29-30 Vic., Cap. 92, 1866.

12 B. E. Hill, The Grand River Navigation Company. . ., *OHS*, v. 63, 1971, pp. 31-40.

13 Elizabeth A. Willmot, *Meet Me at the Station*, Gage (Toronto), 1976, p. 78.

14 *Ibid.*

15 6 Wm. IV, Cap. 6, 1836.

16 Mahlon Burwell to John Joseph, 5 February 1836, in Walter Neutel, *From Southern Concept to Canada Southern Railway, 1835-1873*, M.A. Thesis, University of Western Ontario (London), 1968, pp. 9-10.

17 J. P. Merritt, *Biography of the Hon. W. H. Merritt, M.P. . . .*, E. S. Leavenworth (St. Catharines), 1875, p. 161.

18 Lot Clark to W. H. Merritt, 6 July 1841, *Merritt Papers*, PAC. See also the *Merritt Papers*, v. 29, pp. 5233-5234, 5252-5257, 5281-5282.

19 J. P. Merritt, *op. cit.*, 284.

20 *Ibid.*, p. 285.

21 *St. C.J.*, 16 October 1845.

22 J. P. Merrit, *op. cit.*, p. 359.

23 Donald C. Masters, W. H. Merritt and the Expansion of Canadian Railways, *CHR*, v. 12, 1931, p. 172.

24 *St. C.J.*, 16 October 1845.

25 *Toronto Colonist*, 3 July 1845, as quoted in J.P. Merritt, op. cit., p. 234.

26 J. P. Merritt, *ibid.*, pp. 286-287. See also *Merritt Papers*, Packages 19-20, PAO.

27 George S. Tiffany to W. H. Merritt, *Merritt Papers*, 9 September 1845, PAC.

28 J. P. Gilkison, Secretary of the Great Western Railroad, to W. H. Merritt, in J. P. Merritt, *op. cit.*, p. 286.

29 W. H. Merritt to J. P. Gilkison, *ibid.*, p. 287.

30 *St. C.J.*, 31 July 1845, "from an article in the last *Colonist.*"

31 *St. C.J.*, 16 October 1845.

32 W. H. Merritt to Sir Allan McNab, 8 July 1847, in J. P. Merritt, *op. cit.*, p. 310.

33 *JLA*, 1849, Appendix QQQ. See also *St. C.J.*, 29 July 1847.

34 Letter from J. W. Brooks to R. Stuart Woods, 20 March 1850, *JLA*, 1850. Appendix EE.

35 10-11 Vic., Cap. 117, 1847.

36 16 Vic., Cap. 239, 1853.

37 18 Vic., Cap. 179, 1855.

38 18 Vic., Cap. 182, 1855.

39 22 Vic., Cap. 118, 1858.

40 22 Vic., Cap. 90, 1859.

41 31 Vic., Cap. 14, 1868.

42 33 Vic., Cap. 32, 1869.

43 *St. C.C.*, 6 February 1868.

44 38 Vic., Cap. 66, 1875.

45 57-58 Vic., Cap. 34, 1894.

46 *Order of the Privy Council*, 21 August 1929.

47 4 Edw. VII, Cap. 55, 1904.

48 47 Vic., Cap. 75, 1884.

49 Andrew Merrilees, *The Toronto, Hamilton and Buffalo Railway Co.*, (undated, unpublished paper), p. 1. This paper was made available by J. A. Hill, General Manager, Toronto, Hamilton and Buffalo Railway Co., Hamilton, on 12 December 1977. It has been published in a slightly revised form in *Wentworth Bygones*, No. 12, 1977, pp. 36-44.

50 60 Vic., Cap. 6, 1896.

51 Merrilees, *op. cit.*, p. 9.

52 *Ibid.*, p. 3.

53 *Ibid.*

54 Frank E. Page, *The Story of Smithville*, Tribune-Telegraph (Welland), 1923, p. 57.

55 *Ibid.*

56 *Ibid.*

57 Willmot, *op. cit.*, p. 36.

58 *Ibid.*

59 Peter C. Andrews, The Canadian Shore from Pt. Abino to Erie Beach, *Buffalo and Erie County Historical Society*, (Buffalo), 1966, pp 8-10; see also John M. Mills, *History of the Niagara, St. Catharines & Toronto Railway*, Upper Canada Railway Society and Ontario Electric Railway Historical Association (Toronto), 1967.

60 Andrews, *ibid.*, pp. 9-10.

61 Francis Petrie, Picknickers Covered by Cinders. . . ., *N.F.R.*, 14 March 1970.

62 Ernest F. Ott [et al], *A History of Humberstone Township*, Humberstone Township Council (Port Colborne), 1967, pp. 112-113.

63 *Ibid.*, p. 116.

64 John N. Jackson, *Recreational Development and the Lake Erie Shore*, Niagara Regional Development Council (Grimsby), 1967.

CHAPTER V

1 St. Catharines Board of Trade, *Annual Report for the Year 1900* (St. Catharines), 1901, p. 59.
2 44 Vic., Cap. 73, 1881.
3 62-63 Vic., Cap. 77, 1899.
4 1 Edw. VII, Cap. 76 and Cap. 87, 1901.
5 2 Edw. VII, Cap. 83, 1902.
6 John M. Mills, *History of the Niagara, St. Catharines & Toronto Railway,* Upper Canada Railway Society and the Ontario Electric Railway Historical Association (Toronto), 1967.
7 38 Vic., Cap. 63, 1874.
8 45 Vic., Cap. 63, 1882.
9 Mills, *op. cit.,* p. 4.
10 John F. Due, *The Intercity Electric Railway Industry in Canada,* University of Toronto Press (Toronto), 1966, p. ix. See also George W. Hilton and John F. Due, *The Electric Interurban Railways in America,* Stanford University Press (Stanford, Ca.), 1960.
11 Mills, *op. cit.,* p. 3.
12 *Ibid.,* p. 10.
13 55 Vic., Cap. 96, 1892.
14 William R. Gordon, *90 Years of Buffalo Railway,* 1860-1950, (Rochester, N. Y.), 1970, p. 249.
15 63-64 Vic., Cap. 56, 1900 and 1 Edw. VII, Cap. 86, 1901.
16 2 Edw. VII, Cap. 12, 1902.
17 Wm. E. Blaine, *Ride Through the Garden of Canada: A Short History of the Hamilton, Grimsby & Beamsville Electric Railway Company, 1894-1931,* (Grimsby), 1967.
18 55 Vic., Cap. 95, 1892.
19 1 Edw. VII, Cap. 80, 1901.
20 *Economic History* [*of Niagara Falls*], 1964, p. 20, a background report to Georges Potvin, *City of Niagara Falls: Urban Renewal Study,* Council of the City of Niagara Falls (Niagara Falls), 1965.
21 St. Catharines Board of Trade, *op. cit.,* p. 7.

CHAPTER VI

1 Janet Carnochan, Bridges over the Niagara River, *NHS,* No. 36, 1924, pp. 31-37, and The Queenston Suspension Bridge, *ibid.,* pp. 26-31, provide introductory accounts. Somewhat more detail, together with photographs, is provided by A. E. Parsons, George A. Seibel, James Morden and W. Herbert Kribs in George A. Seibel (ed.), *Niagara Falls, Canada,* Kiwanis Club of Stamford (Niagara Falls), 1967. See also Carl J. Christensen [et al], *History of Engineering in Niagara,* Niagara Peninsula Branch, Engineering Institute of Canada (St. Catharines), 1977, and James C. Morden, *Historic Niagara Falls,* Lundy's Lane Historical Society (Niagara Falls), 1932, pp. 7-25.
2 A recent concise study of railway developments in New York State is found in Robert B. Shaw, A Case of Railway Mania, *Trains,* v. 37, 1977, pp. 22-27.
3 William J. Wilgus, *The Railway Interrelationships of the United States and Canada,* Yale University Press (New Haven), 1937, p. 13; authors' emphasis.
4 George A. Seibel, The World's Most famous Address, in Seibel, *op. cit.,* pp. 52-53.
5 *Communication from the Secretary of the Treasury . . . on the Trade and Commerce of the British North American Colonies . . .,* Robert Armstrong (Washington), 1853, pp. 84-85.
6 See Merritt Papers, Package 35, PAO.
7 J. P. Merritt, *Biography of the Hon. W. H. Merritt, M. P. . . .,* E. S. Leavenworth (St. Catharines), 1875, pp. 279.
8 *Ibid.,* p. 286.
9 J. J. Talman, William Hamilton Merritt, *Dictionary of Canadian Biography, v. 9,* University of Toronto Press (Toronto), 1976, p. 546.
10 *Ibid.,* p. 548.
11 J. P. Merritt, *op. cit.,* p. 402; authors' emphasis.
12 10 Vic., Cap. 112, 1846.
13 *Ibid.*
14 D. B. Steinman, *The Builders of the Bridge: The Story of John Roebling and His Son,* Arno (New York), 1972, p. 157.
15 A. E. Parsons, The Whirlpool Rapids Bridges, in Seibel, *op. cit.,* p. 329.
16 J. P. Merritt, *op. cit.,* pp. 333-334.
17 For an engineering description of the bridge, see Leiffert L. Buck, *Report on the Renewal of Niagara Suspension Bridge,* C. W. Ames (New York), 1881.
18 *St. C. C.,* 21 March 1855.
19 *Ibid.*

20 Parsons, *op. cit.,* p. 332.

21 *The History of the County of Welland . . .,* Welland Tribune (Welland), 1887, p. 339. This book was reprinted, with a new introduction and name index by John Burtniak, by Mika (Belleville), in 1972. See also Francis Petrie, Niagara's 15 Bridges During the Last 140 Years, *N. F. R.,* 11 November 1967.

22 12 Vic., Cap. 199, 1849.

23 James Morden, The Falls View Bridges, in Seibel, *op. cit.,* p. 335.

24 31 Vic., Cap. 82, 1868.

25 Morden, in Seibel, *op. cit.,* p. 337.

26 57-58 Vic., Cap. 97, 1894.

27 Morden, in Seibel, *op. cit.,* p. 338.

28 14 & 15 Vic., Cap. 172, 1852.

29 20 Vic., Cap. 227, 1857.

30 W. A. Thomson to W. H. Merritt, 28 December 1856, *Merritt Papers,* PAC.

31 C. S. Gzowski, *Description of The International Bridge* (Toronto), 1873. See also Ludwik Kos-Rabcewicz-Zubkowski, *Sir Casimir Stanislaus Gzowski: A Biography,* Burns & MacEachern (Toronto), 1959.

32 A. W. Spear, *The Peace Bridge, 1927-1977 . . .,* The Buffalo and Fort Erie Public Bridge Authority (Buffalo), 1977.

33 Charles Evans Fowler, Revision of the Niagara Railway Arch Bridge, American Society of Civil Engineers, *Transactions,* v. 83, 1920, p. 1927.

34 Report submitted to H. C. E. Childers, President, Great Western Railway of Canada, 2 March 1875, in *Report [of the] Lewiston and Queenston Bridge Company, 1875,* [N. p.], 1875, p. 1.

35 *Ibid.*

36 *Communication from the Secretary of the Treasury, op. cit.*

37 Joseph Wynn to W. H. Merritt, *Merritt Papers,* 17 April 1855, PAC.

38 19 & 20 Vic., Cap. 114, 1856.

39 Amos S. Tryon to W. H. Merritt, *Merritt Papers,* 5 March 1857, PAC.

40 Quoted in *Report [of the] Lewiston and Queenston Bridge Company 1875,* p. 2. The lake ridge refers to a former shore line of Lake Ontario (then Lake Iroquois).

41 *Ibid.,* pp. 11-12.

42 *Th. P.,* 16 January 1880.

43 *Ibid.*

44 Alonzo C. Mather, *Buffalo: Its Surroundings, Possibilities and Proposed Plan of Developing its Water Power,* (Buffalo), 1893, p. 7.

45 Alonzo C. Mather, *The Practical Thoughts of a Business Man,* Smith and Colbert, (Chicago), 1893, p. 15.

46 *Communication from the Secretary of the Treasury, op. cit.,* p. 84.

47 37 Vic., Cap. 77, 1874.

CHAPTER VII

1 Barlow Cumberland, *A Century of Sail and Steam on the Niagara River,* Musson (Toronto), 1913, pp. 42-43.

2 *St. C. C.,* 17 January 1855.

3 *Welland Herald,* October 1856, as quoted in *The History of the County of Welland,* Welland Tribune (Welland), 1887, p. 342.

4 Arnold McAdorey, *Niagara's Story of Customs,* Customs– Excise (Niagara Falls), 1960, p. 44.

5 Robert W. Bingham, First Days in Old Fort Erie, in Times– Review, *Fort Erie Centennial, 1857-1957,* (Fort Erie), 1957, pp. 8-9, 34.

6 Marguerite A. Raymond, From 1857 On, in Times Review, *ibid.,* pp. 8, 45.

7 E. W. Johnson, Bridgeburg Story, in Times-Review, *ibid.,* p. 10.

8 *Ibid.*

9 George Tait, Street and Place Names and Early Reminiscences of Bridgeburg, *WCHS,* v. 3, 1927, p. 104.

10 Francis Petrie, Fort Erie's Railway History, *N. F. R.,* 20 October 1973.

11 H. R. Page, *Illustrated Historical Atlas of the Counties of Lincoln and Welland* (Toronto), 1876, p. 16. A facsimile edition was reprinted by Cumming (Port Elgin) in 1971. Pagination refers to the reprint edition.

12 58 Vic., Cap. 62, 1895.

13 62 Vic., Cap. 63, 1899.

14 John N. Jackson, *Welland and the Welland Canal: The Welland Canal By-Pass,* Mika (Belleville), 1975, Chapter 3. See also John N. Jackson, *A Planning Appraisal of the Welland Urban Community: Trends, Transition, Potential,* Prepared for Department of Public Works, (Ottawa), 1974, pp. 11-53.

15 Page, *op. cit.,* p. 17.

16 *The County Town Question to the Rate Payers of the County of Lincoln,* S. C. Smith (Niagara), 1864 and *The County Town Question,* S. C. Smith (Niagara), 1864 express this opposition. Both pamphlets are in the Niagara Historical Society Museum, Niagara-on-the-Lake.

17 W.H. Smith, *Canada: Past, Present and Future, v. 1,* Maclear (Toronto), [1851], p. 153.

18 Francis Petrie, Area Had First Railway in Ontario in 1835, *N. F. R.,* 13 May 1968.

19 *Ibid.*

20 Janet Carnochan to Hon. R. W. Scott, Secretary of State, an undated [1898?] draft of a letter in response to a letter with the same content from James Wilson, Superintendent, Queen Victoria Park Commissioners, Niagara Falls, to Janet Carnochan, 27 August 1898.

21 Hon. R. W. Scott, Secretary of State, to Janet Carnochan, 1 October 1898. This and the previous letter were provided in 1977 through the courtesy of John L. Field, President of the Niagara Historical Society.

22 Ray Corry Bond, *Peninsula Village: The Story of Chippawa,* Lindsay Press (Niagara Falls), [n. d.] p. 76. See also Arthur W. Roebuck, *The Macklems of Chippawa,* Best (Don Mills), 1969.

23 William F. Rannie, *Lincoln: The Story of an Ontario Town,* (Lincoln), 1974, p. 94.

24 J. F. Gross, The Early History of St. Johns, *WCHS,* v. 2, 1926, p. 137.

25 Smith, *op. cit.,* p. 184.

26 *Ibid.,* p. 208.

27 Rannie, *op. cit.,* p. 242.

28 *Ibid.,* pp. 247-248.

29 A. E. Coombs, *History of the Niagara Peninsula,* Historical Foundation (Montreal), 1950, p. 168.

30 *St. C. C.,* 31 January 1855.

31 *St. C. C.,* 28 March 1855.

32 *St. C. C.,* 23 May 1855.

33 See letters by "T. H.", *St. C. E. J.,* 27 June 1872, and 9 July 1872.

34 Smith, *op. cit.,* p. 151. This map is reproduced in Charles P. DeVolpi, *The Niagara Peninsula: A Pictorial Record,* Dev-Sco Publications (Montreal), 1966, plate 36.

35 *St. C. J.,* 8 July 1847.

36 *St. C. M.,* 14 December 1853.

37 Colin Keates Duquemin, *Sequent Occupance in the Lower Valley of the Twenty Mile Creek . . .,* M. A. Thesis, Department of Geography, State University of New York at Buffalo (Buffalo), 1968, p. 91. See *St. C. C.,* 21 March 1855, for a summary of the Wismer case.

38 Correspondence in *Merritt Papers,* October 1854, PAO.

39 *St. C. W. N.,* 21 November 1872; authors' emphasis.

40 *St. C. J.,* 4 October 1855.

41 *Ibid.*

42 Page, *op. cit.,* p. 24.

43 *St. C. W. N.,* 12 December 1872.

44 *Ibid.*

45 *St. C. W. N.,* 6 February 1873.

46 G. P. de T. Glazebrook, *Life in Ontario: A Social History,* University of Toronto Press (Toronto), 1971, p. 131.

47 See Mabel Burkholder, *The Story of Hamilton* (Hamilton), 1938, and other histories of Hamilton.

48 R. W. Camm, The Great Western Empire, *WOHN,* v. 6. 1948, pp. 11-12.

49 C. Pelham Mulvany, *Toronto: Past and Present,* W. E. Caiger (Toronto), 1884, p. 59.

50 12 Vic., Cap. 8, 1849; 13 and 14 Vic., Cap. 64, 1850; and *Canada Gazette,* 1854, pp. 477 and 478, respectively. The western extent of the boundary, which included St. Paul Street West, is depicted incorrectly on Department of Municipal Affairs, *Regional Municipality of Niagara: Municipal Boundary History,* Sheet 3 (Toronto), 1970.

51 *St. C. J.,* 5 December 1855.

52 *St. C. C.,* 21 February 1861.

53 *Ibid.*

54 *Ibid.*

55 *St. C. C.,* 28 November 1867.

CHAPTER VIII

1 G. Lowe Reid, Report of the Engineer to the President and Directors of the Great Western Company, 14 September, 1854, *JLA,* 1855, Appendix YY, p. 161.

2 *Shanly Papers,* 21 December 1857, Box 74, PAO.

3 H. R. Page, *Illustrated Historical Atlas of the Counties of Lincoln and Welland,* (Toronto), 1876, p. 21. Pagination refers to the reprint edition.

4 *Ibid.*

5 *Th. P.*, 30 January 1880.

6 William F. Rannie, *Lincoln: The Story of an Ontario Town,* (Lincoln), 1974, p. 98.

7 *Ibid.*, pp. 273, 282-284.

8 *St. C. J.*, 11 December 1856.

9 William Pay, *Struggles and Triumphs,* (St. Catharines), 1902, p. 8.

10 "Junius", *St. Catharines A to Z,* St. Catharines and Lincoln Historical Society (St. Catharines), 1967, p. [16]. A reprint of newspaper articles published in 1856, and attributed to Seymour Phelps.

11 *Diary of Hugh Neilson,* 1861, PAO.

12 *St. C. J.*, 14 October 1858.

13 Page, *op. cit.*, p. 61.

14 "Junius", *op. cit.*, p. [15].

15 *Shanly Papers,* PAO.

16 Cash books, revenue ledgers and fiscal records of the Great Western Railway were deposited with PAC in 1963. They are housed in the Public Records Division, (RG 30, v. 23-79).

17 *St. C. C.*, 10 January 1855.

18 The surname Shickluna is variously spelled, e.g. Shickeluna.

19 *St. C. C.*, 25 August 1864.

20 *St. C. C.*, 7 July 1864.

21 Pay, *op. cit.*, p. 9.

22 *St. C. C.*, 25 August 1864.

23 *Shanly Papers,* 13 June 1857, PAO.

24 *Ibid.*, 9 April 1858.

25 *N. M.*, 9 January 1856.

26 H. A. Musham, Ships That Went Down to the Seas, *IS,* v. 2, 1946, p. 20.

27 Barlow Cumberland, *A Century of Sail and Steam on the Niagara River,* Musson (Toronto) 1913, p. 38.

28 Shanly Papers, *op. cit.*, 1 July 1857, PAO.

29 *Ibid.*, 2 April 1858.

30 Pay, *op. cit.*, p. 8.

31 *Ibid.*, p. 9.

32 *Ibid.*

33 *Ibid.*, p. 11.

34 *Ibid.*, pp. 11-12.

35 *Ibid.*, p. 12.

36 *St. C. J.*, 19 December 1850.

37 *St. C. J.*, 26 December 1850.

38 J. P. Merritt, *Biography of the Hon. W. H. Merritt, M. P. . . .,* E. S. Leavenworth (St. Catharines), 1875, p. 390, and *St. C. J.*, 15 April 1851.

39 St. Catharines Board of Trade, *Annual Report for the Year 1900,* (St. Catharines), 1901, pp. 6-7.

40 *Ibid.*, p. 7.

41 *St. C. E. S.*, 12 December 1895.

42 *St. C. C.*, 4 April 1855.

43 F. M. Quealey, The Fenian Invasion of Canada West, June 1st and 2nd, 1866, *OHS,* v. 53, 1961, pp. 37-66.

44 E. A. Cruikshank, The Fenian Raid of 1866, *WCHS,* v. 2., 1926, p. 25.

45 *Ibid.*, p. 30.

46 *Ibid.*, pp. 32-33.

47 *Ibid.*, p. 37.

48 *St. C. C.*, 19 October 1859.

49 Robert W. Stretton (ed.), *Dunnville, Ontario: Centennial Year 1950, 100 Years of Progress,* Centennial Book Committee, Corporation of the Town of Dunnville (Dunnville), 1950.

50 Great Western Railway, *Time Tables: Great Western Railway and Connecting Lines — From November 10th., 1879, Until Further Notice,* (Hamilton), 1879. It is of interest that this guide had to be purchased for five cents. The descriptions inside the front cover were written in English, French and German, indicating that Niagara Falls now attracted an international clientele.

51 *Ibid.*, inside front cover.

52 *Ibid.*, p. 32.

53 *Ibid.*, p. 33.

54 *Ibid.*

55 *Ibid.*

56 "Junius", *op. cit.*, p. [13].

57 *Ibid.*

58 *Ibid.*, p. [65].

59 Neilson, *op. cit.*

60 *Th. P.,* 17 August 1877.

61 J. P. Merritt, *op. cit.,* p. 403.

62 "Junius", *op. cit.,* p. [28].

63 *Ibid.,* p. [39].

64 *Ibid.,* p. [40].

65 *Ibid.*

66 Neilson, op. cit., 29 March 1861.

67 *St. C. E. J.,* 19 August 1867.

68 *Ibid.,* 23 July 1861.

69 F. I. Whitney, Assistant General Passenger and Ticket Agent, Chicago, to F. Geddes, Agent in Niagara, 26 July 1884, in Niagara Historical Society Museum, Niagara-on-the-Lake.

70 Neilson, *op. cit.,* 12 August 1861.

71 *Ibid.,* 16 August 1861.

72 *Ibid.,* 2 January 1861.

73 *Ibid.,* 31 July 1861.

74 *St. C. J.,* 29 January 1857.

75 G. P. de T. Glazebrook, *Life in Ontario: A Social History,* University of Toronto Press (Toronto), 1968, p. 134.,

76 Francis Petrie, Telegraph Era Ends With Closing of Office, *N. F. R.,* 27 September 1975.

77 Ernest Green, Canada's First Electric Telegraph, *OHS,* v. 24, 1927, pp. 366-372.

78 Neilson, *op. cit.,* 11 February 1861.

79 Irving P. Bishop, *The Red Book of Niagara: A Comprehensive Guide to the Scientific, Historical and Scenic Aspects of Niagara,* Wenborne-Sumner, (Buffalo), 1901, p. 10. For a history of the City of Niagara Falls, see James C. Morden, *Historic Niagara Falls,* Lundy's Lane Historical Society (Niagara Falls), 1932, and George A. Siebel (ed.) *Niagara Falls, Canada,* Kiwanis Club of Stamford (Niagara Falls), 1967. Francis J. Petrie has written many articles for *N. F. R.;* these are indexed in the Petrie Files, Niagara Falls Public Library. For a bibliography of material, with excerpts, about all aspects of the Niagara River and the Falls, see Charles Mason Dow, *Anthology and Bibliography of Niagara Falls* (Albany, N.Y.), 1921. 2 vols.

80 Francis Petrie, Recount Earlier Years of Michigan Central Railway, *N. F. R.,* 10 October 1964.

81 Francis Petrie, 10 Minute Stop at Falls View a Big Selling Point for Railway *N.F.R.,* 18 September 1971.

82 Quoted in *ibid.*

83 For example, H. G. Acres, *Traffic Study — City of Niagara Falls,* (Niagara Falls), 1963.

84 Neilson, *op. cit.,* 3 August 1861.

85 J. P. Merritt, *op. cit.,* p. 415.

86 "Junius", *op. cit.,* p. [36].

87 Page, *op. cit.,* p. 24.

88 *St. C. J.,* 27 October 1859.

89 A. James Rennie, *Niagara Township: Centennial History,* Niagara Township (Virgil), 1967, p. 94.

90 William F. Rannie, *Lincoln: The Story of an Ontario Town,* (Lincoln), 1974, p. 62.

91 *Ibid.*

92 *Ibid.,* pp. 62-63.

93 *Ibid.,* p. 64.

94 G. M. Found, *Winona Centennial, 1867-1967,* (Winona), 1967, p. 6; the fruit industry is also discussed on pp. 11, 13 and 23. See also *Saltfleet — Then and Now, 1792-1973,* Corporation of the Town of Stoney Creek (Stoney Creek), 1975, pp 44-48.

95 St. Catharines Board of Trade, *op. cit.,* p. 9.

96 John N. Jackson and Carole White, *The Industrial Structure of the Niagara Peninsula,* Department of Geography, Brock University (St. Catharines), 1971, pp. 124-125. See also Gloria A. Martine, *The Role of the Welland Canal in Industrial Location,* B. A. Thesis, Univeristy of Toronto (Toronto), 1961.

97 Jackson and White, *op. cit.,* p. 166.

98 *Ibid.,* p. 197.

INDEX

Incline railways, 23-24, 32
Industrial development, 87-90, 113, 123, 125, 130, 169-170, 183-184, 185-186, 191-194, 197-200, 221-222
International Bridge (Fort Erie), 163-164, 167

Jarvis, 108
Jordan and Jordan Station, 37, 51, 58, 102, 165, 177, 218, 221

Keefer, T.C., 13-15, 32, 94, 194, 201, 221

Lewiston. See Queenston-Lewiston crossing
Locomotives, 2, 25, 41-2, 43, 44, 45, 54, 61, 77, 84, 85, 125, 154, 197, 204
London, 34, 35, 36, 39, 43, 51, 91, 187
Lorraine, 116
Lowbanks, 93, 94

Mack, Dr. Theophilus, 46
Mackenzie Rebellion, 15, 99
Mail service, 211-212
Marshville. See Wainfleet
Mather, Alonzo C., 156-158
McNab, Alan (Sir), 34, 102
Merritt, William Hamilton, 17, 23-24, 67, 84, 98-103, 139-141, 155
Merritton, 49-50, 58, 67, 75, 80, 85, 87-90, 123-125, 165, 182-184, 194, 197, 206, 221
Miles, George Patrick, 65-66
Military use of railways, 53, 173, 203-204
Montreal, Quebec and the St. Lawrence, 15, 19, 21-22, 25, 31, 36, 39, 43, 51, 56, 70
Montrose Yards (Niagara Falls), 107, 163, 214
Moulton, 105

Niagara (Niagara-on-the-Lake), 19, 24, 32, 36, 59, 60, 61, 64, 70-72, 73, 138, 172-175, 194, 198, 206, 211, 212, 218, 221
Niagara Escarpment, 14, 17, 18, 19, 21, 23-24, 35-36, 41, 42, 48-49, 55, 59, 60, 78, 80, 82, 86-87, 103, 107, 111, 128, 194
Niagara Falls, 24, 32, 33, 37, 57, 127, 134, 135, 160-163, 166, 201, 206, 210, 211, 212-215, 221, 222. See also Clifton; Drummondville; Elgin; Suspension Bridge, Niagara frontier
Niagara frontier, 13, 15-16, 19, 21, 27, 33, 35-36, 47, 48, 94, 98-108, 136-138, 141, 157, 194
Niagara Peninsula, definition, 13
    regional setting, 20-23
    settlement pattern, 19, 138
    topography, 16-18
Niagara River, 14, 17, 19, 24-25, 32, 64, 94, 127-131, 136-158, 175, 195. See also Niagara frontier.
Non-developments, 154-158, 180-182

Oille, Lucius S., 118-119, 123
Ontario Lakeshore Plain, 17, 18, 19, 21, 36, 50, 51, 102, 217-220

Pay, William, 85, 196, 198-199
Perry, 212

Port Colborne, 19, 32, 33, 53, 67, 70, 73, 74, 75, 77, 78, 79, 82, 83, 85, 94, 96, 116, 190-192, 199, 206, 210, 221
Port Dalhousie, 19, 31, 32, 33, 53, 54, 67, 68, 70, 73, 74, 76, 78, 79, 80, 82, 84, 85, 89, 120-127, 132, 190-191, 193, 199, 200, 204, 206, 209, 210, 215
Port Maitland, 19, 31, 113
Port Robinson, 19, 63, 78, 79, 81, 82, 84, 179, 194, 206, 210
Point Abino, 197

Quarries, 85, 132, 194-197, 209
Queenston, 17, 18, 19, 24, 25, 32, 36, 119, 126-129, 138, 155, 175, 195-196, 203-204, 212, 221
Queenston-Lewiston crossing, 36, 127, 155, 212

Railway and Rail Road Companies,
    Amherstburg and St. Thomas Railway, 103-104
    Buffalo and Lake Huron Railway, 27, 28, 31, 32, 55, 77, 78, 79, 82, 91-98, 107-108, 191, 203
    Buffalo, Brantford and Goderich Railway, 32, 73, 91-93
    Buffalo Railway Company, 130
    Canada Air Line Railway, 33, 56, 85, 107-110, 168
    Canada Southern Railway, 33, 56, 63, 89, 98-107, 108, 111, 112, 136, 144, 167, 168, 212, 213, 214, 215
    Canadian Pacific Railway, 110, 111
    Erie and Niagara Extension Railway, 104
    Erie and Niagara Railway, 14, 33, 59-66, 79, 105, 108, 144, 173, 206
    Erie and Ontario Railroad, 24-25, 28, 31, 32, 59-63, 65, 67, 71, 75, 104, 196
    Fort Erie Railroad, 63, 104
    Fort Erie, Snake Hill and Pacific Railroad, 33, 116-117
    Grand Trunk, 27, 31, 32, 33, 39, 43, 44, 54-57, 70, 89, 94, 107, 108, 112, 115, 116, 119, 120, 134, 152, 162, 167, 195, 196, 212
    "Great Gorge Route", 33, 128-131
    Great Southwestern Railway, 104
    Great Western Railway, 27, 28, 31, 32, 33, 34-58, 60, 61, 63, 67, 72, 73, 74, 78, 82, 83, 85, 89, 91, 93, 98, 101-105, 107-110, 138, 142, 155, 160, 162, 177-178, 182, 187-188, 195, 196, 197, 201, 203, 205-207, 211, 212, 218
    Hamilton and Toronto Railway, 39, 43, 182
    Hamilton, Grimsby and Beamsville Electric Railway, 33, 132, 202
    International Railway Company, 130
    Lake Ontario Shore Railroad, 155
    London and Gore Railroad, 32, 34-35, 99
    Michigan Central Railroad, 33, 36, 44, 64, 107, 110, 111, 119, 134, 144, 162, 175, 211, 212, 213
    New York Central Railroad, 61, 64, 107, 111, 206, 212
    Niagara and Detroit Rivers Railway, 98-104
    Niagara Falls Park and River Railway, 33, 127-130, 212
    Niagara Falls, Wesley Park and Clifton Tramway, 120, 127
    Niagara, St. Catharines and Toronto Railway, 33, 119-127, 132, 134, 202
    Ontario Southern ("Peg Leg") Railway, 33, 115-116
    Pere Marquette Railroad, 107

A summation of railway achievement in the Peninsula.

John Burtniak Collection

JOHN N. JACKSON

Dr. John N. Jackson is Professor of Applied Geography at Brock University, St. Catharines, Ontario. He was appointed in 1965 as Head of the Department of Geography. Subsequently he has concerned himself with many aspects of development in the Niagara Peninsula, Canada and Europe. His prime academic interests are in the historical evolution and present characteristics of the city, at home and abroad.

He has published five previous books: *Surveys for Town and Country Planning*, Hutchinson (London), 1963; *The Urban Future*, Allen and Unwin (London), 1972; *The Canadian City*, McGraw-Hill Ryerson (Toronto), 1973; *Welland and the Welland Canal*, Mika (Belleville), 1975; and *St. Catharines: Its Early Years*, Mika (Belleville), 1976. Published reports about the Niagara Peninsula include *Recreational Development and the Lake Erie Shore*, Niagara Regional Development Council, 1967; *The Industrial Structure of the Niagara Region*, Brock University, 1971; *The Welland Urban Community*, Federal Department of Public Works, 1974; and *Land Use Planning in the Niagara Region*, Niagara Region Study Review Commission, 1976.

Trained in Geography with a B.A. (Honours) Degree from the University of Birmingham and a PH.D. Degree from the University of Manchester, he worked for local government in England and was then a lecturer at the University of Manchester. He emigrated to Canada in 1965. He first lectured at the University of British Columbia before joining Brock University. He is married with two sons and a married daughter. He has travelled extensively in Western Europe and North America, and saw service in the North Sea, Australia and the Far East whilst serving with the British Navy in the Second World War.

JOHN BURTNIAK

John Burtniak is presently Head, Technical Services Divisions, Brock University Library, St. Catharines, Ontario. He has held various positions in the Library since joining the Library staff in 1965. He also has responsibility for the Library's Special Collections and the University Archives. He obtained a B.A. Degree from the University of Ottawa, and B.L.S. and M.L.S. degrees from the University of Toronto.

He maintains a professional interest in the library field and is a member of the Canadian Library Association, the Ontario Library Association, and the Bibliographical Society of Canada. He has an abiding interest in all facets of the local history of the Niagara Frontier, and including both the Ontario and New York sides of the Niagara River.

He is a member of all of the historical societies in the region, and holds office in the Lundy's Lane Historical Society, the Thorold and Beaverdams Historical Society, and the Niagara Regional Historical Council, and is a Member of the St. Catharines Historical Museum Board. He belongs to the Ontario Genealogical Society, of which he is Second Vice President, the Ontario Historical Society and the Great Lakes Historical Society, and other kindred organizations. He is in the happy position of combining his professional responsibilities with his avocation of collecting, preserving and interpreting the written, printed and pictorial record of the Niagara Frontier. Although born in the Province of Manitoba he has lived in this region from an early age and considers himself to be an adopted son of the Niagara Peninsula.